THE BOOK OF
REVELATIONS

THE BOOK OF
REVELATIONS

A Novel

ROB SWIGART

E. P. DUTTON NEW YORK

Published in the United States by
Elsevier-Dutton Publishing Co., Inc.,
2 Park Avenue, New York, N.Y. 10016

Library of Congress Cataloging in Publication Data

Swigart, Rob.
The book of revelations.
I. Title.
PS3569.W52B6 1981   813'.54   81-3114
AACR2

ISBN: 0-525-03051-4

Published simultaneously in Canada by Clarke, Irwin & Company Limited, Toronto and Vancouver

Designed by Mary Gale Moyes

10 9 8 7 6 5 4 3 2 1
First Edition

This is a work of fiction, and any resemblance to events or creatures living or dead (or in any other, yet unconfirmed, state) is purely coincidental. As in any work of fiction, however, there are numerous connections with the real world and the people and other species which inhabit it, their spirits and thoughts and utterances. I would like to acknowledge some of them here.

Mike and Patty Demetrios, and the staff at Marine World/Africa U.S.A., particularly Ron Whitfield, Jim Mullin, and Tom Hansen, were generous with time, information, and space. I was allowed to meet with the elephants, the dolphins, and orcas; it was an unforgettable experience. Without fail, the people who worked with these creatures did so with humility and respect and a sense that there was still much to learn.

Bob Johansen, Kathi Vian, Carol Westberg and others at the Institute for the Future gave me some experience of what those who think about the future for a living actually do. Their work is, in a sense, the creation of fiction, for the future does not yet exist, and, in fact, never will, for when it arrives it will be the present. That is the essential paradox of their work.

Jacques Vallee, in conversations and in books, gave me some startling and exciting notions about the possibilities of science and its applications to areas of human experience considered, by lesser men, to be inaccessible to rational and skeptical scrutiny. Whatever the future (*sic!*) may reveal about psychic technologies, there were some intelligent investigators willing to take a serious look.

My debt to John C. Lilly and hopes for the success of the work of the Human/Dolphin Foundation should be obvious.

There are others, of course. I thank them, too. It is all connected. Thankfully.

This book is for daughters: Saramanda and Tess. They are, after all, the future.

There is a fine old story about a student who came to a rabbi and said, "In the olden days there were men who saw the face of God. Why don't they any more?" The rabbi replied, "Because nowadays no one can stoop so low."

—C. G. JUNG
Memories, Dreams, Reflections

*Nero wasn't uneasy when he heard
the prophecy of the Delphic Oracle:
"Beware of the seventy-third year."
He had plenty of time left to enjoy himself.
He was only thirty years old. The god gives him
sufficient time indeed
to confront his future dangers.*

*Now he will return to Rome slightly tired,
but exquisitely tired from his journey,
which was nothing but days of pleasure—
at the theaters, in the gardens, at the gymnasium . . .
evenings in all the cities of Achaea . . .
ah, above all, the pleasure of naked bodies . . .*

*So Nero. And in Spain, Galba
secretly gathers and trains his army,
an old man seventy-three years old.*

—C. P. CAVAFY
"Nero's Term"
tr. ROB SWIGART

The universe is a teaching and learning machine. Its purpose is to know itself.

—ITZHAK BENTOV

5:1 *And I saw in the right hand of him that sat on the throne a book written within and on the backside, sealed with seven seals. And I saw a strong angel proclaiming with a loud voice, Who is worthy to open the book, and to loose the seals thereof?*

MONDAY

TURTLES
ALL THE
WAY DOWN

6:1 *And . . . the Lamb opened one of the seals*

"The end of the world?"

"Three more days," the young man said. He fidgeted from foot to foot, his sparse moustache twitching above red, wet lips. "Get ready."

"The end of the world?" Cassie repeated. "Boom?"

"Maybe boom. Maybe not. The signs aren't clear."

"The signs?" Cassie looked up at the fog layer over her head. Would it rain today?

"Madame Glabro has been told about it. I am part of her telepathic network. Now I am telling you." His lips worked damply under the pale moustache; they made a small smacking sound, like a marble dropped into Jello.

"Telepathic network?" Cassie said.

"Telepathic network," the soft lips stated emphatically. "There are dozens of us, all around the world. Well, forty-seven, exactly. Australia, Guam, Lithuania . . ."

"Who are you?" she asked. She was holding the door to her apartment ajar, just on her way to the office, when this *creature* showed up. The end of the world, in exactly three days.

"Oh," he patted his jacket pockets frantically. "Oh, I'm sorry. Gosh, I mean . . ." he pulled a worn business card from a pocket and passed it to her. There was a thumbprint across the name, and she could barely make it out.

"You are Mr. . . . Zsylk?"

He nodded frantically, chin alternately obscuring and revealing his prominent Adam's apple. She noticed for the first time the wisps of blond beard on the chin, like fragments of fog torn by an outcropping of soft rock. "CoreLight Mission," he said. "Of the Visitors' Disciples."

"Mmm," Cassie pulled her own lips in between her teeth, trying to thin them. "And why are you telling me about the, uhm, the end of the world? Ronald." She made out the first name under the loops and

3

whorls of the thumbprint. Yes, there it was, CoreLight Mission, above a pyramid radiating something. An eye in the center. The eye looked a bit sleepy to her, but the drawing was crude; it could be deceptive.

Ronald seemed preternaturally embarrassed; his sneakers jigged unevenly on Cassie's front step, paranoid whispers on the cement. "Oh, the signs," he said.

"Ah," she nodded. "The signs. Yes." She chewed on her lips a moment. "What signs?" she said finally.

"Oh." Ronald looked away, gazed up at the thick layer of cloud, flat and even as a gray ceiling. No signs up there. Perhaps he was picking up a message from his network. "Do you know about the Dalai Lama?"

Uh-oh. "Dalai Lama?" Carefully neutral. After all, Cassie was in communications, wasn't she, and telepathy was a form of communication, wasn't it?

"He's picked by signs. Astrological, mostly. The signs lead the monks to him."

"Are you telling me signs led the CoreLight Mission of the Visitors' Disciples to my house?"

He beamed. The signs had not misled them! "Yes," he breathed. "To *you.*" He pulled from the same pocket that held his business card a spottily Xeroxed copy of a badly typed transcript. "Here." He thrust it toward her.

She took it as she peered out toward the street. Traffic seemed unusually light this morning. Mondays should be more active. She shook her head, let her lips relax, and glanced down at the page in her hand.

A music in the universe, spread lightwise from all Bibbles. The Prindl is just. A number with three times three times three, and downward the light to be carried off with flaming in the music, just before the End, Oh four.

"What is this junk?"

Ronald was baffled. "Junk?"

"Okay. What's a Bibble?"

"Oh." He was clearly relieved. A drop fell from the end of his nose. "You are. I am. Bibbles are the Chosen, to be carried off, transfigured, made negentropic. And this is your address, see. Twenty-seven-oh-four Prindl Avenue. Three times three times three, and oh-four,

4

twenty-seven-oh-four Prindl. A sign." He nodded emphatically. There was no doubt at all.

"Where did you get this?"

"The Visitors. Well, Madame Glabro got it, really, in a trance. Telepathically." He nodded again.

"Oh. Right. Telepathically. From the Visitors, whoever they are."

"Higher beings," Ronald Zsylk said, "from another plane of existence. They appear in UFOs—flying saucers—from another galaxy, come to take us away, those of us who are . . ."

"Bibbles?"

"Yes, yes, exactly. Bibbles."

A car passed in the street, headed up toward the mountains, away from town. Otherwise silence on this Monday morning. It was a quiet street, Prindl Avenue, but not that quiet.

"And the end of the world, which may or may not be boom, is Thursday?"

He nodded more. "March twenty-ninth, yes. The end of the world. For most, for everyone but those who are carried off."

"I am to be carried off. In a *flying saucer?*"

"That's right, a light vehicle."

"Ah. A light vehicle. Swooping through the sky. Give the cars dead batteries, that sort of thing. Blond aliens in black giving cryptic messages."

"You know!" Ronald breathed. "This is fantastic. The signs, the message from Them, it all comes together. There's no doubt about it, you must be ready by Thursday."

"For the end of the world."

"Yes! The End of the World." He put it all up in caps, like a prized vintage car on blocks. "They are blond, the ones I've met, and they wear black. From head to toe, always black. Or silver, but those are the dwarfs."

Cassie was nodding. They won't believe this at the office. Jehovah's Witnesses, yes. Mormons, of course, in shiny blue serge suits. Political organizers, consumer action groups, vegetarians, and SPCA fund-raisers. But not this. "Right," she said. "The dwarfs. They always wear silver, the dwarfs."

"Oh, no, not always. Only when they have on the diving helmets, like in the ancient Peruvian sculptures." He was earnest. Another pearl had gathered at the end of his nose, a pearl of pure ardor and sincerity.

"Listen, Ronald, I've got to . . ."

5

"There will be fire," Ronald said. "That much is certain. Burning, consuming, and thick smoke."

She looked up at the sky. No rain, she thought. Features had appeared in the base of the fog, a pattern of dark and light; sun shining through. It would break up soon. It always did. Another car passed in the street, headed toward town this time.

"Floods in the Midwest," he went on. "The Ohio River valley drowned, the Mississippi, the Missouri, everything from the Appalachians to the Rockies submerged, black waters and ineffable music."

Cassie could imagine the sky filled with alien, swooping lights. She could imagine the shiny metal saucer landing on the slope of lawn behind Investigate the Future and Roddy McDowall stepping out to offer her the stars. She could imagine that all right.

A memory mixed with this imagining: When she was six her father went into a skid on the New Jersey Turnpike right next to a neon sign, green and flickering in a rainy November dusk. A clock, reading 6:47, and curtains of rain sweeping across the road. She caught the clock in the corner of her eye, a round neon circle, the blurred numbers barely visible in the gloom. The hands, crackling neon arrows with stylized barbs. The long hand flickered, and the car went into the skid, a long looping circle and a tilt that sent the sign, the two names like wings on either side of the cloak, Goring and Goring, soaring away into lift-off, a majestic indifferent climb into the cloud-thick skies.

At the time the greenish shape had been to her either angelic or demonic, but it could have been an unknown craft with unpredictable behaviors: an alien science: a flying saucer.

It could have been, but it wasn't. It was an advertisement for a funeral home, tucked away under the elevated turnpike, its roof even with the road, the sign stuck right up there against the guardrail in a gentle irony. A warning, maybe, but ordinary.

"Black waters," she said softly, partly lost in that vision. "And"—briskly then—"I'm going to be late for work. A busy day today, I fear. Especially if the world is going to end on Thursday. Excuse me." She pulled her door shut behind her, felt the lock click tight.

"I'm so glad," Ronald said. "Because, Ms. St. Clair, you are a Bibble."

"Uh-huh," she nodded. "You know my name. And I'm a Bibble. I can't tell you what a relief it is to know that. Especially since Thursday . . ."

6

"Of course," Ronald went on, holding her arm. "Thursday could be the day we are to be carried off, rescued. Friday might be the end, but it will all begin on Thursday. That much is certain. Read the rest of the prophecy."

"I'll take it to the office with me," she said, folding the grimy manuscript carefully. "We study the future there. This will be extremely useful. Extremely."

"You study the future at your office?" At last it was Ronald's turn to ask a question.

Cassie tucked the folded paper in her shoulder bag and looked at him briskly. "Yes. I work at a think tank; the name of it is Investigate the Future."

Ronald snorted. "Very interesting, I'm sure. But they will be out of business soon, eh? Not much future." He didn't seem to think of it as a joke, though Cassie smiled.

"Well, we'll see." She brushed past him, down the walk to her car parked at the curb.

He called after her. "Ms. St. Clair?"

She turned. "Yes?"

"The signs brought us here. We will be seeing you. On the ships, if not before."

She waved, climbing into her car. It started perfectly, fuel in the tank following the laws of physics, the designs of engineering, the constraints of matter, fluid mechanics, chemistry. Warm, familiar, solid facts. She shook her head, curled auburn hair brushing her ears, as she drove away.

In the rearview mirror Ronald Zsylk walked slowly down the steps, watching her recede, toward town. Sun broke through the fog layer here and there.

It was going to be a beautiful day.

It was going to be a long day. She could tell as soon as she walked through the door. For one thing, L.R. was muttering by the status wall. For another there was a look of panic on Joanne's face.

"Dome-shaped glowing lights," L. R. Hubletz said. He was the director of Investigate the Future. Cassie thought he lived in the past. "Big green Dutch ovens. Pah. Silly season."

"What's up?" Cassie asked. The status wall was a bank of television screens, thirty of them, monitoring the world information networks, news, satellite communications, computer conferencing, the works. A keyboard below the screens gave access to the computers, so the status wall could search for key items and organize the information. It was L.R.'s baby, and he was proud of it; it was solid scientific engineering, a tangible event in the life of the office. He owned the patents on it, and several other places had leased the rights. He glowed with satisfaction whenever anyone turned the thing on. All the screens were blinking now.

Cassie hated it. It was an intrusion, a malevolent assault on her eyes and ears. But necessary, she recognized.

"What's up?" L.R. turned to her. "What's up?" His voice rose an octave, appalled at her ignorance of what was up. "What are you working on now?"

"What am I working on now? I'm working on that endangered species project Mr. Brockhurst assigned me. You know, the elephants. It's mainly a literature search, trying to track down the locations of what free elephants are left. Not many, it seems, and one of them is at Brockhurst's place. Harold has the computers working on it. Why?"

"Because we have another project for you, a different one, and because scheduling is getting all fouled up because of it. What do you know about the DLF?"

"Oh no you don't. Uh-uh. No sir, I'm not doing anything with the Dead Liberation Front. Nope, no way. My mother's a member. No, thanks." Cassie poured herself a cup of French roast coffee from the machine.

"Just a minute. There's more to the DLF than you seem to think."

"L.R., I'm surprised at you, really I am. It's a cult, a bunch of kooks who go around with earphones picking up the residues from graves. You know, the world's most oppressed group, the dead. Forced into crowded ghettos, nothing to do, no entertainment, nothing. Christ, L.R., what could you be thinking about?" She sipped her coffee, stared through the wide-mesh drapes at the emerald green lawn sweeping away downhill from the building. The camellias were in bloom, the heavy red and white brilliance unfolding and falling, shriveling. Dead. Cassie had two dead fathers; she knew about all that, and her mother, Martha Bridgeworth St. Clair Malatesta, wandering around the graves with her detectors, her headphones, listening for the technological message from Beyond.

The Techno-mystics were everywhere these days. There was Ronald Zsylk, for instance, with his flying saucers coming to save him from the end of the world.

"Cassie, this project is a little different."

"In what way?"

It was different. L. R. Hubletz told her, because this was big. It was big because a man from the National Science Foundation had called, had recommended most emphatically, the man who was coming to visit, a certain Wesley Millet—had suggested that the project Dr. Millet would be proposing was worthy of serious consideration by the staff. It was big because within minutes Wesley Millet himself had called to make an appointment and had, in passing, mentioned the scope of his project.

"Now, L.R., it wouldn't be the size of the budget that interests you?" Cassie wanted to know. "A good big budget when sources for grants are drying up, perhaps." She nodded vigorously. "Right, good. But the DLF, L.R.? The *Dead Liberation Front?*"

"This is a communications problem, Cassie." The tension was almost visible in his voice. "And," he went on, the sarcasm rising in direct proportion to volume, "your specialty is communications, is it not?"

Cassie glanced over at Joanne, seated at the reception desk inside the front door. The look of panic had not subsided on her face, nor had she moved since Cassie entered. "What's the matter with her?" Cassie changed the subject.

"Never mind that," L.R. said brusquely. "She saw a flying saucer this morning. Nothing important. Nerves."

Joanne twitched, her bland puffy face a discount store notion counter during a fire sale, the details changing rapidly without ever changing at all. There was, at the same time, something indescribably sleepy about her look, a sort of lethargy spread with panic. To Cassie, the effect was eerie. Especially since Ronald Zsylk had brought her the glad tidings. "Nerves, huh?" Cassie muttered.

"Cassie, come *on*. Joanne, why don't you go on home?"

Joanne didn't move.

"Oh, never mind. Cassie, you are interested in communications. This project is ideal. You and Arnold Deleuw are perfect for it. I want you to talk to this Millet, you and Arnold. I want you to listen to what he has to say. All right?"

Was it all right? Do mice like cats? "All right," she said.

It was going to be a long day. Cassie rinsed out her coffee cup absently, turned it up on the rack, went into her office and shut the door. Her mother had been seated beside her that night on the New Jersey Turnpike when the car went into its skid. She remembered the greenish light pooled in her mother's cheeks, under her shadowy eyes; light from that neon clock. The darkness was damp, swept with rain over brown November stubble on the salt marshes. The wipers had been reassuring, clack-clack, clack-clack, a metronome dirge, somnolent and safe. She'd been watching her father's face, his watery eyes peering uncertainly through the rain-streaked windshield, the wash of water sliding down.

"We're going to be too late," he muttered. That made Cassie look back at her mother, a hot wire of fear down her abdomen.

There were the tight lips, the drawn look, the haggard expression, the green light. It was theatrical, that light, corpse light, death by drowning light. But the pain was real, the dark lips compressed with it.

Martha was in labor.

Then came the violent swing, the green angel tilted up and away at impossible speed.

"Bah," Cassie said. "Stuff. And nonsense."

There was a knock on the door. "Oh, yeah," she said.

Arnold Deleuw entered, a long gray figure who approached in sections, sloped shoulders, gangling arms, awkward hips, pipestem legs following a pale face and lank hair. "So anyway," he said.

"Yeah."

"I think you might be surprised," he said.

"I've had enough surprises for one day, thank you very much. Quite enough. Do you know that Thursday is the end of the world?"

He nodded. "Mmm-hmm, I heard that."

That got her. "You did? You heard it? What do you mean, you heard it?"

"Tsk, Cassie. You haven't been spending your requisite ten minutes a day with the status wall, as Dr. Hubletz has ordered. There's this woman, Madame Gabrow, who has something of a following around here. Anyway she's been in telepathic contact with beings from Saturn or something, who tell her the world is going to end. Thursday, you say?"

"Thursday. Maybe Friday. And her name's Glabro." Cassie pulled out the folded paper Ronald had given her. "Here."

Arnold pursed his lips as he read. Then he grunted. "Interesting coincidence."

"I presume you mean Joanne. She saw a flying saucer."

He nodded. "A pair of flying saucers, actually. A red dome-shaped one and a big Dutch-oven-shaped thing, green. Nobody else saw them, alas. She's always been a little . . . excitable."

"Excitable, yes."

"It was early this morning. What she was doing up then I don't know, though I got the impression she was just on her way home, around dawn. Her car stalled on two-eighty, these things buzzed her and vanished into the fog. She's been shaking ever since she got here, but then, there's no telling what she was doing all night. Drugs, or something. No telling."

Carefully neutral, Cassie murmured, "No telling."

He looked up. "Except for one thing."

"Oh?"

"Mmm. It seems others have seen UFOs around the country." He nodded, and his lips twitched slightly. A smile? "It seems the, uh, president saw them. Over the White House."

"Okay, Arnold. A joke's a joke. Are you a Bibble too?"

"No, I'm serious, really. It was on the networks. They're playing it as a joke, true. You know how people are feeling about the president these days, but it's there. And a statue in upstate New York was vandalized."

"By a flying saucer."

"No. By three flying saucers."

"Jesus, Arnold, it's too much."

He laughed then. "Yeah, it is, isn't it? By the way, what's a Bibble?"

"Why, I am, Arnold. I am."

"Oh."

She stroked her computer console, tapping into the networks, requesting the messages she might have from the conferences in which she participated. Log on, give the password, welcomed to the net, with a list of the conferences, number of messages in each. One of them concerned the elephants.

There was a message from Harold, back in Connecticut, where, he said, the weather was foul for March. The New York City toll-takers were on strike and no one could get into or out of Manhattan. Again. But he had completed the literature search on elephants. Results to follow.

The population in the Serengeti was down to less than two hundred, and many of those were older cows, past breeding. Thus the calf population was down badly, the ratio of young to adults the worst since the 1950s. Lake Manyara, the only remaining park outside Serengeti with free African elephants, was down to less than thirty, only one kinship group. Zoos, wild animal parks, and private reserves accounted for the remainder. Less than six hundred in all. The formerly vast herds had vanished, forced out of existence by human population pressures, competition for agricultural lands, necessity.

An old story.

She could prepare a preliminary report based on this information, design the appropriate questionnaire to sample attitudes toward elephant intelligence, and ship it off to Mr. Brockhurst, the elusive founder of Investigate the Future. She filed some thoughts on the questionnaire, notes for the modified Delphi poll they would run, and leaned back in her chair. The CoreLight Mission report lay on her desk where Arnold had dropped it.

It behooved her, as a Bibble, to read it all.

Cycles were inverted, above the awaitments, and all waters rising to musics, where the Bibbles sang, their vibrations coincident with light at 3,700 Angstroms, but harmonic to all galaxies. Precious Bibbles would be there on peaks when crafts came, and entropy declines for all. Suffering must cease! The wasters go beneath fire and wave, with vast detonations and noise. Death inverted.

The communication had been typed with an overused ribbon, and the typewriter put all the *r*'s on an angle. It was both pathetic and uncanny, this message from Madame Glabro's unconscious mind, a mixture of scientific jargon correctly used and utter nonsense. Cults like this had always existed before, of course, and were bound to flourish as a millennium approached and the quality of life appeared to decline.

"The quality," Cassie said aloud, "of electronic copying is certainly declining." This document looked like a tenth generation copy, highly entropic, faint, ghostly.

It was twelve minutes after ten. The seconds blinked in the upper right corner of her CRT screen. The future was coming on as vast and implacable as glaciers.

She thought of glowing red domes hovering in the air above the freeway, darting off into the fogged sky; of green Dutch ovens sailing with a quiet electronic hum in precise formation performing aerodynamically impossible feats, stopping abruptly, receding at incredible speeds. And there was that look of panic on Joanne's face.

Cassie slapped her desk, stood up. "Pretty soon I'll be believing all this stuff," she said to the wall over her desk. A chart of a decision tree stared back at her, logical, precise, rational, boxes containing choices branching to other boxes with other choices until the correct results emerge. A fabulous invention, the decision tree, lovely to contemplate and completely useless.

The decision tree did not answer.

She was singing when Arnold came back into her office. "I'm a Bibble, a Bibble, a Bibble," she sang.

"Is Joanne a Bibble?" he asked.

"Is Joanne a Bibble?" she sang. "No, she is not."

He held up his hand. "Okay, okay, you're probably right. She's gone home anyway. The doctor gave her some Valium. Do you suppose she actually saw something?"

Cassie did not answer right away, instead staring at the chart above her desk. "You know," she said shortly, "I'm going to take that thing down."

She climbed on the desk and pulled the heavy paper from the wall. "It's been here for years, you know, ogling me when I work, telling me to be more logical; *admonishing* me. *Chiding* me. What I need is a nice landscape or something."

The paper pulled away, bent over itself, folding over her hands, flopping on the desk. It was a big chart, and she had trouble controlling it. Arnold stepped in to help, and at last they got it down on the floor, where she glared thoughtfully at it for a time.

"Look," Arnold said.

She turned. He was looking at the wall where the chart had been.

"Unh," she grunted. The words were written in red, a deep red that looked like new ink, although the paint on the wall was faded around the outlines of the chart. The words were *Flaming Music*. "Oh, really," she exclaimed. "This is too much! Arnold, who's playing tricks on me? You didn't send that jerk around to my apartment this morning did you? Ronald Zsylk. No, of course you didn't, you're not the type. But someone in this office has been sneaking around doing practical jokes. 'Flaming music' indeed! Shit."

"I don't know," he said slowly. "I don't think anybody could have gotten under that chart. That tape is old and hasn't been pulled off in years, like you say. Maybe you wrote it up on the wall before you put the chart up?"

"Maybe I . . . Well. Maybe I did." She chewed her lip. "But 'flaming music?' Really. Here," she read from the smudged CoreLight communication. " 'And downward the light to be carried off with flaming in the music, just before the End.' Is this a modern-day Revelation, Arnold? Saint John the Divine squatting in his cave on Patmos seeing fire running in the firmament and all that? The whole thing is simply not *healthy*."

Arnold smiled. "I'm a systems analyst, Cassie. I believe in numbers, trends, extrapolations. Facts. Left brain, logical, rational thinking. This really isn't my bailiwick."

"Nor mine," she answered, not smiling back.

14

"But we are old-fashioned futurists," the systems analyst told her, "if we are not open to the intuitive. The right brain, you know. I have no talents there, really. I prefer facts, and that's a fact. You, on the other hand . . ."

"Because I'm a woman, do you mean?" The question was coy indeed.

He put out a chalky palm. "All right, we can change the subject. There are other things to talk about.

"For instance, Brockhurst called. He wanted to put his own endorsement on you and I doing this DLF project, he said. Just a gentle shove in the direction yes. Not an order or anything like that. Just a suggestion."

"What about this elephant project? Am I supposed to drop it?"

"He didn't mention it."

"You know," she answered his earlier question. "What if she did see something? Something real?"

The phone rang.

It was an ordinary Touchtone telephone in basic black. It sat on the corner of her desk where it had always sat, a mute plastic object with the capability of connecting her to anyone in the world within seconds. She took it completely for granted, as did everyone else in the world who lived with this device. It was an arm's reach away, available, ready.

It rang again. Why did the sound fill her with dread? Something about the timing. She picked it up.

"Yes?"

"My dear," Wilbur Stapleton Brockhurst drawled, his voice a deep and extraordinarily slow rumble, close, yet somehow thin, a ponderous bass, tenuous as prayer. It came, they said, from talking with elephants.

"Mr. Brockhurst," she said. Brilliant, she thought. The sense of unreality grew stronger, that vague itch of displacement, time out of kilter, a scrim between her and the present.

His voice washed in, rumbled, fell, made deeper and deeper valleys in sound.

"You are concerned about the elephant project, my dear." He made a statement she did not answer. "Do not be concerned. The project will continue. I have something more for you, however."

To Cassie's ear there was the faintest of echoes, more overlapped more more*more,* a slight delay in the microwave amplifiers perhaps, a subtle loop in circuits struggling to handle a voice this deep and low.

"What . . . is it?" she said, forcing her own voice through a thickening veil of darkness.

"Tomorrow I want you to go down to La Jolla. L.R. has the particulars. It is very important, Cassie, that you go. You will meet with the . . . cetaceans. Whales, dolphins. It has been arranged."

"Does this have something to do with the elephant project?"

"Very important," he was saying.

She turned to Arnold as she cradled the phone. "Is the world getting stranger or is it my mood today?"

"The world," he said, "has always been strange. And we are in a peculiar business, Cassie. People pay us money to think about the future. At times I find that very odd."

"Yeah," she said. "And people pay Madame Glabro to think about the future, too. And what does she predict? The end of the world. No more future."

"Well," he grinned. "No more future for some of us. You Bibbles, on the other hand . . ."

She threw a pencil at him.

"You'd think it would be an earthquake. After all, this is California. We've been expecting the coast to fall into the ocean for eighty years."

Cassie was in her car, listening to her radio; a man had called into the station by telephone. The guest on the talk show was Madame Glabro, leader of the CoreLight Mission of the Visitors' Disciples.

The caller was faintly hostile, angry; his question had belligerent overtones. Yet he wasn't questioning the basic premise at all; he assumed the world was going to end. What concerned him was the *manner*.

Madame Glabro expressed assurance, an imperturbable confidence mingled with patience. "The world," she said in even, dulcet tones, as familiar and soothing as a set of Nutone door chimes, "is going to end. There will be fire and flood. There may also be satellites or meteors falling from the sky, nuclear meltdown, epidemic, plague, collapse of society, loss of faith. And earthquake. It doesn't matter, really. The fact is, the world will end. Thursday."

There was a long silence, filled with faint radio-frequency hiss, speaker hiss, an ether stuffed with energies. Finally the moderator broke in: "Let's take another call from the South Bay. Go ahead, please, you're on the air."

Cassie reached out to switch the radio off, but her fingers missed the knob, and she pulled her hand back as if it had been bitten: The hiss was serpent hiss, the venom already flowing in her, the numbness rising through wrists and ankles. The caller's voice was so familiar, ancient, that serpent-strike of recognition, though it was impossible, of course, that her father, thirty years dead and gone, would be calling in about the end of the world.

But it was his voice, filtered by telephone and radio, submerged in cosmic background noise, George St. Clair himself, myopic, absent and meek, patting her on the head when she was seven, or eight, and her sister Izzy, born that night of the sweeping skid in New Jersey, was toddling in diapers.

"This is George, in San Jose," the voice said.

"Yes, go ahead," the talk-show host urged, and George, in San Jose, went on, into an involuted question completely unlike her father, who was aware of his surroundings dimly perhaps, and not particularly good at inventing things, but who, nonetheless, had a way with words. This George, in San Jose, was not her father, George, at all, groping as he was through thickets of words, seeking the core of his own question, which appeared to be related to the economic situation, and had little to do with the end of the world.

Madame Glabro agreed. "Economics are irrelevant," she said primly. "By the end of the week there will be no economics to worry about, sir. If I were you I would be getting ready. Only the Bib . . . those chosen will be rescued."

"Then what, I mean, if the world is going to end," George began, faltered, started once more, faltered again, put on a spurt of speed, finished: "What should I do to be ready, then?"

"Oh," said Madame Glabro, and a vagueness swept through her tone. Cassie could see her wave her hand, dismissing the mundane. "I

17

don't know. Get some food together. It is said, 'Precious Bibbles would be there on peaks when the crafts came.' The world is faithless, Mr. . . . George. Only the Bibbles . . ."

"We have to take a break now," the host said quickly, cutting Madame Glabro off before she wound up into her patter. Cassie's hand made it to the off knob this time, and silence filled the car. Physics reasserted itself, the engine purred. But then, the engine of the family sedan had purred on the turnpike, too, before the tires squealed in a looping spiral over three lanes, and the car ended up ticking wisps of steam into November darkness all those years ago.

Her father, George, not this resurrected voice floating in the airwaves, but a solid daddy George, had died awkwardly, myopically, grotesquely, his left foot twisted in slick shower residue, head pitched forward against the toilet bowl.

Most likely he had said nothing as he fell, for he was always very quiet, and when he spoke it was almost always to himself. Yet there he was, neck broken, staring in bemused astonishment at the ceiling fixture.

"Where's Daddy?" Cassie asked, and in her throat she could feel the nine-year-old high pitch.

"Your father is gone." Martha was prim disapproval, brows sewn together.

"Gone?"

Martha had sighed then, a cold wind blowing across a desolate prairie.

"He's dead, Cassie. An accident."

She had thought then, of that neon sign, Goring and Goring, the funeral home under the turnpike, tilting on its side and sailing away into the November evening. A premonition.

Oddly, she easily found a place to park. Traffic was light, she noticed. She went in, changed, and spent her lunch hour performing the strenuous spirals and circles of aikido. She blanked her mind, concentrated on her movements, forgot her wide hips, her father's broken neck, the phantom memory-voice on the radio. She forgot the vanishing elephant, her future trip to La Jolla, the Dead Liberation Front. She developed an ignorance of the nature of time itself, attempting to feel in the muscle and bone of her body the cycles, inverted or not, of the world.

She grew unaware of the silence in the room, the scratch of bare feet on the mats, the soft undercurrents of breath, the movements of heavy cloth against her skin. For once she felt balanced, relaxed, in tune. They practiced *irimi-nage,* the entering throw, guiding the attacker into a tightening circle, lifting the lead arm and letting gravity relax it down into the chest. Done right, it was a very powerful throw; done wrong, as it usually was, it did nothing.

Today she did it right, relaxed and poised, weight distributed over her feet, her center down and her energy flowing where she wanted it.

Afterward she sat stretching, and talked to Kit.

"Have you ever had one of those days?" she asked, clasping the sole of her foot with her left hand, breathing into the stretch.

"You mean a day filled with coincidence?" Kit asked back, stretching too; Cassie could see the slender muscles on the back of her neck as she bent down, forehead to knee.

"Yeah," Cassie said. "One of those."

"Yes."

"I mean," Cassie went on. "I'm leaving for work and this wispy man shows up to recruit me for salvation from the end of the world, which, by the way, is going to be Thursday. I'm going to be picked up by flying saucer."

"Super," Kit said, laughing.

"Don't laugh. Then I get to work and the receptionist has seen a flying saucer. She's in shock and has to go home dosed up with Valium. Then I take down a sign in my office written on the wall and there's two words from this message from the stars the wispy guy gave me. Then on the way here I'm listening to the radio and the woman who has predicted the end of the world is on a talk show, and some man who sounds just like my father, who died in 1961, calls in. The phone rings at eerie times. I'm going to work on a project for the DLF, of which my mother is a kook member. One of those days."

Kit laughed again, leaning back on her arms. "You know the Sufi story about the man with the inexplicable life?"

Cassie shook her head.

"Mojud, a small official, runs into Khidr, the Sufi guide, a sort of elf figure dressed all in green. He tells Mojud to jump in the river, which he does, thinking to himself this is a pretty weird thing to do. He floats down the river, is fished out by a fisherman, goes to work for him for a couple of years. Khidr appears again and tells him to leave. He runs into a farmer, goes to work for him for a few years. Khidr shows up again, tells him to go be a merchant, then a grocer. He does these things, and as he does them, he gets tuned in to the mysteries, starts healing people, that sort of thing. Philosophers come, want to know how he learned all this stuff, how he started his career. "As a small official," he says. "You gave it up to devote yourself to self-mortification?" they ask. "Nope," he says. "Just gave it up." His biographers come and complain. "This doesn't explain where you got your strange gifts," they say. "Sure doesn't," he says. So they make up a wonderful life for him, because saints have to have wonderful lives. Listeners demand that. Anyway, the Sufis aren't allowed to talk about Khidr directly, so this story isn't true at all."

"Wonderful," Cassie said. "That's a terrific story. Do you think I've been running into Khidr?"

"I don't know," Kit said. "But I sure like the story."

"So do I, but have you noticed that there aren't many people here today? And traffic is light, too."

"No. Some days are like that."

"Yeah. Some days are like that."

It continued to be like that, full sun on the pale gray streets, serendipitous and gay, lights turning green as she approached, unaccountably smooth transitions, cars pulling away as she appeared, leaving her the spaces she needed. She shook her head. Banks of flowers bloomed in front of the stores, yellow acacias dusted the streets with golden pollen. The shade from pepper trees dappled the sidewalks, and a sweet eucalyptus smell filled the air. Twice she saw orioles flicker in the bushes along the road as she climbed toward the Palo Alto Hills and IF.

"IF," she said aloud. " 'If you can keep your head . . .' "

She got her cottage cheese from the refrigerator at the office, sliced an avocado onto it, and spooned it in, let the smooth creamy textures saturate her tongue, while she stared at the wall above her desk. The *Flaming Music* glowed in the brilliant afternoon light. The telephone sat mutely on her desk and refused to ring. She had no thoughts, no schemes. Her spoon clacked hollowly against the cardboard container as she scooped the last curds. A shaft of sun fell across her desk, and she watched the dustmotes dance in the currents of her breath. She put the cheese container down next to the pencil she had thrown at Arnold earlier. A Scripto, yellow, with a worn eraser. The point had broken when it hit the wall.

Cassie drifted. Idly she thought of her training on the Alpha-theta machine. Hypnogogic imagery, the reverie state just before sleep, associated with creativity. And, she ruefully thought, with episodic rage, psychosis.

20

A number of the researchers at IF had taken some biofeedback training on the machine, which picked up theta brain waves and fed them back to the subject as sound. Theta in the right ear, alpha in the left. Alpha was easy, relaxed alertness. Theta was harder, more elusive, but she'd been pretty good at it.

Images. The dustbeams danced before her, bright points in the air. Let them go. Hear the theta spike, don't jump at it, it was just like meditation before aikido practice, let all thoughts go. Whatever comes into the mind, notice it and let it go. Images. Dustmotes. Dance, spirals and circles, the curl of dustdevils in the desert, a wind. She felt a wind rise, a distant howl among the wires that slapped back and forth. Mountains in the distance, coming closer. There was a face, an old face with a slack mouth and open, staring eyes. It turned to her, the eyes were hollow. Not hollow, empty, pits in the skull, flickering with dark fires. A hand stretched out to her, cupped, and in the palm, a crystal, glowing with an inner light, a crystal coiled and multi-sided, geometric. The light was a power, herself. She was underwater, her own face, her own mouth open as her eyes, staring emptily. Her hair swirled slowly around her head, a random current, drowned.

She shuddered, and Arnold stuck his head through the door for the third time that day.

She stood slowly; her hand fumbled for the edge of her desk. Motes swirled in the sun, sparkled light danced behind her eyes, floaters glimpsed and gone as blood rushed to her head. The reverie images shredded and blew away, leaving only the aftertaste.

"You look like you saw a ghost. Are you all right?"

"A ghost? No, I . . . it's nothing. I was trying theta. Never mind." She swept her palm through a shaft of sun, and the dust scattered easily, past her hand, and rejoined the dance. "What is it?"

"Conference call. A Wesley Millet, the DLF project. In the conference room."

L.R. was there, to make the introductions, and then hurry off to Reggie's office to discuss a health care project.

Millet's voice, amplified though it was, sounded tinny and unreal, as though his adenoids were packed with used Reynolds Wrap. Cassie felt a high buzzing in her nose, a sympathetic response, perhaps. Or the early warning signs of a sneeze. She put her hand to her face.

"Egzguze me," she said.

"What's that?" the tin voice asked.

She sneezed.

"Sorry," she said.

There was an awkward silence. She and Arnold could not see their client, so they stared at the tiny amplifier on the desk instead, waiting for something to happen. Cassie imagined Wesley Millet staring at his amplifier as well, waiting.

"You have a project for IF," Arnold said at last. Inane, but something.

"Yes."

Another protracted silence; by osmosis a vague foreboding filled it.

"Could you give us some information on the nature of this project?" Dr. Deleuw urged.

"Communications," Wesley Millet said shortly. Cassie got the impression his attention was elsewhere. Abruptly his voice became stronger, more forceful. "A significant announcement to the world, a research breakthrough. An announcement that will have . . . implications. Consequences. There are social forces at work, special interests, even, shall I say, evil people who wish to manipulate events to their own ends. We need to have a precise idea of the nature of the consequences of our announcement, to understand how it might be used by others."

"Could you describe the nature of this announcement?" Cassie asked.

"No. Not just now. We have some matters to clear up first. You will be making a prediction for us . . ."

"Forecast," Arnold murmured.

"Eh?"

"Forecast. We don't make predictions, we make forecasts—trends, possibilities. Potentials. Dr. Deleuw means you will not get a definite, precise prediction."

22

"Yes, yes," Millet snapped peevishly. "Forecast."

"Any matters outside the scope of the project—negotiations about rates, proprietorship, and so forth—must be taken up with Dr. Hubletz. Now in terms of time, do you want a long-range forecast, or is this a local matter, temporally speaking."

"Oh, quite local," Millet assured them. "You have until Monday."

When Millet had rung off, Cassie scrutinized her fingernails, lips pursed. She grunted softly, picked at a fleck of foreign matter under her index nail. She sniffed; another sneeze was coming on. She tried a smile at Arnold.

Arnold tried a smile back. Neither felt particularly successful.

"Well," she said.

It was his turn to grunt. "Unh."

"The DLF," she said. "The Dead Liberation Front. A very old-fashioned name."

"We are old-fashioned people," he said. "Left brain people."

Cassie shook her head, hair flying. "No good." She sighed. "I spoze we'd better get to work. Sociometric analysis of DLF, attitudes toward. Belief systems, credibility, acceptance or rejection. Blah blah blah."

He too sighed, pushed himself up from the table. "I'll go set up some parameters for PEST."

She snorted. "Did you name that damn computer?"

"Tsk tsk. It's not a computer, it's a computer program. Project to Establish Statistical Truth. A very sophisticated futures modeling program, thank you. And yes, I did name it."

"It is a pest," she said.

He smiled then. "I know."

She ran the computer search. Information flowed across her screen; the DLF had many earmarks of a cult: monolithic leadership, a complex hierarchy with an inner circle. A list of names followed this fact, names not to be trifled with. *Who's who* names. A number of front organizations appeared to be part of the structure, but there was no definitive evidence. She ran some correlations. Key words emerged, merged: pronuclear groups (More nukes, less kooks); Protein for People; Right to Life.

None of it made much sense. On impulse she tried Glabro, Core-Light, Visitors' Disciples. Meaningless information scrolled upward. Size, geopolitical distribution, demographics, financing.

"Pah." She turned to stare out the window. The sun was setting behind the hills out there, gathering a twilight gloom, deeper on the

23

lawn that swept away toward them. The sun was faltering there above the mountaintop before snuffing itself in the Pacific, an orange egg laid by a blue-feathered sky.

There were no lights flying, no unidentified objects, no blond aliens in black suits. Further up was a crescent moon, a paring, twin-horned moon. Nothing unidentified, just sun and moon out there.

It didn't look like the end of the world at all. Just the end of yet another day.

She turned back to the console, tagged certain information for hard-copy printing. When she got to Madame Glabro again, she sank back in her chair, nibbling on her thumbnail. It reminded her of something.

Down on El Camino, a fifty-mile strip of car lots and fast-food restaurants, theaters, and stereo stores, a neon palm reached out, as though admonishing traffic to stop. Madame Glabro: Psychic. Palms, Tarot. Your Fortune Told.

Blue neon. When she passed at night, she noticed distantly that the lifeline in the palm crackled from time to time.

That made her smile. A shorted lifeline. The palm beckoned, come in, come in, I will tell all, though the future is short, it holds no secrets, not from me. Nor ether, nor ectoplasm, tea leaves, I Ching, speculum and crystal, stars and aura, time's arrow does not fly straight, *I* can see into the unknown; all things coexist. There are no mysteries, no impenetrable darknesses. I have friends in high places. All Bibbles. Come in and see.

Cassie shook her head, smiling. "Right," she said aloud. She looked out her window again. It was growing darker. The twin horns of the moon just showed themselves above the ragged fringe of trees on the coast range, bright arrowheads of white light. As she watched they dimmed faintly orange and sank. The sky was empty again, save for the brightest stars.

She might be a Bibble, but there were no galactic brothers up there watching over her. Nothing but empty space for unimaginable distances, meaningless trillions of miles, parsecs of hard vacuum with raisins of matter embedded within them, specks of dirt so distant from one another that if there was intelligent life there it would be years and years before a voice traveling at the speed of light could arrive with its faint greeting.

"We will be seeing you," Ronald Zsylk had said. "On the ships, if not before." There were no ships.

24

But there was a light, intolerably bright, a brilliant white glow over the hills, dagger sharp. "Uh-oh," she said softly. The light was moving, falling down the sky toward her, growing larger slowly, slowly.

She laughed. "Oh," she said aloud. She could hear it now, the rumble of jetliner engines on approach for SFO. It's landing lights vanished overhead. "I must be spooked," she said.

"What's that?" Arnold asked, head through the door again. "Hey, it's quarter of seven. I thought you might like some dinner?"

The boat of tofu floated in her soup, the clear broth in which a few sprigs of green onion twisted. For some reason, as the light glanced off the surface, and she considered the questions she wanted to ask him, the boat reminded her of a story.

"There was a crescent moon," she said abruptly. "Did you notice?"

He shook his head.

"It reminded me of the helmets the warriors in medieval Japan had, with crescent moons on them. There was a famous battle, at Dan-no-ura, told in the Heike legend. The Heike clan and the Genji were fighting for control of the country. The Heike had been running things, behind the scenes; they were a mariner clan, experienced with the sea. But at Dan-no-ura they misjudged the tide and were routed by the Genjis, who were from the mountains and had no experience with sailing. The Heike were smashed on the rocks or swept out to sea. They had the child emperor, Antoku, with them, eight years old, and when they saw the battle was lost his grandmother, Nii-dono, carried him overboard in her arms, telling him they were going to a fabulous capital under the sea."

Arnold didn't say anything. She carefully lifted the rectangle of tofu from the broth with her chopsticks, but the fragile white flesh broke, and two pieces fell back. She shrugged and ate one of the halves. "What about you?" she asked.

25

"Ah. Who am I, you mean? No one special, really. One of life's walking wounded. Had the expected midlife crisis. Got the expected divorce at the median divorce age, after two point seven children. Lived with a graduate student of mine for a while, then alone. Packed up and left my furnished rooms in New Haven because Brockhurst offered me a project and it looked more interesting than more anonymous students passing through my life, more papers to grade, more repetitions of the same material. I felt stale. I had a perfectly mapped life, but I ran out of map."

"That's *all?* Ha. Are you telling me you've *met* Brockhurst? Actually *met* him, in person?"

"Sure. He was around. I saw him a few times."

"What's he like?"

"Old."

"He'd be in his nineties now. I looked him up once, and all I could find was one old World War Two photograph. He was going in the door of an airplane, a big one—I couldn't tell what kind, just the door—and had just turned to wave at the camera. He was smiling, and the light from the flashbulb had caught his eyes so they looked weird, dark and empty with bright centers. Of course, it was real grainy, the picture, and it was hard to tell things, like how tall he was."

"Small."

"He invented something. Radar, something like that."

"Sonar. He holds some sonar patents. What about you?"

"What do you mean?"

"What about your life?"

"Oh. 'Bout like yours, I'm afraid. I was a brainy girl, and no one likes a brainy girl. Came from New Jersey, then Cincinnati, then college in New Jersey."

"Princeton." He grinned at her.

"How'd you know?"

"I looked it up. I was a brainy boy. Have you been married, Cassie?"

"Hasn't everyone?" He was a jogger, who ran around the lake over and over, lap after lap, before breakfast and the law office. He had a plump face and sweated freely; his jogger smile was shiny when he came back from his morning run, up before her and out of the house, running, leaving small waffle-squares in dust, mud, or the snow beside the road. He took her arm when they went out, proprietary, and guided her

26

deftly through the shoals life threw in her path. He could take her arm and joke as easily as he jogged. She would try to laugh, pretend she wasn't smarter than he was. He had his own law offices now and flashed around the world, jogging after the sun and slowly gaining, one of life's marathon winners, despite divorce.

"I know the type," Arnold said. "I used to be one."

"He was really very nice, in his way," she mused.

She swirled the leaves in her tea. "Can you read leaves?"

"No. Do you?"

"I see," she said, peering into the diminishing spirals of leaves, "the end of the world."

"Ah. And how is the world to end, then?"

"Circles. The world is to end in smaller and smaller circles, until there is nothing left."

He laughed. "Want to hear some music?"

"Sure."

The group at the Space Academy was called Up and Down Red and Yellow. Cosmic Rock: hard vacuum music for the twentieth century's end.

Inside, lighting shimmered with high-tech gloss, pipes, tubes, tables, and floor reflecting like a fun-house mirror. Everyone was a Bug-Eyed Monster: bulging, sagging, melting. The BEMs were dancing, dragging slow feet on the hard actinic floor while subsonics throbbed through their bones. The music was not loud, and the band barely moved on the stage, but it was the music of Anxiety, a low growling sound. Downer music, the music of technological death; the dance was called The Bummer.

"What do you think?" Arnold asked when they found a small table as far from the band as possible.

"I think we should be a lot more worried than we seem to be. Madame Glabro may have a point."

The couples pulled themselves across the dance floor without lifting their feet. They stared into unfocused distance, where the nightmare music made a tailored reality for each one. Cassie's attempt at humor was lost in all that desolation. She watched the band, and images of her own face, drowned in ghastly bluish light, hair swirled around her empty eyes, flashed before her.

The band was catatonic, their eyes as empty as the music they were making, its simple rhythm, monotonous lack of melody, almost robotic.

She saw again the image of the coiled crystal, facets gleaming with dull milky light. The music grew like a crystal, by accretion, adding layer after layer of misery.

"I've lost interest in dancing," Arnold said in a mock funereal voice, and Cassie tried to laugh, but the slow unpleasant beat stifled it.

"They're on something," she said. "The band."

He could barely hear her, his teeth on edge with the gritty vibrations. "Downers. Yellows. The name of the group. Up and Down Red and Yellow. They've been on television but you miss the subsonics, fortunately. I didn't realize they were this dreadful."

"Listen."

There *was* a song of sorts in all that torment and sullen rage. It was called "The Death of the Large Mammals." When the singing started, the dancers stopped moving and stared into the black-light spaces. Elephants drifted across their grazing lands, were shot from helicopters, poisoned at their watering places, sterilized, anesthetized, ambushed, rotted bones scattered so food could grow where they once roamed.

The black light flickered obscurely and the huge whales were harpooned, detonated, rendered. The sperm whales, the blues, the whites, and the dolphins were ripped with a depressed savage monotony akin to joy, but not joyous. Radioactive wastes were buried in the deepest seas, and whales rotted alive, skin peeling away in ragged flaps as big as houses, small teeth softened, eyes turned to milky pus, ulcers filling their bellies and mouths.

Cassie stared too, feeling suffocation and decay closing around her, mesmerized by the implacable hypnotic power of the music. The lead singer began to scream and abruptly burst into flame. The scream turned subtly to agony as the conflagration rose around him, as thick smoke rose above the bandstand, and red fires flickered at his black vinyl clothing.

The crowd in the huge room, fascinated by this illusion of immolation on the stage, did not move. Cassie breathed "My God" as the smell of that black smoke began to spread through the room, and a restless understanding came over the audience. As suddenly as lightning the dancers started screaming and clawed their way toward the doors. Two or three of the band members also started hesitantly offstage, stopped bemused to stare at their leader blackening, burning, his flesh crisping *in reality*. This was no illusion, the scream was an authentic suicide shout of exultation and despair. By now the floor around him was crackling, electric fires rippled in sheets across the metallic floor, and the amplifiers shot static and flame.

The ventilation system spread the stench of burning flesh, the thick greasy smoke, and then, abruptly, it all stopped. The lights came up, and the lead singer took a bow to the crowd, a lethargic, disinterested bow. The dancers who had been fooled stood foolishly by the door, grinned, came faltering back into the room, sought their tables. The band was taking a break.

Cassie and Arnold sat for a long time without saying anything. He fingered the ashtray on the black tabletop, twirled it, stopped it, twirled it again. It went around in circles. The circles grew smaller and smaller. The ashtray stopped by itself.

"Flaming music," Cassie said softly.

He nodded. "Let's get out of here."

After the fragmented murk of the Space Academy the streets appeared regular, geometric, clear. The air was fresh, the sky pale black above the lights. They walked and breathed together.

"Where are we?" Cassie looked around.

"Moving into the future at a steady speed. In fact, we're not far from a health club I belong to. Kind of a pretty place. Like to see it?"

She shrugged, sure, and they walked on, footsteps soft on the pavement, through pools of streetlight and ripples of darkness; the scents of spring flowers drifted around them, daffodils, and pittosporum, jasmine and wisteria. "What's your brand of health?"

"Mostly I swim. Long muscles, you know; I did a bit of swimming in college, distance, mainly. They have exercise rooms too, a gym, saunas, and *furo*."

"Japanese bath? Not your basic California hot tub?"

"Hmph. Same thing, only different. How about you?"

29

"I do aikido, a form of self-defense. Like all the Japanese martial arts, it's also a way of life. It's based on circles, and spirals, waves and wind."

"Good. You'll like this place." He bowed her through an entrance, a Japanese *torii* gate.

"Fantastic," she exclaimed softly. Pine scent filled the air, reminded her of something. Heavy stone lanterns were scattered around the small entrance garden. Black pine, a grassy mound, here and there a mugho beside a boulder. Running water somewhere out of sight splashed through the resin smells. They crossed a small wooden bridge, and to her right she could see lantern light reflected on the black surface of water. They passed through a bamboo grove, another small gate, stepping from flat rock to rock in a meandering path. He opened the gate with a ceremonial air, and they stepped through into a courtyard.

"It's beautiful," she said. They were on an elevated walkway of narrow boards, and the courtyard contained a sand-and-boulder dry-landscape garden, raked to resemble waves. Heavy chain hung down from the gutters at the four corners, to carry rainwater to the drains concealed under the sand. "What is this place?"

Arnold opened the door and they entered. "Originally," he said, "it was a Nichiren Shoshu monastery. They were a Buddhist sect that was very powerful in this country for a while."

"I remember. *Näm-myo-ho-renge-kyo.* Adherents of a rather aggressive form of conversion."

"Shakabuku: 'break and subdue.' "

"Yes. It was all very militant and bigoted—unlike the rest of Buddhism."

"Well, now they're gone. No more salvation through chanting. Salvation through better health, now."

The floor was tatami and springy under foot, the colors muted earth tones. A Buddha statue, eyes crinkled in amusement, homely face convulsed in nearly painful laughter, stood beside the door. "Look," she said, pointing. "His belly's shiny from rubbing. It's good luck." She rubbed the Buddha's belly. "What do you suppose he's laughing at?"

"He knows something we don't. You know, on the Extended North Carolina Scale for measuring the depth of hypnotic trance there is a stage that starts around fifty, pretty far in, called 'Awareness of the Joke.' By that time the experimenter has become just a voice, peacefulness has become a meaningless concept, time has become meaningless, even the sense of identity has begun to submerge in a feeling of oneness and infinite potentiality. The 'joke' seems to be that the subject should engage in such strange activities, and some 'higher' aspect of himself is amused at it." He gestured at the laughing Buddha. "Maybe he's hypnotized."

"Or maybe we are." She went on across the room. One or two other people came through on their way out, but said nothing to them. She stared at a scroll, a landscape that unfurled vertically, down jagged cliffs of hard-edged rock where determined pines twisted in their effort to hang on. A path wound through that mountain, and a waterfall that appeared and vanished again, to fall at last into a river, and beside that, a pavilion. Two small people, half obscured by the railing of the building, were chatting inside.

Arnold pointed. "Look." A tiny man, bent with either the effort or years, climbed the path where it swung into view for a moment between boulders. He had planted his staff firmly on the path, and pushed himself ahead, a wide-brimmed hat low over his eyes.

"He's left the other two down there in the pavilion," she said. "Gone on alone, up the mountain."

"He'll never get anywhere, either. It's a picture."

"That's the point. Always on the road. You know, I went to Machu Picchu once, years ago. The pines outside reminded me."

As the train had thumped up the steep mountain, most of the passengers were staring at the floor between their feet. Outside was frightening; the train crawled along the edge of cliffs, mountain falling away on the left, rising precipitously on the right, close enough to reach out the window and touch. It was more comfortable to watch the other passengers, which Cassie did, and made up stories about them. An American couple with a young boy, about eight. He would be well-traveled. This year Machu Picchu, next to Sri Lanka.

An elderly couple from Peking, wearing Mao jackets, sat in the front, holding hands and staring out the window. They were the only ones to look out at the cloud tops, dark pines, and jagged rock on the left. He was a T'ai Ch'i master, she thought, his face serene, his unblinking eyes taking in the rugged peaks, so similar to Tien Shan, the soft greens and browns tattered by cloud and fog.

No, he was probably an electrical engineer who had spent most of his life in a laboratory, wore thick glasses, and had bad lungs. (His glasses were put away now, and the landscape was a blur, which was why he wasn't frightened.) His wife would be the T'ai Ch'i master. Cassie smiled. She liked that scenario better.

31

"Well?" Arnold urged.

"Well, the train broke down. It took three or four hours before the engineer could fix it, and I started talking to the old couple. The only thing I got right was that they were from China."

"Happens to me all the time, can't even predict the present. So they were not T'ai Ch'i masters?"

"No, and he wasn't an engineer, either. He was a stone mason. He was sent to Machu Picchu because the masonry of the ruins is exceptional. Incredible, even, considering the Incas didn't even invent the wheel. And his wife was a poet, an expert on Li Po, a T'ang Dynasty poet. She was reading Neruda in Chinese, a poem called 'The Heights of Machu Picchu.'"

"Neruda?"

"A poet. Anyway, it was like that." She put her finger close to the bent figure struggling up the mountain. "The train made a lot of noise, and I was sitting there, watching the Chinese couple because they were the only ones looking outside, and I got this feeling, a premonition that something was about to happen. It was very strange, eerie, but I had just looked out myself, and down, and I thought that was it, that I was scared. And then the noise stopped. Silence, just like that, no engine. And the train started to roll backward. Nobody said a word then, but you could feel it run through the car, through the people, the shock of it, like wind over wheat. Everyone just stared stright ahead, tense, expecting the worst. Everyone but that old Chinese couple. They just stared out the window as though nothing had happened. She had her Neruda open on her lap, her hand resting on it. Such thin, delicate fingers. I was across the aisle from them, on the mountainside, and could almost feel the rock and dirt flying past the window beside me, flying the wrong way. And that old couple just sat there as though going backward down the mountain out of control was a perfectly normal part of the trip."

Arnold had been watching her attentively, his head tilted to one side, so the lock of gray hair fell across his forehead. "That's quite a story. What about the feeling you had, that something was going to happen?"

"Oh, like I said, I thought it was fear. I'd looked out the window, past the couple, and seen cloud tops, distant peaks. That's all." She turned her back on the old hermit climbing the steep path.

"Still, perhaps you're psychic."

She laughed, a short bark. "Don't be silly. I've been tested. I'm not psychic."

"I wouldn't be so sure. It doesn't often work in the laboratory, you know. Motivation is low. But it is related to coincidence, and you've had one of those days."

"Hmph."

They took a walk, around the grounds, through a series of courts, more gardens, hills, streams, stones, water. Luminous carp drifted through the water under an arched bridge, bamboo rustled its leaves in the light breeze.

"Quite a contrast to the Space Academy, isn't it?" she said.

"Yes," he answered. "A contrast."

They wandered back into the building, back to the scroll. A man was bent over it, peering at the pilgrim through thick glasses.

"It's a lovely scroll, isn't it?" Cassie asked, and the man jumped, turned. His look was frightened for a moment, and the look frightened Cassie. He looked so much like her stepfather. Arnold took her arm, reassured her.

"Yes," the man said, taking his glasses off and rubbing them. "Lovely. Hello, Arnold."

"Dash. This is Cassie St. Clair. Cassie, this is Dashwood Crowley. He's a Satanist."

That surprised her. "A peculiar profession."

"Oh, Arnold is kidding you. I have a degree in magic and thaumaturgy is what he means. From Berkeley. I study what used to be called the 'occult.' That is, I study it scientifically, or try to. It's really a branch of sociology, though. Belief, you see, has power that appears magical at times."

"Do you think the world is going to end Thursday?" She couldn't resist.

"Ah, you refer to Madame Glabro and her group. If the world doesn't end, hers will, in a way, won't it?"

She laughed. "You have a point there."

"Yes, I do." He pointed at the figure in the scroll. "You see that man? He's a student of the same things, a Taoist sage, very powerful magician, but very lonely. It's hard work, studying mysteries, and hard to keep friends. Not like those two down there. Bureaucrats! They stayed behind, drinking rice wine. They don't care about magic."

"Are you a Taoist sage, then?"

33

"To tell you the truth, I wasn't looking at the painting at all. I have a toothache, and I was pressing my jaw, here, and trying out an old spell against toothache. Johann Weyer's charm, from the 1568 edition of *De Praestigiis Daemonum et Incantionibus ac Veneficiis:* 'Galbes, galbat, galdes, galdat . . .' "

"Fantastic!" Arnold exclaimed. "Did it work?"

"No, alas, it didn't. So then I tried an old Accadian incantation, the seven gods of the great heavens, great earth, igneous spheres, and so on. Malevolent gods, phantoms, conjure, conjure! I called on Utuq, Alal, Gigim, and Maskim, the Chaldean talisman against the entrance of demons, but they failed to show up."

Cassie and Arnold were both laughing, now.

"Fortunately," the mage went on, "I always carry my magic vial," producing it from a secret pocket and opening it, "which contains a magical substance known as 'aspirin.' " He put two in his mouth. "Tomorrow I will go to a shaman called, in this culture, a 'dentist.' "

"Wonderful, absolutely wonderful. Can you read the future also?" Cassie asked.

"Depends," Dash said. "But if you'll excuse me, I must get home. This tooth hurts like the very devil . . ."

"Perhaps I have led a sheltered life," Cassie said, "but there always seems to be something that surprises me."

"How do you mean?" Arnold took her arm, and it was the way her husband used to take it. Quickly now, Cassie suppressed her annoyance. They walked this time in a different direction.

"Well, I am in the futures business, so to speak, and should be prepared for anything. Yet tonight I met a magician in the heart of the scientific age. There's always something. Every time you think you've grasped the nature of the world there's something else underneath." She slid her elbow out of Arnold's grasp, and asked, "Where are we going?"

34

"Thought you'd like to see the pool, some of the other rooms."

"Okay. Do you know the story about William James and the turtles?"

It was his turn to be surprised. "Where does that come from?"

She shrugged. "I was just thinking about it, layers of meaning." She lost herself in the story, in the atmosphere of gas lamps and potted palm fronds, in the Victorian clutter of horsehair furniture and bewhiskered men, in tassels and bric-a-brac and dark velvet.

"A woman came up to Dr. James after the lecture he had given on the nature of the universe. 'Oh, Dr. James, I did so enjoy your lecture, really I did,' she said. 'But I'm afraid you've got it all wrong. The universe isn't like that at all. Not like you said, no.'"

They stepped from tatami to tile.

Cassie tossed her hair and looked, forgetting for the moment her anecdote. The pool was very blue and filled with people, even at this late hour. A volleyball game was in progress, and the room clattered with the peculiar echo of large, enclosed, flooded spaces. Shouts banged off the walls, doubled, fell dead in corners. Laughter riffled up the tile walls. Someone shouted "Damn!" and although it must have come from one of the players, since she could see the missed goal, it sounded from behind her, and she turned.

"What?" she shouted into Arnold's ear, her voice lost even in that small distance.

He smiled and pointed around the room, mouthing Can't hear. She thought for a moment he'd said something else, but a ricochet of squeals danced past. She thought about what it would be like underwater and about tomorrow, in La Jolla. She would try to talk to the whales. Their world would be so different, would give them strange ideas. Even with the primitive communications established with them so far, elaborate as the equipment, the technology was, no one really understood them.

More images drifted through her mind. She felt a distant fear, one she could observe as well as witness. The sea would be rich in sounds. Creaks, pulses, and thuds—these were all clean information with a definite source, and a meaning, she knew that. She saw an orca pause to feed, casually. She could see the unnaturally pink, very human interior of his mouth.

Distantly she felt that annoying tug on her elbow again, saw her ex-husband's face, and she shook her arm, briskly this time.

"Cassie!"

35

"Oh," she said aloud. She smiled at Arnold and they stepped back onto tatami, leaving the baffling mingle of sounds behind. "So William James said, 'And what exactly is the universe like, madame?' " James had been putting the woman on, Cassie knew that, but her own universe was fragmented just now, a babble of shouts and echoes, odd light spiking off the choppy pool water they had just left behind.

"Okay?" he asked.

"Sure. A little dizzy, is all."

"Yeah," he said. "Loud in there. You get used to it, when you're playing the game. I know a place we can sit down."

The room was quiet, filled with abandoned exercise machines. She wiggled her toes against a metal plate, which vibrated gently against her arches, soothingly.

"Why Dr. James," the woman had said. "The earth rests on the back of a gigantic turtle. Everyone knows that. We don't live on a ball that rotates. We'd fly off. Absurd!"

"Do you believe the earth goes around the sun?" Cassie asked.

"How could it?" Arnold said. "The sun rises, doesn't it? And sets. So it must go up and down, like a yo-yo."

"A yo-yo? Is this a joke, Arnold? Did you tell a joke?"

"Well, it's a very big yo-yo, so it takes all day. Celestial mechanics, you see. Simple, really."

"What does it do at night, then? Got you there."

"Oh, no. It spins, hits bottom and spins all night. It's called 'Cradle the Baby' or something. A little tug in the morning and back up it comes."

"Ah! Who tugs the string. William James tried that too. 'If your theory is correct, madame, what does the turtle stand on?' 'Why, another turtle, of course,' she said."

Arnold grinned at her. "You were named after Cassandra, correct? The gift of prophecy. Cassandra, dragged from the altar of Athena by Ajax the Locrian, dragged away from her sacred duties and raped. Tsk, tsk."

She saw her face, staring eyes, drowned hair swirled around her face, and the fear stabbed through her. Her stepfather's face grinned at her, a malevolent leer, leaning into a circle of light. She threw something, a hairbrush, and glass broke. Ajax the Locrian. Dragged from the altar, a coiled crystal, aglow with milky light.

She took her feet off the metal plate. "No," she said, very far away. "It's just Cassie. Cassandra was given the gift of prophecy for that rape,

36

a terrible gift, because no one would believe her. It was a curse, and I wouldn't want it. Besides," she turned to him, "you didn't answer. Who tugs the string?"

"Oh, that," he said. "Nobody."

"All right, and William James said, 'What does the second turtle stand on?' She answered, 'Why, the second turtle stands on the back of another, larger turtle, of course.' "

Arnold nodded. "Yes?"

Her fear receded, faded, vanished. " 'But, madame, what does *that* turtle stand on?' 'Oh, no, no, no,' the lady crowed. 'It's no use, Dr. James. It's turtles *all the way down!*' "

TUESDAY

RAPTURE OF THE SHALLOWS

6:3 And when he had opened the second seal I heard the second beast say, Come and See.

She took the new airship shuttle to La Jolla, a strange triangular dirigible that floated almost silently above the cortical folds of the mountains. Not as fast as the jets, but more economical, roomier, more generous with time and space. Light glanced off the observatory dome at Mount Hamilton, high above the shreds of fog still hovering over the bay, the dense building, and traffic-clogged streets. She leaned back in her seat and gazed out the window at the hills dropping away to Monterey Bay: white fishing boats on the blue surface.

A mockingbird had flashed white and gray as she walked out to the aircraft, a flutter of motion amid fog-damp scents and early light. Now she stared out at the leisurely passage of landscape. An orca moved through blue gray waters with the same leisurely precision, an identical lack of expression.

She had instructions from Dr. Hubletz; too brief, too enigmatic. Go to La Jolla. Meet Mr. Bade. Talk to the cetaceans you will meet there.

Not much to go on.

"Excuse me." The steward leaned over her. "You have a call, Ms. St. Clair. The booths are in the back, number three."

As Carmel vanished astern she stared out the port of the telephone booth at the empty horizon: water all the way to Japan. Distant haze blurred the edges of sky and sea, blending them, blues fading together. She picked up the handset.

"Hello." Here the soft susurrus of the turbines was more insistent, though damped with insulation. She could feel the high vibration in her body, a tightening in her chest.

"Good morning, my dear." Brockhurst's slow drawl crawled over the distances between them. It wavered in and out, frail and uncertain.

Cassie stroked her cheek lightly with a fingernail, barely aware of a phantom itch.

"You've met Wesley Millet. Now you will meet the cetacean." Cassie did not answer Brockhurst's statements, instead listening to the rush of silence between them. "I call to tell you ... to pay attention. Things are not as simple as they appear. You know that, of course. Things are approaching a cusp, events ... Well, just pay attention. Don't judge, not yet. Listen behind what the orca says." He fell silent again; it was as close to incoherent as she had ever heard him all these years of occasional phone calls.

Where was he? She nearly spoke out loud, something to fill that silence stretching taut between them, but instead remembered her family moving from New Jersey to Cincinnati, the rolling green hills and a thick brown river. The spring in Cincinnati was filled with strong smells, the heat lifting water from the river to drench the air. Cassie used to find baby rabbits in burrows on the hillsides. The long grass had been filled with insect whine.

She frowned, hearing the blend of sounds the turbines made, the rush of air, the whir of blades turning inside metallic housings. "I'll try," she said into the space.

"That's all I ask." Brockhurst hung up.

She listened to the disconnected tone absently. Far away monks were chanting, and she had to tilt her head to discern the language. For a moment it seemed like Latin, then it was gone, only a dial tone, and in front of her eyes the empty Pacific, vast and void as sky. She went back to her seat and watched the coastline drift by, past Big Sur, where cliffs tumbled sheer to the sea. Four thousand feet below she could see tiny surf break on fractured rock, frozen by distance, flat as the back of a turtle. "All the way down," she said aloud.

"Pardon?" The stewardess passing.

Cassie smiled. "Just talking to myself."

She leaned back with a sigh, the short night's sleep catching her. Her eyes dropped closed. She saw Arnold Deleuw, driving her home through the late streets drained of traffic under a dark sky. Her feet still tingled from the foot massage machine; the fragmented water of the pool, the laughter and shouted echoes still rattled in her mind as the car thumped under pools of streetlight and shadows. No moon. No chance to meet. She thought of her lover seeking out her house in the darkness, no moon to guide him. He would carve his name in her gate a hundred

42

nights proving his devotion, for she was a lady of the court, and not for just any man, though daily her beauty faded like the pale flowers.

He came every night, through seasons, all the nights but one, for he died then, and her soul was unforgiven, would wander forever. That was the way the Nō drama told of her, an old woman, withered and lost, wandering, desolate and sick, until his shade would forgive her, the Buddhist monks would chant the proper sutras for her rest: no moon. No chance to meet.

She had written that poem, her brush hissing against the rice paper, drawing the smooth connected *kana* down the page, a court lady famous for her beauty. It was a pun in Japanese, a play on moon and chance, the same sound: no moon, no chance. They could not meet, and she combed her long black hair endlessly, with a tortoiseshell comb, in flickering oil light, her shadow leaping on the white shoji paper with each brush. Her name was Komachi, and her life was a path, across a bridge of dreams.

Cassie loved Komachi's poems, their melancholy and pathos, their delicacy, their complexity in the classical Japanese. She breathed deeply once in her sleep, the dream of Komachi filling her with that very sense of transience, impermanence, the flickering of days that had never happened, had happened to someone else, would happen to her. The shadings of those alternations of light and dark became the smooth thrust of flukes and the silence of rest after, drifting near the surface, the soft flutter of one eyelid closing on itself and the brain dreaming, herself dreaming, the whales dozing near the air, rising easily to blow and breathe, asleep and dreaming.

Her own eyes fluttered open, and the green shape tilted swiftly on its side and flew away at an impossible angle and speed, flashing lights, a chromatic arpeggio in her eye, and she was filled with a profound paralysis, a sad lethargy that pinned her to her seat, eyelids drooping, a helpless and paradoxical kind of sadness and joy.

When she awoke again it was all a dream, of course, and San Simeon was drifting astern. She watched lazily out the window: Moro Bay, San Luis Obispo, Point Conception. The sun blinded her, and she drew the shade. Breakfast arrived, and she ate.

The orca too had dozed and now fed, slashing rapidly through a group of dolphins, tearing one apart and feeding. Then he dove and screamed, deep this time, across the Pacific along the temperature interface. Then he rose into the air, felt the position of the sun, water

43

temperature, the moving plankton as it drifted downward in response to increasing light. His screams were answered, a rapid dialogue with long pauses.

The dolphins grieved and played. Two he ordered to follow him, and they did, rubbing now against his vast black side, his white belly, playing sensual games with him, chattering laughter. They were his heralds, his scouts.

He was implacable as he moved through the water, indifferent to the dolphins' games. When his answer came from the Mariana Trench there was a sense of something vast, imponderable, and ancient in it; if he had had a flexible neck he might have nodded at that answer, but instead he creaked and turned toward the coast, trailed by the dolphin pair. The water now tasted thick with human spoor and waste as it shallowed.

When she awoke again, the dirigible was drifting dowward into La Jolla, and all the elements of her dreaming merged, the orca-sense, the whirling rapid chromatics outside the window, the persona of Ono no Komachi whose lovers languished and died for her; merged, and vanished utterly.

At La Jolla she walked through the lobby of the airport toward the exit, passing the ProNuke table. The ProNuke lobby's motto: "Feed Jane Fonda to the Whales," riffled through her mind as she deftly side-stepped the earnest, neatly dressed and well-scrubbed young man handing out literature, and her eyes met someone else's. She felt, for a fraction of a moment, a sharp stab of recognition: some sense of urgency, a threat she did not understand. Then it was gone, the contact broken.

Beside the front door to the terminal the Friends of the Sea were handing out their own literature. A sheaf was pressed into her hand, and she took it absently, still puzzling over the man she had just seen, the aura of familiarity about that heavy, athletic face.

"Are you aware that nuclear power plants are killing the whales?" a voice asked.

"What?" She had paused at the door and hadn't understood.

"The ProNuke people," a young woman gestured back, to the interior of the lobby. "They want to kill the whales. Whales are intelligent, and nuclear power is dangerous. Did you know that those people want to build power plants on the ocean floor? They say it's safer there. Safer for them, of course. Safer for people. Not for the whales."

"Yes." Cassie smiled absently. "I know."

The young woman was bitter. "Do you know what they say? They say, 'More nukes, less kooks.' Us kooks, we want to protect the planet. They've been saying it for years, and they just won't learn."

"Yes, it's terrible," Cassie agreed. She stuffed the literature into her bag and went outside.

Sun glanced crystal-bright off the water, and she sweated in the unfamiliar heat. The sea was still empty before her, as it had been from the aircraft window.

"Have you ever talked to them before?" the man said. His name was Bade, and he turned away even before she said no, leading her down the steps toward the end of the Scripps Pier where the tanks were.

"We call this the embassy," he said. The rectangular concrete building was painted a pleasant blue, soft and soothing after the harshness of the sunlight backing off the waves coming in.

"Ah," she said. "Embassy. Theirs or ours?"

He shrugged. "Both?" Lifting an eyebrow. "A place where we can talk together." He looked at her more carefully now. "Why do you ask that?"

"Talking is tricky business. So much can happen to information between transmitter and receiver, especially when the two are as alien to one another as we are. I wondered if it was important to the cetaceans, whether this place was ours or theirs; and whether, if this is their embassy, we had one underwater somewhere."

"Hmm. This way."

The door opened softly, and they entered the embassy: dim-lit vestibule, a turning to the stairs, and at bottom the room, huge glass wall facing into the blue depths of the tanks, south and west.

"He isn't here yet," Mr. Bade told her. "Won't be long though. The gillis came in a half hour ago, so he'll be here soon."

He pointed into the west tank, and she saw them, just surfacing and plunging down again, crossing in front of the glass. They saw her there and reversed, rolling on their sides, twisting. Hidden speakers burst into a high-pitched chattering: Delphinese. "What are gillis?" she asked, waving to them.

"Pacific bottle-nose dolphins, *Tursiops gilli.* It's like calling us saps for *Homo sapiens,* but that's what we call them. They seem to be very bright and energetic, but it's the orca you will spend most of the time talking to. It's not . . . easy, talking to them. I suppose you know that." He looked embarrassed.

"Not really. What do I have to do?"

He looked at her curiously then, his pleasant, confident, and uninspired face expressing a detached interest. She felt bad news in that look somehow, apprehension. "Why, you have to get in with them, of course." He waved at the tank, where the dolphins hung, staring at the two of them. The speakers filled the air with extremely high-pitched chittering and creaks.

"In with them?"

"Not for long, just enough for them to 'see' you, or rather, to sound you out."

"Can *you* understand them? Really understand them, I mean, not just words?"

He thought for a moment, considering. "No," he said at last. "No, I don't think so. Their language is ultrasonic, of course, and we need the computers to get even a rough idea. There is a lot we don't know."

"Then why do I have to get in with them? I'll need the computers even to talk."

Oh, she knew why, the sensual medium of ocean water making contact real, a pervasive, no, *invasive* understanding for them and not for her, awkward air creature. She knew why, but she wanted to keep this man talking, keep the human contact, tenuous as she knew it to be.

"They need a sonar picture of you," Mr. Bade was saying. "They can, we believe, read your mood, your intentions to some extent, in the picture they get back from your body. They won't talk at all unless they get that picture. Some people won't get in and don't get anywhere. Sorry." He laughed. "I'm afraid they don't think we're very bright. It's a feeling I get from time to time."

"It's okay, I guess. I'll get in with them." She looked around the room, thinking of the pool at the health spa, the confusion of sound, uneasy echoes, turbulence; a contrast with this soundproofed, comfortable room, the clear blue water with the two dolphins now racing in circles, playful. "Where's all the machinery, though? The computers and stuff?"

He nodded. "There are twenty-five remote pickups in this room that triangulate the speaker, in case there is more than one here, analyze the language, translating automatically, for the most part, into Cetacean. Or, more precisely, the semi-Cetacean we have worked out with the dolphins and orcas. I don't know if we will ever really understand them completely, no matter how sophisticated the computers get. The machines are mostly up at the institute, and the people who work with them. It's sometimes done by feel, the translating, like an art or something. I don't know, I'm not a linguist. But they can vocalize in three different ways, for example, all at the same time, and a large part of their communication system is made up of three-dimensional sound pictures, re-created sonar echoes and so forth; sometimes stereo, too. Very intricate and difficult. We've only had a few years of actual communication with them at all, and it's still pretty primitive, I'm afraid. There's a lot of work to be done yet." He paused at a soft chiming sound.

"That'll be him. Shall we go up?"

It was just like that, a phrase that sent her tumbling: "go up." She was seated on a platform in the dark. It was underground, the air filled with earth smells, mingled with smoke and vapor. She was preparing to go into a trance, her back straight, lids drooped over her eyes in spite of the absolute darkness.

Outside was the hot day, the hard light, and in *here,* in her skull, the river valley of her childhood, thick with forsythia in spring. In her skull too was the child-emperor Antoku sinking under the waves of the Inland sea, bloody water closing over his head, salt filling his mouth as he tried to cry out in spite of all his stoical training; and the memory of herself, dead eyes staring, hair swirled slow-motion around her drowned head. Fear.

A scream rose in her throat; she wanted to cry out, to struggle; for a moment it was salt water, bloody water filled with pain, rushing into her mouth. Then it was earth, damp moldering earth, burial ground. This chamber was too small, too close, suffocating. There couldn't be enough air, she couldn't breathe. Her mouth opened, her throat tightened with the scream.

There was no sound. She held her muscles tightly for a moment,

47

the jaw joint clenched tightly, temporomandibular, and the scream was stillborn. Then she inhaled slowly and fell into the trance, just like that, as easily as falling asleep.

The darkness filled with shapes, forms, deep color. She saw the Persian fleet forming a bridge across waters that surged against the wooden sides of the boats. They rocked uneasily, the water troubled, thick with turbid currents.

The fleet vanished, swept away in the muddy air. Now she saw far below, in the tiny harbor, the water grow calm, reflection smooth, and Apollo swam into that clear lagoon, his smooth gray sides gliding, a dolphin then, come to name his shrine up here, and she was his prophetess, seated cross-legged in the earth, the cramped cave. She was the Delphic oracle, reading futures in the earth, the vapors.

Apollo was alongside the Cretan boat, sailing up the Gulf of Corinth, moving easily through the waves, and she waited in the dark, watching the shapes, unable to distinguish past from future, unsure even there was a distinction to be made. She saw herself from a vast distance turn away from a glass wall and move toward some stairs, following a man.

That vision blurred as well, and she saw suppliants threatening, turning away with curses hard in their mouths, despair dragging their steps, offerings of gold and bronze abandoned, a thousand lives entangled inside her.

Her divine trance faded, the Persian fleet gone, the swift dolphin-shape Apollo gone, the Cretan ship and all those anxious suppliants, shredded away into patterns of light and shadow, abstract and meaningless. She uncrossed her legs and straightened, an ordinary person who forgot as she moved everything she had said, all the cryptic words, the phrases priests puzzled over. She climbed out, into the light.

"You can change here," Mr. Bade told her, pointing to a room off the vestibule. She nodded, dreamy from the vision.

The wet suit was thin, elastic, and light. When she came outside he whistled approval, quickly stifled. "You look good," he said.

"Thanks," she said. Body heat was warming the suit, and pricks of sweat started on her back and ribs. "But will he think so?"

He smiled. "I suppose it depends on his sonar, and what he understands about people. Are you ready?"

"Yes."

He led the way to the south pool. The two gillis were there, waiting for her.

48

"Where's the orca?"

"He's on his way, don't worry. This meeting is to be at one o'clock, and they have an uncanny time sense when they want. He'll be on time. For now just get in with the gillis and let them get to know you. They'll pass it on."

"I don't get it." Sweat tickled her lower back, but she shrank away from the water.

"Orcas are big. Up to thirty feet. It's easier for us to relate to creatures more our own size, at least at first. Dolphins and people have a long history together. Not always good, of course, that history, not on our side at least, but for some reason they don't carry a grudge toward us. They seem, in fact, to, well, to *cherish* us. You've heard the stories I suppose, times when dolphins rescued shipwrecked people, that sort of thing."

She nodded.

"Good. Then you know the dolphins won't hurt you. The orcas are predators, though, and we still don't really understand them. But it is clear the dolphins pass on information to them, do some interpreting for them and so on. When they can keep their minds on the work, that is." He gestured toward the pool, where the two gray bodies were involved in an intricate and obviously erotic three-dimensional dance.

"I'm afraid they think about sex most of the time." He smiled apologetically.

"Maybe they know something we don't," she said.

"Hmph." He looked out to sea. "There he is."

She followed that look and saw the black-and-white shape leap once and smack the surface.

Even from this far away she could see that Bade was right. The orca was big, more than thirty feet, she guessed. She turned and dove abruptly into the pool.

The water closed around her and she fell through blue patterns, eyes closed against salt. Her wet suit absorbed the moisture, warming, enfolding, and she rose through the multitude of bubbles to break the surface. When her vision cleared she saw the dolphins, heads in the air, tilted in a humanly quizzical way, watching. The eyes were small, brown, and bright. One of them lowered beneath the surface and gently nuzzled at her legs. She kicked lazily, moving over the surface.

She could feel pulses in the water through her suit, could hear very faintly, at the upper limit of hearing, the high-pitched whistles as the pair dove and swam around her. Slowly she relaxed, let the water cradle her, let the muscles of her stomach and back relax. She rolled onto her back and floated there, staring up at the sky, mind empty. Her hands trailed in the water, fingers cupped downward, pale jellyfish. Soft waves rocked her.

The sun was high, dazzling, in a sky as empty as her mind. Hunger approached her, nuzzled at awareness, receded. Gray bodies of an incredible tough smoothness skimmed under her limp fingers, along her legs, thighs, a light caress, a distant tickle. Rocked, enfolded, stroked, held warm: The blending was slow, the transition unnoticed, as sounds pulsed through her flesh, reflected off bone, air in her lungs, the smoothing turmoil in her abdomen. At each exhale her body sank, and one of the dolphins would lift her up again, coasting under her back. She floated away on a long tether of dream, softly jostled, supported, so what she saw against her closed eyelids, the orange light there, was like the past, but was not past. She drifted into it, a time that might be future and might be fantasy.

She should know these people. They were familiar, something in the postures, the set of shoulders. The faces were drawn, solemn, exhausted, the eyes hooded. One wore dark glasses, and when he took them off she could see the eyes then; they were blind, uncertain, moved but did not see. She knew him, but could not recognize. He spoke to her, voice low. "Lead me," he said. "Lead me."

He reached out his hand, and she took it. The fingers were hard, warm, gnarled as roots, and strong. She could feel that strength in them, not physical exactly, but confident; it made her doubt the pleading in the voice, the dependence.

Even as she said "Where?" she thought this was daydream, reverie, this man, these shadowed faces, and even as the hand pointed toward a distant circle of light where others were waiting, she thought this was a curious fantasy, this sense of leading an old man toward light, this wish for that kind of power. She held the thick, twisted fingers carefully and led the way. He followed easily, trusting her. A voice annoyed her. "What?" she said aloud, opening her eyes into the bright sun.

"I said you can come out now. He's waiting for you at the breakwater." She squinted up into Mr. Bade's face.

"Ah." She climbed out of the pool, stroking the dolphins as they passed her, lightly down the dorsal ridge, though she could not feel spine under that tough, resilient skin.

They chittered and nodded at her as she stood on the cement.

"They like you," he said, wrapping a towel around her. She dried her face and hair. "That's strong approval, as strong as I've seen."

They pushed vertically out of the water, nodding their stiff neckless heads and bodies, whistling, making raspberries from their blowholes. She wanted to think they were smiling, that that fixed grimace was a warm and human gesture, but resisted. They were alien, too different, though she felt their approval.

In the shower she turned, letting salt sluice away from her, steam rise around her. She saw that blind old man once more, holding out his hand. Now he was holding something, a small, coiled white object, milky texture shifting inside, but she couldn't tell at first what it was. Too much steam here, too much mist in the air. It was faceted, coiled, the crystal. A feeling of power in it, of focus just out of reach.

"Bah," she said, turning to let the water slide down the front. "Damn crystal. Doesn't mean anything."

Once she was an experimental subject in an ESP test. The experimenter had tried to teach her how to train her talent, but it hadn't taken, she could never really believe in the stuff—it was always coincidence, she felt, that explained the curious dovetailing of her reveries and reality . The experiment, as far as she was concerned, had been a failure, though the psychologist told her that her failure to predict cards had been statistically significant, that a kind of negative talent had been operating. She didn't trust statistics, though, and hadn't gone back.

It was something to live with, this sense that what she had was a kind of occasional luck at predicting, a subconscious rapid data processing (or something) that let her see, in what she knew were inspired guesses, a bit of what was coming out of the future. Guesses, and a lot of data, theoretical knowledge, painfully refined methodology, and an overactive imagination.

Which never explained the absolutely sharp *reality* of these visions, the unpleasant certainty that they were not hallucinations, memories, daydreams, or wishes. So she said "Bah" once more, warm water cascading between her breasts, over her belly, and thought, pleasantly, of Arnold Deleuw instead.

He was too sallow and undernourished, in spite of his health spa, his swimming and foot massage. His hair was lank, gray, lifeless. He needed more exercise. Perhaps she could take him to aikido practice . . .

"Watch it," she said aloud to the tile walls. "You're too old for thoughts like that." She twisted off the water, brisk and no nonsense. She stood in front of the hot air drier and wondered instead, deliberately, what the dolphins were saying to the orca, what they really thought or felt about her, what being them would be like, having no hands, seeing everything mainly through their ears, 3-D and with altered time sense, with strong connotative overtones, emotional information more significant than factual, external data.

"Still talking," Mr. Bade told her when she got down to the conference room. "Here's some food for you. They like it when people eat with them, for some reason. A meaningful ritual even for them. Do you have any psychic abilities?"

The question was so abrupt it startled her, and for a moment she stared at a sandwich on the plate without answering, her hand stretched out toward it, although she had not thought of eating yet. That momentary pang of hunger she'd felt in the tank returned then, and she allowed her hand to continue, pick up the food, and put it to her mouth. She chewed thoughtfully for a moment, swallowed, and looked at the liaison officer. He appeared slightly embarrassed again.

"I don't know," she said shortly. "The evidence seems undeniable that some people have an ability, or that some phenomenon exists—it's all around us, in UFO experiences, precognitive dreams, and so on. But I find it difficult to really believe. That affects any talent I might have,

52

so . . ." she shrugged. "I don't know. It doesn't seem very useful in my case, since whatever suspicions about it I might have get in the way of reliability. I once had it checked, and the statistics said I had a talent. But I don't trust statistics. Why?"

"I'm not sure. I suppose because communication with them is so difficult at best, that any little extra talent for it would help." He waved at the glass, and just then the orca slid past, rolled halfway over to reveal white belly-markings, broad fins, the flat blades of his flukes.

"My god," Cassie said.

"Yeah." Bade grinned.

"I knew he was big, but up close . . ."

"Not the same. He's old, you know. Really old."

The speakers burst with muted squeaking, buzzes, clicks. "Would you like to listen for a while? He's still talking to the dolphins I think, but that was his greeting to you, that pass. Just be a few minutes more. This button here keeps the original going through the speakers. Switch it off and you get simultaneous translation, or what passes for it. The orca will fade but not disappear. Sort of like the UN."

"How accurate is the translation, anyway?"

He lifted his hands in a helpless gesture. "Like I say, I'm no linguist. But even between two human languages the chances for misunderstanding are enormous, and humans share brain structure, language centers and linguistic structure, vocal apparatus, similar cultures anyway, not to mention the same physical environment; and hands, naturally. There are some who say anatomically cetaceans are the same as us, but they do in fact have different brain structure, different vocalizing equipment, no hands, a sonic range that nearly does *not* overlap with ours, and a different medium to carry it, not to mention the way they would see the world. So I would say not very accurate at all. We have to take a great deal on trust."

"On trust," she echoed. "Yeah." She thought of that night, running down the corridor. A hard rectangle of light on the hall carpet, from her bedroom door. She had thrown the hairbrush, swinging and letting go. Her stepfather calling "Wait!" and the brush leaving her hand, the light fragmenting, shards of glittering mirror falling, broken glass everywhere behind her as her stepfather, Anthony, called out to her. Her long hair flew around her shoulders then, as she ran. It was short now, and the curls no longer concerned her.

That was a memory; it haunted her, recurring at odd times, inappropriately. She shook her head, throwing it from her with violence, gazed at the glass, where the enormous face looked back at her, black and bland. The huge mouth opened, and she saw how pink and human the color was inside. Conical teeth grinned, the mouth closed once more, and sounds came faintly from the hidden speakers.

Then the human voice of the translator came through loud and clear.

"Hello," the orca said.

It was momentous and absurd, that greeting, a word so ordinary and important that she felt she was standing at the edge of a cliff that fell away before her.

For days there had been lights in the skies, moving, large as the moon. The people were filled with apprehension, nameless fears. Armies were on the march, gathering in the mountains, in secret. Savage storms groaned, roared, shattered the land with lightning of a strange red-orange color. Banners whipped in the gusty wind.

She stood on bare rock, hard and uneven under her bare feet. The rock shone and fell away. Only a few yards to her left was another promontory, gray orange and shining in the momentous violet light. Between them was the gorge, plunging eight hundred feet straight down to the Castalian spring.

She could see the world in fitful glimpses: The lights flashed in silent swiftness southward from the plain of Honshū, over Kyoto, reversed, and sped north again. On the third day earthquake and fire. Armies flowed across the plains, clashed, retreated, clashed again. Clans met in secret, made deals, changed sides, treachery walking among them all. No farmer knew if his crop would reach harvest. Rain flattened the seedlings.

There was earthquake at Delphi, too, a crack like thunder, and two vast boulders split from Mount Parnassus and fell upon the Persian army, destroying it. And the Euphrates, the Yangtze, the Nile all overran their banks, drowning the land. Beneath the island of Thera magma pushed at a weakness in the earth's crust, pressure mounted, broke through, and the volcano showered ash on the Mediterranean, tsunami and hot wind rocked the land, empires fell, smothered in seconds. The air darkened. The end of the world.

She stood there, at that edge, hesitant, as the images flew. Then she nodded.

"Hello," she said, her voice digitalized by computers and translated, emitted into the water as ultrasonic squeaks and clicks. She considered for a moment, and said, "Do you know who I am?"

The huge alien head tilted, turned slightly away, and the small, brown, seemingly melancholy eye looked at her; the mouth opened slightly, and again she could see the small conical teeth, carnivore teeth. She noticed a faint coil of smoky fluid drifting away from the eye; protection against the salt, but it looked like weeping into the ocean.

"I have heard. Not all." The mouth did not move, of course. He vocalized internally, inside his nasal passages.

Heard. Heard her sonar pattern, knew her feelings, her soul. The precipice gaped at her feet, great danger just beyond control, at the far side of vision. She said nothing, hesitant.

The silence grew, stretched. She had forgotten food, joy, even fear. She was talking to Leviathan, and felt, if anything, absurd and trivial.

So she said, "Nothing bad, I hope."

The eye rolled gently in its socket. Then the body tilted very slowly sideways. Faintly she could hear chittering from the speakers. The human voice broke in over it. "He's laughing. That's what we *think* it is. There are overtones of pleasure and approval. He thinks you told a joke."

"Joke?"

The whale body rolled upright, the mouth opened, and the smooth pink tongue curled there. Buzzes, squeaks, clicks from the speakers.

"He says your shape is ... 'delicious' is the word we have for it, having to do with the satisfaction of hunger. In balance with your age and in health. You have some uneasiness, apprehension, confusion. He says you are coming down with a respiratory disease. A cold. You are curious, interested, and yet detached, something pleasing to them, the dolphins and orcas."

The orca watched her through the glass. She rubbed her palms against her pants without noticing. He turned abruptly and swam away. She could see him circle the far side of the pool, his immense black body moving smoothly through the water, white side markings brilliant when they caught the sun.

"Why did he leave?" she asked the ceiling.

"Don't know. They do that often, though, so don't worry about it." The disembodied voice from the speakers did not reassure her.

When she was small, it was dark in her room, only faint moonlight making contorted shadows in the bookshelves. The pale light seemed to move. Where were her parents? She climbed carefully from her high bed, rolled onto her belly, and slid backward to the floor, cold under her feet. There was a sound, a creak. Downstairs. Terror filled her. Someone was sneaking into the house.

She crept out onto the landing, huddled into her nightgrown against the banister, watched through the bars. The front door was immobile there. The house creaked and whirred to itself, a mouth, a huge beast, devouring her. Light flooded the landing.

"What are you doing there?" her mother shouted, light from her bedroom blinding her. That shout sent an impenetrable blackness rushing in her which pinned her in place, froze her against the banister there, so she could not answer. She had done something wrong and did not know what it was.

She was punished for her incomprehensible wrong and did not notice at first that he had returned. He had no expression to read when she did notice, and when he spoke, when the speakers came to life again, she had trouble following. Only a sense of wrongness and fear.

She wiped her palms against her pants once more, trying hard to listen.

"We returned to the sea long ago," he was saying. "Many millions of years in your numbers. During the time of dreaming, when the universe made itself, and fixed the cycles, set custom. We all must maintain the dreaming. I spoke to the human Brockhurst yesterday, he has told me of you, that you are a specialist in communications, in the talking, and in the dreaming. A cycle is changing now, the dream is changing, for the shape of the sea is becoming different, since man began to hunt. These are things we can understand, even the singers and the grazers. You are our cousins, young and jealous. There is a rightness to this, but the cycle is changing. So the dreaming must change also, and humans have been slow to understand. So we need each other." The translator fell silent though the orca sound continued.

Then the interpreter interrupted and spoke to her. "Ms. St. Clair, I've asked him to stop for a moment. We did the best we could there, but it doesn't make too much sense. It was fast and complex." She watched the huge shape drift away from the glass, watched the body sink languidly to the bottom, resting on its flukes. His head rose slowly to the surface to blow. The sound of it came to her, muffled by the speakers.

The interpreter went on. "There is something very *definite* about what he is saying, a certainty to it. There are seventy-four overtones the computers can't handle, though, harmonics, whistles, and the like for which the data banks have no meanings. Primary meaning is vocalized on the left, which is right hemisphere, of course, giving an aesthetic or gestalt overtone. In the thirty to forty kilohertz range. The others are way up there. Sorry, but we can't do too much more; he's saying a lot more than we can give you. All that stuff about dreaming and cycles has come up before, and appears to have something to do with a metaphysic, but we can't figure out exactly what."

"Never mind," Cassie said. "What did he mean by yesterday? Is that literal, or a general time parameter?"

"Ah, general. We think. Their sense of time is different from ours. I suppose he means in the past, his own past."

"All right. Ask him to expand on 'the cycle is changing.'"

Her words were translated, and the orca lowered his head in the water. "Regrets," he said. "There is a seriousness about what will happen."

"What *will* happen?" She hit her hand against her knee. "What do you mean?"

"You must . . . listen, I mean see, watch what is happening among the people. It's not so much for cetaceans, although that is important also. The cycles are unhappy."

She forced herself to relax, let the silence between them grow. Leviathan hung in the water, watching. She felt confusion, frustration. Let them go, let the coils of doubt, fear, excitement, all go. Her hands fell open in her lap, and she watched the orca watching her.

He rose again, and blew, a puff lasting less than a second. She heard it, the rapid expelling of air, the deep inhale, and he sank again, just below the surface. He made no sounds, not even sonar.

She dropped thought and sat. She was listening to the dial tone after Mr. Brockhurst had disconnected. Before her the Pacific was an empty plate. She could hear monks chanting, a presence in the air of incense and reverence. She tilted her head, testing the sounds for words, for language, but meaning eluded her. It was as if it were on the tip of

57

her tongue, that language, but refused to coalesce into understanding. Not Latin, though the rhythms had something of Gregorian chant, solemn and somehow very sweet.

She was sitting on a couch, facing an alien mind in a huge, slow, powerful, and very beautiful body that had no hands, had never manipulated the physical world the way she had, and could not objectify it the way humans did. At the same time there was that solemn chant, at the edge of human hearing. Japanese? No. She thought this was what was happening, she was listening to a whale speak, and could not quite shape what he was saying into meaning.

And he was waiting for something.

A minute or two must have passed as she listened passively to that chant, low and polyphonic, because he rose to breathe once or twice more. She noticed then that he was very slowly rolling onto his side, then his back. He hung upside down, watching her for a moment, assessing it seemed the intensity of her attention. Then, slowly and extremely deliberately, he winked.

The gesture was so incongruous she didn't believe she had seen it. It was far too human a gesture, too familiar and intimate. The chanting faded from her mind, leaving a melancholy debris that slowly faded as well.

Suddenly she laughed, leaned forward slightly, and winked back, giving him a leer. With one powerful lash of his flukes he propelled himself through the surface of the water and twisted sideways to smash the surface with his side. Waves crashed against the sides of the pool, and water sucked away from the glass for a moment, leaving teary trails. When it settled again, the whale was gone and she was hungry.

She'd forgotten the sandwiches, and fell on them ferociously now. She was about to eat her fourth when the whale reappeared, mouth open in a grin.

"He wants to eat also," the interpreter told her.

"Wait," Cassie said. "I'd like to do it. I'll be right up."

Behind glass he looked big, but somehow safe, contained and separate from her. From above he was a presence in the water she could not deny, a black floating body she could have walked on, and she felt an apprehension with him she had not felt with the dolphins, who after all were cute, lovable creatures, nice people to know.

Mr. Bade approached with a bucket of butterfish. "Frozen, I'm afraid," he said. "But he'll like them anyway. Do you want me to . . . ?"

"No, I'd like to give them to him. It seems important, though I'm not sure why. They used to be called killer whales, didn't they, the orcas?"

"Yes."

Ten giant steps from rostrum to flukes. More than ten meters. His brain was four times the size of hers, and as complexly convoluted and structured. He had no natural enemies and was afraid of nothing, not even man. And she felt fear, knew he would know her fear instantly.

She sat by the edge of the pool, slipped off her shoes, and put her feet in the water. Her slacks soaked moisture up to the knee, but she kept her feet in.

The orca was waiting at the other side of the pool, head out of the water. She took a fish and held it.

What happened was so sudden she had no time to react. One moment he was hanging languidly in the water, his tiny eye, not much larger than her own, watching her, the next the water was boiling in his wake as he streaked toward her, mouth open. Horror filled her totally, followed by panic. The mouth slashed violently at her naked foot; she could hear the teeth clash together, the sharp snap of the jaws, but felt nothing. She jerked her legs from the water as soon as panic let her.

It took an enormous effort not to scramble away from the edge, even as she heard the liaison officer cry out a warning, too late. She caught herself halfway, and looked at her foot. It was unmarked. She felt weak, terror wailing at her, but forced herself to sit once more and put her feet back into the water. She tensed but did not move as he charged her once more, mouth open, teeth pointed and ready to slash. She tensed involuntarily as the mouth raked and snapped closed. She could feel the surge of water against her foot, could feel through the skin the shock of jaws snapping shut.

He circled the pool, charged her again, snapped his mouth shut, then raised his head from the water and grinned at her.

Her fear was gone. She held up the fish she had been clutching and he gently opened his mouth a little wider. She threw the fish into the pink mouth, which closed and instantly opened again. The fish was gone.

"Hello," he said, air puffing from his blowhole. The word had whistles in it, and pops for the *l*'s, but she understood him. "Hello," he said, in English.

"Hello," she shouted joyously. "Hello." She held up another fish, two fish. He opened his mouth again. She threw them in.

"Hanks," he huffed, ducked his head once more and nudged her

59

naked sole with his tough upper lip. She wriggled her toes, and he bumped gently against them.

He pushed her feet up out of the water, rose after them, and made a rude noise, playing. She laughed delightedly. He opened his mouth, and she tipped in more butterfish. He gulped and whistled.

He moved back, away from her, and blinked. Then he began making sounds in the air, a slow whistling with buzzing underneath, creaks, clicks. She was away from the speakers, from the interpreter, and did not know what he was saying, but he understood her dependence on the machines, so what he was doing must be deliberate. She listened without thinking, without trying to analyze.

And then she understood: He was singing to her. The rhythms were strange, slow, and seemingly uneven, but there, a pattern she had never heard before, a kind of refrain, a motif repeated again with variations, then with pauses.

Hesitantly she entered the song, singing nonsense herself, "La la lalala," trying to copy, vary, harmonize.

He answered, copying her variations, introducing more of his own, putting rhythmic clicks and squeaks under her sections, answering her back once more, a duet. She hummed, sang, began to introduce words, "My name is Cassie, what is yours?"into her lalalas, and he whistled and sang in return, without words she could understand, in the orca language, if it was a language, if it had words. There were subtle differences in his singing now, as if he had moved on, as she had, to meaning. She thought he understood her, what she was saying, and was answering her, telling him his name, what he was called, for there was a phrase repeated often, and she lalalaed and tried to introduce that sound into her patterns, a quick-rising, slow-falling whistle and creak.

Back and forth the duet went, and gradually she realized he was correcting her, *teaching* her his name, repeating what she had said, then repeating it correctly. She redoubled her own efforts, listening more carefully to his vocalizing, trying harder to match his sounds. She had always been good at languages, knew a lot about human language, about clicking languages and tonal languages and syllabic and stressed languages. But all of them presumed a larynx and mouth and tongue like hers.

She had a lousy accent in orca. No doubt about that. But he understood her.

Thinking about it later she knew that never in her life had she been so concentrated, so focused on the present moment, so free from interruptions from her unconscious, her memories, her reveries and fugues, her sense of déjà vu. But that was later, for now he started to chant, and a shiver went through her swift as light through ice, and as hard and sharp and touched with shattered color, for this was the chant she had heard coming down this morning, a low, sweet chant without words at all, and she knew why she hadn't been able to tell what language it was.

The chant began in the middle and ended in the middle, without clear boundaries for beginning or end. It stopped so abruptly she was startled, and he turned under the water and glided swiftly, effortlessly, through the entrance and out to sea, where he leaped once, sounded, and was gone from sight.

"That was beautiful," Bade told her as the orca vanished. "We got it all, the whole song. That kind of duet has happened before, of course, but I've only seen it once, a long time ago." He shook his head. "I should have recognized him."

"What do you mean?" she asked. Her eyes were unfocused, on the water.

"There's a forward tilt to his dorsal fin, and a shape to his head patch. He's the one I saw before. He's bigger now."

She looked at him now. "What happened, that other time?"

"I was just out of graduate school, my first job as a marine biologist. We were on a ship, the *Dreambridge.*" He gestured at the ocean, glittering under the afternoon sun, the small chop flashing random symbols. He was under them somewhere."

"*Dreambridge.* Isn't that Brockhurst's boat?" She stood with her back to the offshore breeze, hardly aware of the chill in her lower legs where the air was drying her slacks.

"Yes. How did you know?"

"I work for him, in a way." She caught the question in his expression. "I work for a think tank he started, Investigate the Future. We specialize in communications research and futures studies. I must have heard about his ship somewhere, the name, anyway. I don't remember. Was he on the boat?"

"Yes, on the boat. Way up in the bow, where there's a platform built out over the water for observation. He was seated on a zafu, a meditation pillow, and he sang with that orca." Bade gestured at the vanished whale again. "It was a calm day, not like today at all, and later in the afternoon. The water was glassy, tinged orange by the setting sun. We were out of sight of the coast, and the horizon was clearly defined, a perfect circle with us as the center. No haze, like now. Blue sky, darker blue water. The orca floated about ten meters off the bow, facing Brockhurst.

"I was up in the cabin, where I could see him, but I couldn't hear what they said to each other. He had a closed channel, the translations going through satellite to Scripps and back again, just to him; there was just a sense of all that technology, even cruder then than it is now, sonographic analysis, computer language programs, data banks, and all the rest just beginning to make sense. They were talking. I could just hear the old man's voice, very low; he was speaking into the microphone, of course, and I couldn't make out any words. I started down to the deck, to see if I could get closer, hear what they were talking about.

"There was a funny sensation in the air, a kind of suspension, like before a thunderstorm, or what people sometimes call 'earthquake weather,' a strangeness. I got closer to him, where I could hear some of his words. I think they were talking about death, and some kinship expressions, but I never could figure out how the two went together. Brockhurst always spoke at length, and the answers, of course, were extremely rapid, only a second or so. It was eerie, hearing those creaks and clicks, watching the old man tilt his head listening for a long time to the translations, and then talking back.

"I remember the heat, that flatness of the air, and shivering. I'd never seen anyone actually communicating with them before, though I'd read all the literature, seen the films and tapes, even heard the tapes of their speech, and all the theories about communication with them. This was different. I don't really know how to explain it."

He stopped talking and stared at her.

Cassie felt an absurd awkwardness, a desire to retreat from his earnestness. "That's why you asked me about psychic ability. You had that feeling. I've had it too."

"There's more to it than that. The feeling had a huge, almost overwhelming *expectancy* about it, as if something important were going to happen. I wanted to shrug it off, thought for a minute I was getting the flu or something. And then something did happen. The old man, sitting out there cross-legged, staring out over the water at that whale, started to . . . sing, I suppose. Chant, anyway. A sort of liturgical sound. His voice was very deep, reedy, too, like an old man's. Of course, he is an old man, but the power in it was surprising. No words, just sounds, chanted. The orca settled in the water, flukes sinking, and lifted his head, listening. Brockhurst did not have a beautiful voice or anything, but it was amazing. That feeling of something about to happen left me, I felt fine then, just listening."

Cassie felt a chill then, too; she was getting a cold, the dolphins were right about that.

"Anyway," Bade said, the spell broken, "they had a duet like the one you just had. There was that same sense of profound communication, or maybe communion is a better word, taking place, with no concept of what kind of information was moving. Do you think he's coming back?"

"Hmm? Oh, I don't know. I think so, but I don't know. They are so different. We should wait awhile, I guess." She hugged herself against the breeze. "What time is it?"

It was late. She slid into it easily, saw dust rise over the plain, where the armies clashed. The sounds of their warfare were faint, the shouts, the metallic clatter. Dust boiled, billowed, lit by the afternoon sun. She was above it all, on a height, nodding. It was as she had told them, the armies down there, the dying, the grief. Just as she had foreseen.

It had been this same time of day, with the same quality of light, that she had warned them all, told them about the treachery, the murders, the battles, and the fall of empires. They nodded gravely and left without hearing. It was often that way, they listened but did not hear. Cassie stroked her cheek with her fingernail. What was she seeing down there? It could be Plataea or Persia, or even Sekigahara. It was too distant and confused to make out the banners, the armor they wore. Only the reek of blood in dust, the distant shouting came to her here.

Bade said, "Three-thirty."

She shivered. What did it matter? The vision was too generalized to be meaningful, too often repeated in the history books to be useful. "Are the dolphins still here?"

"Sure. Would you like to talk to them?"

They were circling the other pool, porpoising smoothly, pink-gummed mouths open. When she said hello, they swam over to the glass and looked in. "Hello," they said, their greetings overlapping. There were two translators on duty.

"I'd like to ask some questions," Cassie said.

"Ready."

"Do you fear the orca?"

"It is . . . unclear." The interpreter broke in. "They don't understand the question."

"He is bigger than you. Are you afraid of him? He's a killer, after all."

The pair circled in apparent distress. Then one drifted to the glass and looked straight into her eyes. "When he's hunting, we will try to avoid him. Is that what you mean?"

"Not exactly. What if he catches one of you?"

"Then he will eat." They had an advantage over her: They could read her meaning in her body attitudes, at least when she was in the water. She could read nothing from the translation.

"Aren't you afraid to die?"

They chattered for a moment, and she heard whispered consultations over the speakers, then only the Delphinese, what was audible to her. Finally they turned back to her. "Why?"

"Because we are, I suppose. Do you know about the Dead Liberation Front?"

"We have heard about it. We have the term."

"What do you think of it?"

"Why should we think about it? You should ask the orca, orcas think about things like that."

They shot through the surface and slapped the water, rocking it against the glass; they chased each other around the pool, chattering loudly, all the previous discomfort gone. She could hear their high squeals through the glass, as well as over the speakers.

When they calmed down, she asked them why dolphins and whales seemed to like humans so much, why they were so gentle with them.

"Humans are fun," they told her. "They are clumsy in the water, and they like to play, and sometimes they need us. So we help them. You could ask the orca about it. He has different reasons."

"Will he come back?" She gave his whistling name, and one of the pair streaked out of the pool. He returned almost immediately.

"On his way," the gilli said.

"Good. I'd like to ask him all those questions." She thought about

Brockhurst, seated cross-legged on the bow of his boat, about the *Dreambridge* and what it might mean. He must be very old now, his rough, gnarled hands resting on his knees, singing in his ancient, cracked voice to the black-and-white killer in the sea, and the whale singing back to him.

After the orca arrived she asked her questions, and when he answered she tried to follow Brockhurst's advice to listen behind his words; but there was nothing she could grasp there, nothing useful, or intelligible, or discrete. Only the alien face, describing for her events and sensations that made no sense. She was a scientist and what did the dreaming across growing of his mate, who had fallen ill and died, have to do with her world?

She presumed grief. Did he grieve? He didn't understand the question. Of course he grieved, but then comes the dreaming, and the new cycles, as it should be. And there always the pleasant illusions of drifting up and down the coast, the feeding, the singing, the pauses at power nodes for necessary event boundaries.

She was caught in the surface of it. "What? What are those things, power nodes?"

"We have difficulties," he said, huge head sinking in a ponderous nod. "That is not my phrase. Places, in the sea, and of course the land as well, that made themselves during dreamtime; they have great—you would call it spiritual—power."

She had an impression of the frustration he was feeling, the computers and machines inadequate to the alien concepts he was using. "Yes," she said absently. "We have them on land . . . Delphi, Dodona, Tien Shan."

He was not impressed. "Those, yes. And many, many more. Such places are everywhere, although not for everyone. Connections are there because of birth, conception, concern, enormous efforts at communication. Many reasons. All from the dreaming that is done, the wishing, and the believing."

What was he talking about? She sniffed, aware of a grating in her throat and nose, the first tentative hints of the cold he had mentioned. And what was behind all these words?

"Language is a new toy," he said, in answer to her thought, and she started.

"Eh?"

"It is 'play.' Isn't that right? For us, using these sounds in this way, a pleasure. But not important. Distracting. They take attention and awareness away from what is important."

"What is important?"

"The dreaming, of course."

She tried to think of human correlates, cultures in which dreaming had a powerful reality, Australian aborigine, American Indian. It did not seem quite the same as his meaning, though. Listen behind the words. She could feel the muscles cord at the back of her neck, the fatigue of effort pulling at her.

He was watching her, brown liquid eye seemingly mournful. Another illusion, she was sure. He changed the subject. "The sea changes slowly, even with man in it. What happens, *is,* and we have no hands to give us the illusion of power to do the changing. Only in the dreaming is there that strength. What you do has little meaning."

"What *I* do?" English pronouns were shifting their meaning. Plural, singular?

"Yes. The future has no meaning. The sea is sometimes clear, sometimes not; sometimes we can hear where the fish or seal is going, and when we will eat. At other times the water is troubled. But you want to know with certainty what is not understood yet. In the air, it seems, is little certainty. But you, Cassie, have special qualities."

"Hmm. I have hunches, sometimes. And a good mind. I work hard. But it's nothing unusual, nothing others don't have."

"That is not your special quality. Listen: The ocean is large, and the surface often rough and quick. Events occur quickly there, storms and wind and waves. When that happens we go down, and there it is not rough, events move slowly, as always. Go below." He fell silent.

She waited for him to go on, but he was finished. So as he rested languidly in the clear water of the tank, she thought about what he had said. *Go below.* Was he speaking about a level of reality beneath the events she thought made up her history, the history of her species?

66

There was apprehension in those visions of vast armies, clouds of dust, but she didn't know whether they were glimpses of a coming future or scenes stolen from films she had seen.

For some people the past was fixed, congealed, locked into place forever but not for her. For Cassie only the present seemed fixed, the place where the past emptied into the future, fresh water flowed into salt, and both were changed. At times she had her back to the past, and at other times the future, so that one became the other.

What she had wanted was a certainty, and what she got was ideas, concepts, models, that changed under her scrutiny, that refused to stay put. She wanted her talent to be sensible and authentic, but could not believe in the statistics.

The orca had talked about dreaming. But dreams had no "reality," they were purely internal.

What were all her theta visions but dreams? Sometimes approximate depictions of what happened *out there,* sometimes not. She saw, for example, on her wedding day what was going to happen, yet what she saw was not herself, but her father and mother, George and Martha, till death do us part, I do, the scent of flowers heavy in the air, as strong as the funeral flowers when her father, George, lay heaped with blossoms, gone, and her husband, Cassie's husband, even as she said *I do,* even as she turned to accept the kiss that was to bind them, had begun to widen the distance between them.

His face was there, open, handsome, ruddy. A very appealing face, all in all. A good match. Martha had said so often, a good match, Cassie, urging the marriage. Their children would be gifted, handsome, clean-limbed, intelligent, the product of old-fashioned midwestern eugenics. But Cassie knew there would be no children, no future in it at all.

She had stood there, right hand in his left, her left holding the bouquet of baby's tears and forget-me-nots and smiled at the photographer, who would lock that particular present into silver nitrate and paper, and even then she wondered who this man was she had just married.

He was not a vast black-and-white body with small brown eyes who *dreamed across growing* of a mate fallen ill, whatever that might mean. Not a mate to spend a lifetime with, till death do us part.

Even that particular past slipped away from her, intangible as dream. The whale in the water saw her attention return.

"Sorry," she murmured. "My mind wandered."

"Good," he said. "Go below. And now, good-bye, Cassie. We will meet soon." Slowly, and deliberately as spring, he winked at her once more, his lid closing slowly over that small, melancholy eye, trailing tears. He opened his mouth slightly one last time and gave her that peculiarly human grin.

"Good-bye." She whistle/clicked his name. "See you."

He surfaced and said, clearly and distinctly, "Cassie," into the air, then swam leisurely out to sea.

She stared into the empty water for a time, thinking, See you soon, wondering if that would be in the dreaming or the world.

Then she stood. The lower parts of her pants' legs were stiff with dried salt water, and she patted them, feeling the slick, greasy salt on her hands. It was not unpleasant.

"How was it?" Bade asked her when she rejoined him.

"I wish I knew. Puzzling, to say the least. What's the time?"

"After five. Dr. Hubletz wants you to call him."

"Okay."

She tried to shake away a sense of unreality before dialing the office. Dr. Hubletz seemed very far away in space and in time. Then she shrugged and dialed.

"Millet brought in the contract today," L.R. told her.

"What's the announcement?"

"He wouldn't say. Not until we sign. They will be more than generous—we did talk about financing. With the tight money on grants these days, a project like this could be very good for us. Very good. And with NSF support."

"The announcement, L.R. What's the goddamn announcement? What are they going to do to the world?"

"Well, I think it has something to do with life after death or something, probably. Some kind of breakthrough . . ."

"But you don't know."

"No, not exactly."

"Can we control the release of the report? Or will we have to doctor it when we finally do know what's going on?"

"Well, it'll be their report, Cassie, DLF will be paying for it. You must understand, though, that they want everything—religion, social impact, economics, the works. It's very big, this project, and we need it."

"We don't have time. It's due Monday. Besides, they could refuse to release it at all, couldn't they? If they wanted to?"

"Mm, they could. So what? As long as they pay for it . . . and it will be ready. The entire organization is working on it. Anyway, that wasn't the main reason I wanted you to call. Arnold put what we have from Millet into PEST, just a trial run, you see, to get a preliminary projection, rough of course. He used the notion of some kind of communication with the dead as the basis for the announcement. After all, we do specialize in communications, so it's a natural for us."

"And?"

"And it all went according to program . . ."

"Yeah?"

"There was something about it that bothered us a bit."

"Yes?"

"It's too much according to program."

"I should think that would please you, L.R. Things are seldom so smooth."

"Ordinarily it would please me. But even I feel a bit uneasy about this one. Cassie, there are *always* surprises in any projection. We allow for them, expect them. It's our business. There were no surprises here at all. Everything was thirty percent this, twenty percent that, in perfect bell curves. That's not right. If I didn't know better I'd think someone was finagling the numbers, or had tampered with our data base. These projections are meaningless."

She scraped her cheek with her fingernail, phantom itch back. She cleared her throat, feeling the scratch in it. "Will Millet think they're meaningless, do you think? We could do a run on the release of a meaningless report, see if it has an effect."

"I don't know. But I don't like it. When do you get back?"

"I'm on the seven o'clock shuttle. It gets in at——"

"Seven-forty-five," he interrupted. "Would you mind stopping by here when you get in? I'd appreciate it."

"Jesus, L.R. I've been up since six, and talking to whales and dolphins all day. I need some time to think it over."

"Just for a few minutes, Cassie. Please."

L. R. almost never said please. "Oh, all right." She saw herself drowned again, knew it was not a literal image. She was not going to drown in water, but in something else.

She hung up and turned, biting her lip. "Of all the stupid . . ."

Bade was watching her. "Oh," she started. "It's nothing. Just work. Makes for a long day."

"Sure."

She nodded.

Her bag lay on the table before her, contents spilled across the surface. Leaflets for the Friends of the Sea, some mimeographed pages, some glossy brochures. On the cover of one a gray whale lifted from the water, caught in momentary aerial suspension. A red bar slashed across the page: whales extinct ahead. But the whales were already protected, already acknowledged as potentially intelligent. After all, they talked.

Of course, this was a gray whale, a mysticetus, not a toothed whale, and therefore, not, perhaps, intelligent.

She tossed the paper aside, and a small corner of cream-colored envelope caught her eye. An envelope was an alien presence amid these public documents. It implied personal communication.

Her name was typed neatly on the front; nothing else, just "Cassie St. Clair."

"Where did this come from?" she asked. She slipped out the contents, a stiff sheet of formal note paper with these words: *Wretches, why sit ye here? Fly, fly to the ends of creation.*

She showed it to Bade.

"I don't know," he said. "What is it?"

"The Delphic oracle. Advice to the Athenians, who were faced with a Persian invasion. The Athenians stayed, though; they refused to take such a negative suggestion back to Athens. They assured the oracle they would die in Delphi first, so the oracle gave in, provided them with another pronouncement, this one about wooden walls. Themistocles took it to mean they should build a fleet, which they did. Beat the socks off the Persians, then."

"I don't get it," Bade said.

"The point is, someone sent me this knowing I would recognize it. But it doesn't seem like the Friends of the Sea would do it, and I have no way of knowing if it was among their literature or not. I wasn't paying much attention." She began to pace nervously. "The first prediction was unacceptable. The DLF? Oh, hell." She stopped, looked hard at Bade for a moment.

"I'd like to get in with them once more," she said.

"In with them?"

"The dolphins. If they're still around."

"I'll see," he said, and disappeared down the stairs once more.

She stood watching the empty opening into the dark earth where the priests had vanished. Wisps of vapor twisted faintly above the irregular entrance, the damp, visionary exhalations of the earth herself. She held a sprig of laurel leaves in her left hand; the leaves drooped, trailing over her fingers. Her linen robe was very white and clean. She was naked underneath, and the touch of the cloth on her bare skin was almost irritatingly sensual.

She shivered. The Pythoness was waiting, down there in the darkness, drunk on the vapors, entranced. Dimly she remembered being the oracle once, but now she was a suppliant. For her the future was dim and unreal, a mist thick as the clouds around Olympus where the gods were hidden from men. She had to know; it was of supreme importance. It was not clear why she had to know, or exactly *what,* but the significance of it drove her. She took a step toward the opening.

A shift in the light caught her attention for a moment, a sudden silence, as if the world had drawn its breath and was holding it; then thunder, abrupt and brief and awesomely loud, followed by a deeper silence. She looked back at the dark entry into the earth. The priest was emerging.

Far away she heard for a small moment the sounds of rhythmic drums, reed pipes, ritual music, as she watched the priest climb into the light and air. It was Bade coming up the stairs. He beckoned, and she went down after him.

She knew before she went down that the dolphins were waiting for her. They were circling, leaping, slapping the water, and whistling, every now and then charging one another, jabbing each other's bellies with their beaks and cackling.

"Is the translator still working?"

"Yes, Ms. St. Clair."

"I want to ask a question."

He nodded at the dolphins. "Go ahead."

"Hey!" The pair slid effortlessly back to the glass and watched her. She thought they were laughing. "I want to ask something."

The male nodded.

"You've been in the ocean a long time, longer than we have been on the planet. But for us, a long time ago, there were stories ... You have a reputation for being friendly to men, human beings, and helping them when they get into trouble in the water, shipwrecks, things like that. Why haven't we ever talked before? Surely with all that contact a language could have been worked out."

They both stared at her. "We thought you knew. We have talked before."

"I don't understand. We've talked before? Do you understand me? I don't mean us, personally. Men and dolphins." It was important, that urgency was upon her. She had to know.

"Of course. It was not ... yesterday. Many lifetimes."

"How many?"

"Many. Numbers are not important to us. Orca might know, but we don't. Your numbers aren't real."

"All right. Many lifetimes, then. Where, what part of the world?"

"Yes." They chattered together. Then: "Crete. You call it Crete. An island from the dreaming."

"Thank you," Cassie said. "I'd like to join you for a few minutes before I have to leave."

They burst into a raucous creaking and clicking, and began to swim once more in an intricate three-dimensional pattern together. Before she turned away from the glass she could see there was room in the pattern for her.

When she slipped into the water and checked her mask and respirator, she could still sense the opening in the pattern, the incompletion. They were performing a three-body dance, using the circular forces of the water rolling off their bodies to simulate a third body: hers. She floated on the surface for a minute, letting the water level jog up and down on her mask. Then the smooth gray mottled body of the male slid between her legs and lifted her; she slid smoothly back until she bumped against the front of his dorsal fin. Then he dove.

She held on to him gingerly and felt no fear. Her hair swirled around her head. Her eyes were open. Her expression must have been joy.

He braked, and she flew forward, over his head, and did a forward roll under the water until she was facing him. Both the dolphins were there, bodies radiating outward, forming an equilateral triangle parallel to the surface. They hung there for a long time, the three of them, looking at one another.

Abruptly, in an unvoiced mutual consent below consciousness, the dance began. It wove, that dance, in the intricately clear water, a limpid pattern moving through time and space filled with nosings and stroking, slow passes and rapid charges. The dolphins flicked their flippers softly against her cheek, her thighs, her feet. They turned over and presented their bellies to her, and she let her fingertips trail along the soft skin there, along the genital slit, off the smooth fluke, and that touch also was irritatingly sensual, the dance they were doing somehow chastely erotic, inevitable, and serene.

For a time. She thought of Arion carried to the Cliffs of Taenarum in safety, in Pelops' Land, nurtured, nursed, breast-fed, and Aphrodite riding to sea on the dolphin's humped back, trackless in the depths, and the Greek word *Delphys* the same as *delphis,* or womb, but these thoughts, these "professional" digressions, were distant and without substance, for it was the touch of warm sea-flesh, the unfathomable smoothness of it, that was there in all that was serene and pure. She hardly noticed when they grew rough and the butting of their beaks against her legs, her belly, made deep sounds in the water. She thumped them back as best she could, slowed by the water's resistance, hands slowed, her air-body clumsy and slow, dragging in the water.

The female dolphin slithered between her legs, nosing her, lifted her head and Cassie felt a fierce pleasure. She twisted and circled the dolphin body with her arms, behind the dorsal fin, her hands trailing down the pale belly, caressing violently, and holding this way, the male pursued her in turn, nosed her as she flew behind the female. She gripped the male's head with her thighs, and the three of them sailed through the water, circling, diving, rising through the thrashing surface to plunge again, the human female in the middle, gripping hard with hands and legs, until her face mask slipped and sputtering and coughing she had to break and rise to the surface and rip away the mask and feel the multiple bruisings of her body.

She coughed and spit water and laughed, resting on the surface, the two dolphins at her sides, supporting her and chattering. The dance was over.

She leaned her head back, and her brown hair spread across the water in the late light. Her hands rested on the backs of the dolphins, and she could see only empty sky, deepening to violet as the day waned. She breathed softly without thought, her torso rising and falling gently with each breath. Her feet trailed away into an unfelt distance, buoyant as all unborn in amnion.

Finally she sat up in the water, supporting herself on those two gray backs, felt inexplicable sadness that stopped her breath entirely, and together they swam her to the side of the pool and nudged her out, onto the land, dry, hard, scaled, safe, and unpleasant to the touch. She sat on the edge, hung over her supporting hands, and sighed once, good-bye.

They begged her, and she put the soles of her feet against their beak ends and pushed them backward toward the middle of the pool. They raised their heads and smiled, then lowered them beneath the surface, and she watched their long gray bodies glide through the baffled opening and out to sea, gone, toward the lowering sun.

She found it difficult to believe the whole dance had taken less than one hour. Much later, falling into bed, she moved effortlessly through blue water, her smooth body gray and delicate and sensitive to the touch, and all around her the shallows sang and rang with voices she could not understand, and although she felt afraid, there was also a terrible rapture.

WEDNESDAY

LI PO

ON

MERCURY

6:5 *And . . . I heard the third
beast say, Come and See.*

So the night sang. The telephone when it rang was high song from the wave tops, spindrift spray in which she dove and rose.

The ringing pulled her out at last. She shook her naked body and fumbled down the handset, "Yes?"

"Good morning lovely person," Arnold's voice in her ear. She breathed in a clean, dry, chalky smell. "Yesterday you were missed."

"I was missed?" She kicked sheets away and stretched. Gray light filtered through the curtain stuff, north light drawn thin and far too early. "My god, what time is it? I was dreaming about the sea."

"Yes. It is six-forty-seven precisely, as our Dr. Hubletz would have it. He tells me today is a very big day in the future."

"I talked to the orca, Arn. And swam with dolphins."

"I want to hear about it," she could see him nodding in assent, of course. "And what do you know about elephants, Cassie?"

"Six-forty-seven in the *morning* you want to know what I know about elephants? No, Arnold, no more large mammals, not just now. You didn't hear me, maybe? Whales. Big black-and-white sea creatures too weird and lovely to make sense of. What's the meaning calling me at six-forty-seven in the morning anyhow? Not that I don't like to hear your voice, you understand, but even the birds aren't calling this early."

He laughed, "Oh, it's a very big day, Cassie, a parade for our delectation and delight, elephants and all. For example," he sounded like a carnival barker, "we have Wesley Millet, feared and revered leader of millions who yearn to breathe free, or breathe at all, or at least those who wish to talk with those who do not breathe for reassurance that they also will sail on into the energetic universe with memory and self intact somehow, living forever in a world without gods. If that is in fact his motive, to live forever, to talk to the dead." Arnold's tumble of words fell through the wires into the gray-lit room like a litter of squirrels poured from warm nest into her hands.

"Stop, stop," she laughed feebly.

"Okay, I'll stop. Really I will. I say no more, ask no more. You may loll about your pillows while the rest of us toil in the vineyards of the future, tilling and planting, posing and solving."

"Arnold, have you been smoking something?"

"Ha ha," he said, a sinister chuckle. "Who knows . . ." he drew the word out, lingering, "what e-e-evil . . . lurks . . . in the hearts of men."

"Hey, you must be *old*," she said, and over the phone he blew her a kiss and cackled horribly. "Okay," she said. "I'm getting up."

She smiled as she climbed into the chill. She smiled as she pressed the heater switch. "The power to cloud men's minds," she said to the radio, and turned it on.

It scanned, found her a station. She smiled when she heard the song for her, a folksy old Yeats poem set to electric sitars:

> There all the golden codgers lay,
> There the silver dew,
> And the great water sighed for love,
> And the wind sighed too.

She dressed, inexplicably sunny herself, though the day continued gray, a thick fog hanging above city hillcrests where the night before last the horned moon had dipped. The sitars spangled and trilled, droned and hummed. A pure soprano let the words rise over them:

> Straddling each a dolphin's back
> And steadied by a fin . . .

She dressed in gold and red, becomingly, she thought, and put a scarf around her soft brown hair. And earring hoops of gold as well.

Water boiled for coffee. Sitars sang. "News for the Delphic Oracle" was the song. Her mind was clear as still water, clean sand. She had no premonitions, no pasts disturbed her, the futures were filled with wonders certainly. It was a good day despite the fog, which after all would clear, would burn away without an ash.

> Intolerable music falls,
> Foul goat-herd, brutal arm appear,
> Belly, shoulder, bum,
> Flash fishlike; nymphs and satyrs
> Copulate in the foam.

"Whew," she said aloud, a whale-whisper in her kitchen at the ending song. "Whew and double whew. In the foam."

She ate, and stared at green tendrils of dill in her kitchen window; sipped from her ceramic cup. Her fingers found the depressions in the cup, traced the chased bamboo.

Chased, she thought. Not really the right word. Intaglio? Or chased?

Chaste, she thought, wry smile playing in her face at this idle thinking. Oh, I've been very chaste, I have, and now I'm chased, and *copulate in the foam* went through her mind.

How long could such things last. Already the cloud over her home began to break as she stepped through shafts of sunshine and cloud shadow from one spotlit pool to another. She looked over rooftops toward the bay and saw, all that way across, the westward slopes of those eastern foothills dipped in purple shadow. The day seemed glorious. She had danced with dolphins, sung with the whale, and Arnold Deleuw had called. She could not be angry for the early hour, no.

Her little car sputtered on alcohol. The radio popped into life, and there it was again, that song, sitars moaning. The day continues synchronous, she thought. It doth continue. She did not think of elephants, or of the DLF, though an image, mercury-quick, of Wesley Millet rising from a bowery bed to checked plus fours and a goofy hat flashed through her mind.

Her little car swam through the morning light.

It was only when she had wheeled silently into the parking lot outside of IF and braked, and parked, and stepped out into this brilliant sun, that the man in the airport yesterday morning, the decadent heavy face, low voice in her visions, renewed itself in her awareness. She stopped solid-fast and rooted, right foot lifted for the first step, hovering over the concrete, eyes unfocused though aimed at the door where *Investigate the Future* was etched in glass, and a subtle, sour shock went through her entirely. It all rushed back, the thick whisper, the open face with that moment of eye contact at the ticket counter, the moment when she first saw that face; the morning coffee soured in her stomach, the morning sun turned dull and flat and cold, and she felt again the raw crackle in her throat, the building pressure in her head, the painful tickle of her cold.

She stood there in midstep, staring hard at something not there at all, at the very edge of her peripheral vision: nothing. Nothing at all. The song returned:

Straddling each a dolphin's back
And steadied by a fin,
These Innocents relive their death,
Their wounds open again.

"How do you do that?"

"What?" she turned her head and lowered her foot, upraised over
the cement.

"You've been standing like that, with your foot in the air over the
step for a good thirty seconds. I wondered how you did it, stood so still
and off-balance like that." Arnold was on the walk just below and
behind her, back turned to his old diesel parked just there, dull paint in
this early light.

"Oh." She placed her foot carefully on the step. "It's T'ai Ch'i. The
Leaping Crane position."

"You do T'ai Ch'i as well as aikido?"

"No, not really." She laughed, embarrassed at her slight joke. "But
they are related. I made that up about the Leaping Crane."

He smiled Okay.

She shook her head then, serious. "It can't be," she said, soft and to
herself.

"Can't be what?" Arnold asked her, catching that mood.

"A man in the airport yesterday. And Wesley Millet's clothes." A
wan smile twitched her lips. "Peculiar, those clothes. Anyway, they
seemed connected just then, the man and Millet."

"What man?" He took her arm, a shy proprietary gesture.

"Oh." She hugged his hand to her side, elbow tucked in, and rested
her head momentarily on his shoulder. It was a sigh.

The fog was gone now, vaporized into the clarity of this early
morning air. Emerald green was all around them. A camellia bush

against the wall of the building was heavy with red blossoms, the ground around it littered with them. Cassie St. Clair moved away from Arnold Deleuw's corduroy sleeve, caught a minute by the dry, chalky natural scent of him.

He noticed, and she felt a slight stiffening in him as she moved, she tried to cover the disappointment by talking, and the moment passed. "A man was following me, I'm sure of it. An athlete gone to seed, heavy face, a smile so pleasant it was nasty, that kind of smile—you know the type?"

"I think so," he answered.

"He looked familiar somehow." She looked at Arnold, tremor on her lower lip. "Anyway, I had this feeling . . ." she trailed off, lower lip caught between her teeth, shook her head. "No, it's silly."

"Tell me," he said, turning to face her. They stood on that first step still, outside the offices of IF, in chilled sunshine and the heavy brilliant colors of spring. "Please."

"Wesley Millet talking on the phone, to that man. I had a feeling the man was following me to prevent us from taking the DLF contract, but that doesn't make sense, because it's Millet's contract, you see?" She shrugged, helpless.

"Mmm," he frowned looking down. "You should trust your intuitions, you know."

"Ha." Her laugh was brittle, uncertain, and a little wild. "I'm a left hemisphere person, Arnold. Languages, logic, that's the stuff for me. No psychic talent, or no belief, anyway. It's only an overactive imagination I've got."

He shook his head no. "You've got something else, Cassie. Everyone knows it but you."

"Well, if Millet arrives dressed the way I imagine . . ."

"Tell me what you see," he said, seeing her eyes. "Blue gray," he said aloud.

She tilted her head, quizzical. "Blue gray?"

"Your eyes," he muttered, looking down. After a pause he took her arm again. "Try an experiment?" he asked, guiding her to a picnic table under a magnolia tree, shaded, a little dew-dampened.

"What?"

"Close your eyes, visualize it again, the way you just did, and tell me everything, okay? Everything, just the way you imagine it. Go on, get relaxed, you know how to meditate, listen to the breathing or whatever you do, focus. Let it drift back up to you, don't force it."

"Arn," she said, but doing what she was told. "This is silly. We should be inside, at work."

"Don't worry about it. If it's a waste of time, so what? And maybe it isn't. We're a research facility, after all."

Dreamily she nodded, disbelief around her lips and eyes. "Okay, Arn." Her knees crossed, hands folded into the circle, thumbs lightly together just below her navel, she began to breathe. After all, she did this every day before aikido practice, ten minutes of meditation. She never felt she was particularly good at it, but it was relaxing, and it was early in the morning, and there were special damp and chilly scents rising from the ground. The sunlight was warm on her eyelids, now closed. Her breathing fell into a regular pattern, a smooth in-and-out without pauses. The turbulence of her thoughts slowed, grew still. She considered Wesley Millet:

Wesley Millet, all things sharp and glittering, swinging spindled shanks over the side of his elaborate awninged bed, calf muscles falling sadly away from shinbones in spotted lumps, stretched his arms straight out, away from his mottled, pucky chest, and there too the muscle seemed to fall into separate groups, triceps here, brachialis there, the bicep itself an apparent meeting of mutually hostile elements, a stringy mass that writhed serpentine around the humerus.

He was skinny and small, his face a pointillist fever-dream. His nose was sharp though subtly bulbed with a slight bend sinister. His sharp chin stubbled with spraggled hairs. Lips were thin, dark near to black in this morbid light, for the drapes were thick and drawn, a rich funereal brocade.

An eccentric dresser, even for these eccentric times; he favored what was wide, and large, and old-fashioned. Today he pulled on plus fours, gathered just below the knee; pants that flared widely in broad black-and-gold checks. There was a small silver buckle at the back to adjust the waist, and she saw him smile an artificially shy smile as he pulled these vast pantaloons up his shanky legs. He relished this dash of clashing color.

A silver shirt glittered in this muted room, slithered over that spindly chest, and he put on cuff links (cuff links!) *argent,* skull and crossbones, hideous grin. Carefully she saw him knot a tie in a flamboyant four-in-hand. "Hose," he said, pulling them on, the abstract clocks on them delicately crosshatched; they had been specially made for him by a family in France (Cassie imagined the family working late).

He ran an electric depilator across the spraggly chin stubble and the hairs were singed to dust and ash.

"Dust to dust," he murmured. "Ash to ash."

He drank his breakfast then, sucking a thin vegetable soup through crooked, age-stained teeth; tiny chips of browned enamel tumbled haphazard into his gums.

His coat was a rough and tweedy brown of Scotland wool, shagged and padded at shoulders, sticking out beyond his skinny arms and lumpy shoulder joints like Gothic gargoyle wings. It was double-breasted, and had a number of silver buttons and green silk piping at collar and pockets.

He paused at his heavy carved-oak door and mused over the visitors who had come through that door, the professionals who came to curry favor, politicians looking for votes he could deliver.

He stared at the hat tree beside that door, gazed over the collection of headgear gathered there: panama, fedora, borsolino, pork-pie, caps, top hat. No two hats were alike.

His telephone buzzed. He picked up the phone in his paneled den. "Yes?" he said.

The voice was a muted, waspish twitter she could not hear.

Wesley frowned, dark narrow face bunched together, lips pursed downward for a moment. "Are you sure?" he asked. The words puffed out, and the knob of his upper lip flapped with a soft *plop* sound after "sure." In Cassie's mind it sounded obscene and flatulent.

"Did she know you?" Wesley's whisper voice asked after a brief listen.

"You shadowed her?" Wesley was asking. "Shadows are invisible at night, Tom. In the day they stand out." He listened, then spoke again, "All right, all right, go on. Next time avoid eye contact though."

Wesley stared at the photographs on his desk: himself shaking hands with presidents, ex-presidents, present presidents, future presidents, the president of the Sixth Republic of France (where his hose were made).

The voice had been whisked away into the electric void. Wesley put the telephone down.

Shrugging, Wesley and the Gothic wings of his coat rose and sighed. He walked thoughtfully back to his door, looked blankly at his hat tree. The hats glowed in all their colors and patterns, fructuous and abstract; he seemed lost in thought a moment.

"He he," he tried a laugh. Then he took the hat he wanted, a large, eight-sided, brilliant lemon yellow golfing hat with an overbearing brim that canted out over his narrow eyes like a granite overhang, and put his face into a shade so deep his eyes appeared as two basilisk stares, indifferent and assessing. Satisfied with the effect, he opened the door and stepped into the brilliant March sun.

"So," Arnold said, smiling at Cassie's vision. "You see him in turn-of-the-century golfing pants, baggy ones in broad checks? And a funny yellow hat?"

Cassie was smiling too. "I told you it was silly."

"Well," he shook his head low and shaggy. "We'll see, won't we? He'll be here this morning."

"Oh, Arnold, you don't believe all that. I just don't like the DLF, so I make fun of him in my mind. Nothing psychic."

"What about you standing there in the Leaping Crane position a while ago? Don't tell me that was just imagination that made you freeze like that?"

"I don't know."

They went back up the steps. When she stumbled, he reached for her absently, stopped himself. Her hand brushed the back of his as she reached up to tuck a stray curl under her scarf.

"Well, it's a test," he said. "When Millet arrives we'll know. But how did it *feel?* Was the quality different from ordinary reverie?"

She finished tucking the curl and lowered her hand partway, reluctant suddenly to bring it down past his. Her fingers opened slowly like a time-lapse flower blooming. She watched her own hand, fascinated, and said, "I just don't know. It might have been, but I might be imagining the difference."

She noticed he was watching her hand too, rapt. And their eyes met then, an abrupt awareness, tension discharged, and they both burst into laughter.

"What the hell," she said, and seized his hand with that aimless wandering one of hers.

"Yes," he said, squeezing hers in return. They went up the stairs and through the sighing glass doors.

Inside L. R. Hubletz leaned over the PEST computer console, his empty pipe clenched between his teeth. The muted thuds of the high-speed printer rose around him smoky and dim. He hunched his shoulders and stared at some flimsy print-out.

"Hi," Cassie called cheerfully.

L.R. grunted. "Where were you?"

84

"Was I?"

"Last night. You were going to stop by. I called you at La Jolla."

"Sorry, L.R. I just couldn't do it. I would have called, but a lot of things happened yesterday, and I simply crashed, out cold. Did you call?"

"Several times."

"I didn't hear it." She shrugged. "Sorry."

L.R. grunted again. "Well, look here." He pointed his pipestem at the print-out.

"I bet it's a bell curve," she said without looking. "And I bet you're worried, and that's why you wanted me to come by last night, but there was nothing I could have done. There isn't anything I can do now. Is there?"

"Ah." L.R. seemed to be practicing his grunt.

"What?" she asked.

"PEST has gotten too good, I think." Arnold spoke slowly, but he was looking at her with a sly humor.

"How do you mean?"

"He means these projections are meaningless, that's what he means. Too good, indeed."

"Sorry, I know that. Why are they meaningless?"

Arnold flickered another smile at her.

He gestured at the wall. "PEST is a model," he said. "A model, as numerous people have observed, and as many have forgotten, is not reality, a map is not the territory. What appears to have happened here is that our model-maker, PEST, has discovered in all its idiot complexity, that the model is not the reality, and hence can have no effect on the world. So it has given us projections that will have no effect. In a nutshell, PEST has sophisticated itself out of existence."

"Bullshit!" L.R. exclaimed. "I won't believe it."

"Well, not believing might work," Arnold said dubiously. "But I suspect it's not that simple."

"Oh?"

"First of all," Arnold ticked off his fingers, "there is, perhaps, and I wouldn't bet on it, some kind of external environmental reality that we cannot perceive except in fragmentary, distorted ways. Then there is consensus reality, the one we all agree on, and act as if it were all of reality. Then there is reality as seen through senses—visual, aural, and so forth. And then there is mediated reality, seen on television, over the computer networks, the Dow-Jones averages, statistics, and so on, edited, selected, with blind spots and misdirections, subject to the ambitions and fears of us all. Then there is our model, our admittedly artificial constructs we pretend are real. And then there is belief. And probably psychic energy, which can alter reality. And concepts like time, space, love, no more real than any other concepts. There is the uncertainty principle, which says that as we observe something, like, say, the present and its events, we change the behavior of what we are observing, for we are part of the universe in which that behavior is taking place. And, I fear, so on and so forth. Our immediate problem is that PEST is a bust."

L.R. was watching the DLF contract slip away to another institution with a better model, a bigger program, a more competent staff. "I won't believe it," he repeated. "We'll get the programmers to fix the damn thing. We simply can't have this."

"Just a minute," Arnold urged. "Before we start ripping out subroutines and tinkering with the programs, let's give this a bit of thought."

"We'd better do it in a damn hurry. Wesley Millet will be here soon. We signed this DLF contract yesterday and he is entitled to daily updates. These," he shook the flimsy print-out, "are as silly as the ones yesterday."

"Will Millet know that?" she asked quietly.

L.R. was startled again. "Why, I don't know. I see what you mean. He might not know our major tool is eating itself, I suppose. Yes, I think you're right; I do think you're right. Arnold."

"So," Arnold said to Cassie as their boss stumped off, muttering. "So what we need is a surprise. Something unexpected. A little random something to get us going in the right direction. Logic is not much help here."

"Mmph," Cassie agreed.

Behind them PEST hummed and burped, meaningless chatter. The day grew warm, mist cleared from the loam, breathing out. The status wall winked and flickered, the phantoms of present events. There was Dow-Jones falling, inflation rising, lights in the skies, rains of blood or mud, clear-sky hail, two-headed calves, interest groups, cults, pollution, species extinct forever and others threatened, energy sapped along with will. Ten years away the millennium waited, an open mouth filled with teeth and random, uncontrolled technologies.

"Might be," Arnold murmured, not looking at her.

"There are other things, too. The cetaceans, for example. Mr. Brockhurst must have intended something when he sent me there. I get only glimpses, something huge, limitless it seems, moving events in ways just out of reach, ways we can't control."

"Yes. We can't quantify the future." He gestured at useless PEST chattering. "So we have to develop all the other tools. Intuition, ESP, systems, holism, whatever. The ecology of time. You may have a talent you don't really believe in yet."

"Well, when Wesley Millet arrives, we will find out."

There was a noise at the entrance doors, and they all turned. A man was standing there, ridiculous in tweedy knickers, guffawing heartily. He whipped his enormous hat from his dark peaked hair and slapped it against his thigh. The yellow screamed bright.

"Turn-of-the-century golfing pants in broad checks and a yellow golfing hat. I'll be damned," Arnold breathed in.

Cassie was startled as well. There Millet was, just as she had imagined him: the brown jacket, the silver shirt, the creamy hose with abstract clocks, the hat. A sharp shaft of fear fixed her to the floor. She had *seen*.

She did not want to see, not like that, not with that kind of clarity,

87

that certainty; it was obscene, a fat, white, grubby, obscenity. She turned away and walked stiffly to her office.

Behind her she dimly heard L.R. greeting his client. She closed her door.

"He's a golden codger," she said aloud, absurdly. " 'There all the golden codgers lay.' In the song. He's a golden codger, that hat." She sat and stared at the blank top of her desk, its dull polish. Light from her window glanced off the surface. Her eyes filled with liquid, fractioning the light into an abstract dazzle in which she saw a crystal, coiled at the bottom of the jar, multi-sided, glowing with a dull white light. Whales swam through it, serene and smooth.

She wanted to shut it out this time, to deny it, to say this was not as she had seen, this was coincidence, this yellow hat, those absurd trousers. She preferred the safety of her ordinary consciousness, of her occasional fugues into memory or fantasy (as she had always considered them), of sleep and dream.

Yet there was the crystal, and whales swimming, and dreaming of things that happened or seemed to happen.

Her hands were gripping the edge of her desk, the knuckles blanched, and a luminous pattern through the moisture in her eyes shone off of them as well. She allowed them to relax, the fingers, so they lay serenely, side by side on the dark wood.

Slowly fear left her. She took deep breaths, slowly exhaled, drifted into meditation again, and without noticing her consciousness changed once more, and she was somewhere else. There was tension in her neck, distracting her. She let go.

"Dash," she heard. "Dash, come on."

He groaned, deeply.

"Dash, wake up."

He shuddered; his swollen tongue stirred obscenely in his numb mouth, the flat tip questing blindly at the ranks of teeth.

"Come on, Dash. You'll be late."

This is the Satanist I met at the Japanese health club, Cassie noted, detached observer. This is Dash Crowley.

He groaned again. "I hate dentists," he said. His eyes opened. To Cassie it was like a dream, being both him, with his point of view, and not him, outside.

"I hate dentists," he repeated.

"I heard you," his wife answered.

88

"They are an affront to dignity," he said. "They do what magic should do better and doesn't."

"Yes, dear."

"I dreamed I was casting spells. Can you understand me? My tongue is numb. I dreamed I was holding a Jerusalem artichoke shaped like the dentist in my left hand, left for sinister, you understand. In my right hand I had some henbane, a little sprig of it, you know, and was breathing it in, smelling it. Very powerful and real, that part. An unpleasant odor. I stroked the artichoke with the leaves, and said things like 'Coridal, Nerdac, Degon.' But my lips were numb and I couldn't get the words out. Success was that close, you see, I almost had that dentist where I wanted him, writhing in agony, but my mouth wouldn't work. I moaned, croaked, scrawked, gargled, but I couldn't get the damn words out. It was awful."

"I can imagine."

He sighed. Her overripe breasts swayed inside her nightie. Large, pink-tipped, fructuous breasts begging to be tweaked. What was going in his mind? Temptations of the flesh, black mass, inversions, thick smoke, and everything upside down. Heavy goat-smells, leaping firelight, the veil of the future partially rent, revealing a vision of this plump and comic thaumaturge atop his ample wife, plump bottom squinching and bobbing.

"Anything you want," she said, lifting her nightie.

Cassie opened her eyes. The wall above her desk was still there, blank since she took down the decision tree. There was still a very faint outline of the rectangle, the wall slightly sun-faded around the spot, and the two words: *Flaming Music.* Afternoon sun splashed into her office, but not now. No sun in here just now, no flame, no music. The hills out the window were visible, though, and they were crowned with light.

Her fingers were still lying inertly on the desk top, thin, not altogether beautiful fingers, but serviceable. She flexed them, humped up over the desk edge, relaxed them again. Curious embarrassment glowed in her belly, for she had imagined something between Dash and his wife that must have come from her own needs or desires.

She closed her eyes: Dash Crowley lying in bed, beside his wife, who at this moment is tugging at his earlobe, giving it a little affectionate tug. "Nice, Agnes," he said.

"Oh," Cassie breathed to herself, backing off again, within a fraction of opening her eyes again.

He sat up, his doughy belly forming three loose folds above the blanket edge, hiding his navel. Adam had no navel, but magic properties instead.

Agnes too sat up, her navel open, belly forming a slope so it was held cuplike upward by the gentle roundness. Very soft and sweet. Then she stood up and walked away, while Dash watched. It was a desirable bottom, dammit, and Cassie felt his smile.

She got out for sure this time, by staring widely at the blank wall.

There was a soft knock on her door.

"Yeah."

It opened and Arnold peered around it. "Hi. Are you all right? You looked pale."

"I'm fine. Come on in. I was just having a little fantasy about that magician we met the other night, Crowley. The feeling was different from this morning, though—real fantasy, not vision. I'm learning. I was imagining him putting a spell on his dentist."

"You can tell the difference?"

"I think I *can* tell the difference. It's as if there were a flag there, a notice of some kind saying, this is reality, or this is imagination, or this is memory, or this is déjà vu. All slightly different from one another. You advised me to trust it."

"So I did, so I did. But come on out, now. We have Wesley Millet on our hands, and he wants to meet the whole team working on the DLF project. That's you and me."

"I'd rather not, Arn. Isn't there someone else who could do it? I don't really feel right about this one."

"He asked for you, especially." He held out his hand. "Come on."

"Why me?" she asked as they walked to the conference room.

Arnold shrugged. "It'll be all right," he tried to reassure her. "Really."

Millet was frowning at the print-outs lying on the table before him and did not look up when they entered. L.R. hovered nearby, fluttering, as if he were not sure whether to put his pipe in his mouth or not. Finally he smiled weakly at Cassie and Arnold.

Millet looked up. "Ah," he stood, reached out his hand. "Ms. St. Clair, so nice to see you once again. So nice." His hat lay on the table, large, eight-sided, yellow.

She shook his hand briefly and murmured something congenial. He bristled with energy; it sparkled off him in all directions. His absurd clothing, peculiar narrow face, his glad-handed manner were a ruse, she felt, to put people off his scent.

"Now we are all here," Millet said, looking around. He nodded and sat abruptly, gesturing. The others sat as well.

"These projections you have given me, from your PEST model. They don't seem to mean much, ah?" He looked at L.R., who shifted uncomfortably in his seat.

"Ah. As I thought. Here, this doesn't seem to indicate much of an impact on the public consciousness from a major DLF announcement. The DLF is a large organization. An announcement of the sort we are about to make would have a profound effect. Even without knowing what it is precisely, you must be aware of that. So what exactly is going on here?"

The question was followed by a lengthy silence. Cassie stared at her nibbled thumbnail, then spoke, slowly and deliberately. "Yes, Mr. Millet. But we have something of a complex problem here. Without knowing more about the precise nature of your announcement we really can't do too much more for you."

Millet nodded. "You all seem pretty disorganized around here. You give me a bunch of mindless computer print-outs and expect me to go away satisfied . . ."

"Now, Mr. Millet . . ." L.R. began.

"Don't now me, Dr. Hubletz. The DLF is asking for immediate, intelligible, useful results, and paying well for it. We have a right to expect something better than this." He slapped the stack of paper in front of him.

"That's quite true, Mr. Millet," Cassie said. "But we need more information. And as for disorganization, you must also understand that what we do is advise those who are making plans for the future. We make forecasts based on the best available information, including that provided by the client. Your information is, in fact, the most important of all. 'Major announcement' is useless to us. And furthermore, we do our forecasting with the aid of right hemisphere abilities—gestalts, intuitions, hunches, even—to the extent we can. We are synthesizers, holists, systems analysts, aided by logic and computers, their models and simulations." She paused to look at him.

He stared back, unblinking.

"Now we do have some information, of course. What is available publicly. We do know, for example, the DLF researches life after death, and we do know that large groups of people yearn for reassurance, certainty, survival; so an announcement of importance in that area would certainly appear to be desired enough to have significant impact, whether it was a proof of survival or of no survival—positive or negative. However," she held up her hand, "the world is so fragmented, specialized, compartmentalized, and disjointed that it is quite possible such an announcement would have no impact whatsoever, merely because there is so much information competing for attention, and so much of it is surprising that people no longer are surprised by anything, despite their hunger for what is new and magical."

She could see L.R. looking at her with a turgid gratitude in his eyes. She smiled. She was getting good at this kind of thing.

"So," Millet said.

"So."

"I suppose you would like me to tell you what the announcement will concern?"

"It would help."

"You are on the right track."

"And?"

"And I will have to check back with my people."

"Mr. Millet, I presume you wish to make a plan, right?"

"We are working on a plan, yes. We want of course to maximize the effect of our announcement. As you have stated, Ms. St. Clair, the world is in a fragmented, unhappy state. The DLF means to do something about that. If, as you say, our announcement would have little effect on that fragmentation, then we must plan a way to increase that effect. We must prepare the world, and it must be soon. We will need it by Monday."

"But this is Wednesday," L.R. protested.

"An acute observation, Dr. Hubletz. Wednesday indeed."

"Mr. Millet, do you know about McTaggart's Paradox?" Cassie asked.

He shook his head.

"John McTaggart Ellis McTaggart proved, logically, that there was no such thing as time. A philosopher's game, perhaps, but it does give one food for thought. But never mind that. What do you know about Li Po on Mercury?"

"This had better be good," Wesley Millet snapped.

"All the craters on Mercury were named after writers and artists," Cassie said earnestly. "Homer, Shakespeare, Bach, and so on. A lovely idea, isn't it? Well, Yeats, who wrote 'News for the Delphic Oracle,' is seven degrees due south of Li Po. Li Po was drowned trying to pull the moon from a river when drunk, so they say."

Millet stared at her, eyes squinched tight, small glossy highlights glancing off the black, depthless pupils. "So?" he said.

"Please. Li Po was eighth-century Chinese, Yeats twentieth-century Irish. Yet they are neighbors on Mercury, a Roman god whose cult began around 495 B.C. in southern Italy—the god of thieves and tricksters, commerce, science and technology, eloquence and the arts. Patron of travelers and athletes. But above all, commerce. See?"

"No, I can't say that I do." There was an irritable snap to his voice, and she noticed for the first time how dimensionless his voice was, how thin and devoid of overtones, as if over a bad phone line.

"The point is, Mr. Millet, all that naming is metaphor. When an organization like IF attempts projections into the future, creates forecasts, simulations, or models, what we do is create metaphors, not realities. Metaphors clustered with beliefs, intangibles. Li Po, a Chinese poet, Yeats an Irish one, Mercury a planet and a Roman god, all coming together, a capsule history of human culture. Mercury is a planet very like the moon, whose reflection Li Po was trying to grasp. And all these ideas, these beliefs and lores, these interconnections are metaphors, moving along with us into the future through the present moment."

"You are not making a great deal of sense, young lady," Millet snapped, and she suppressed the desire to tell him she was thirty-eight, and not all that young.

"Let me put it this way," she went on, glancing first at L.R., who had a comic mixture of confusion and alarm on his face, and then at Arnold, who was watching her with a dry amusement: He knew what she was saying. "No one could have predicted what the committee of astronomers who named the craters would use for names when NASA mapped Mercury. No one. Yet the names are perfectly logical, if anthropocentric. IF is in the business of tracking events like that, a small thing, but a factor in the whole, which includes things like astronomers, and planets, artists, writers, ancient gods, everything connected in hidden and subtle ways, you see? We attempt to make those connections, some of them important, others less so, but all interconnected. All projections are crude at first, and very inaccurate. More data helps, for a time, but finally, data stops helping, and the leap must be made that connects it all into the system."

She sneezed, then, a harsh, grating sneeze that sent a bow wave of shock and pain up her throat. "Sorry," she said, pulling a Kleenex from her pocket. "Excuse me." She left the room.

She went to the lounge to get aspirin.

"Are you all right?" Looking up, she saw Arnold in the doorway.

"I lost track." She was sitting on a couch, staring into her cupped-hands.

"Oh," he sliced the air with the edge of his hand. "It's only been a few minutes. Sounds like you're getting a nasty cold."

"I took some aspirin. Arn, yesterday I swam with those dolphins, and now I can barely remember it. All this dailiness is getting me. Millet, DLF, PEST. It must be the cold, but I feel light-headed and remote from it all, like it isn't important, that what is important is right at the tip of my tongue, or just at the edge of my vision, and I can't pin it down, though it has something to do with the whales. I think."

"Trust that," he said softly.

She smiled then. "Okay, I feel a little better. Back to the arena?"

He squeezed her hand. "This won't last much longer. Millet has to go back and talk to his people. All he'll say is that the announcement has to do with the spiritual realm, as he calls it."

"Yeah."

They went into the conference room, where Millet and L.R. were passing pages of the contract back and forth; it seemed a ritual exchange, an activity to fill the time. After all, it had been signed yesterday.

She looked around the room. Carved cornices, rich paneling, side table with telephone. She had talked to Wilbur Brockhurst on that telephone, but had never seen him. She'd heard a thousand reasons why—he was ill, something came up, next week he would come in, or the week after. Somehow he never did, and remained a low, slow rumbling voice on the phone, thoughtful and patient and remote.

Wesley Millet was on his way out; he paused to say to her, "I wanted to thank Ms. St. Clair for her words. Very thought-provoking, I'm sure. I will be getting back to you, later today, I suspect. About the announcement, it's precise nature, that is. I have taken your point." He slapped the table with his yellow hat, and then set it carefully on his narrow head; his eyes disappeared into shadow beneath the brim, and he sauntered out. The door sighed shut behind him.

The aikido exercise drove the fuzzy visions from her head, brought sweat down her forehead and back; spins and throws were smooth and easy, without thought. The headache receded too. When she got back to the office it was quiet; she ate cottage cheese and stared out her window. This was going to be a busy week, that was clear. IF was one of the twentieth-century technological oracles, but it worked slower than the one at Delphi had. Five more days to come up with a plan for the DLF. At Delphi they would have said, as they did to Croesus, "Attack and a great empire will be destroyed," and that would be that.

Croesus took the oracle at face value and attacked Cyrus. He crossed the Halys River, marched against the Persians, and was destroyed. His own empire fell. The oracle was right.

Cassie thought Croesus held the wrong values: If it had been important to him to preserve great empires and prevent suffering, he would never have attacked. And the oracle would still have been right.

Perhaps they needed an "IF" statement here, for the DLF? "If you make an announcement, a great organization will be destroyed."

She drifted, filled with a sleepy satisfaction, fed and exercised and replete, able for the time to ignore the scratching in her throat, the headache. A warm current lifted her and carried her gently, dozing in the sunlight pouring through her window. There was a distant

95

chiming again, in her memory, very clear. She drifted, did not think of rings or hoops of metal. She saw Anthony Malatesta for a moment, the network of exploded veins across the fleshy greater alar cartilage at the end of his nose. He was leaning toward her, a strange expression gleaming in his eyes. She backed away, felt the chair press against her spine.

Saw Goring and Goring. Calling up the dead. George St. Clair died when she was nine, left her in that house with her mother and baby sister. She saw Buddy's face, unformed and adolescent, above her. Where was her first lover Buddy, after all this time, these years, her marriage and divorce? Fragments were blowing through her mind, speeded as though pushed by a cold and ghostly wind. What was that sound? The bells. Goats, grazing on a sun-drenched hillside in Greece, the earth dry, brown, dusty; it was not far from Eleusis, she felt the ruins nearby, the marble worn, pale, warm under her palm. She was looking up the hillside at the goats, not thinking about that tinkling sound until it came closer, grew louder. She turned, then, saw the source, a gypsy caravan approaching her, drawn by a sleek black mare. Greece was filled with gypsies this time of year, despised and feared with their strange language and filthy ways. This was a memory, this caravan, tagged with time and place in her mind, carefully filed, retrieved now and displayed for her. The gypsy was a fortune-teller, one who pretended to see into the future.

And then Madame Renata Glabro, whose neon palm beckoned. The lady psychic, graduate of many weekend workshops, seminars at Esalen, retreats with witches' covens in Vermont, a professional seer.

Cassie sighed, deeply, hauling air into herself with an almost desperate greed, letting it go reluctantly. She felt the chair back, pressing against her spine, and forced a relaxation. But she did not open her eyes, did not come up just yet. There were more images waiting there for her. There was the orca, floating before her window, in the air above the daffodils, black-and-white brilliance against the green. The sensuous flow of ocean water along her own sides, the tough, resilient feel of dolphin skin, the creaks and whistles of orca talk and dolphin chatter. Li Po on Mercury. Yeats. Human history, blended, rewritten, revised, connected now inextricably with cetacean history.

Arnold touched her shoulder and she opened her eyes.

And saw the Devas seated, glowing, amid fiery mandalas. Saw their hands, fingers curled in mystic mudras, circles, cups, and lilies. Saw the light, the serene and stern expressions. Saw one of that saintly company lean toward her from a great height, lean low, bowing at the waist though seated, suffused with light, all the powers and dominions and saints of higher being circled behind her. Saw her mouth open, blurred light on the teeth pulsing, a brilliant white. Heard words spoken to her alone, although the words did not seem to synchronize with the movement of those lips.

"They laugh at us, you know," the Deva said. Cassie knew she meant the animals, the whales and elephants, the vast and shambling hulks, and she cried out "Why?" in her mind, but the figure was receding with incredible swiftness, until it was indistinguishable from all the others, seated in that vast semicircle, eyes half-closed in deep meditation.

Light formed around them, a gauzy cloud that dimmed the figures into itself, folded over and over until they were gone completely into petals of light.

She was looking out the window. An ordinary window, rectangular, with aluminum edges painted brown, and double panes of solar glass. There was spring sunshine out there, and daffodils, and green mountains. She was looking through wide-meshed drapes.

"Arnold," she said.

"Yes," his hand on her shoulder.

"I'm scared."

"Yes." A slight pressure, and his thumb pushed its way down between her collarbones, seeking the pressure point. She felt herself relax.

"I keep getting them—visions, fugues, I don't know. I can't think about anything, I just see people, things, places. I yearn to go back to the dolphins but I can't, that seems to be closed to me now. A weird crystal comes up, about four or five inches long, coiled like a snake at the bottom of a jar, glowing with a sluggish light. I don't know."

He said nothing, hands on her shoulders now, thumbs pressing in. She reached to touch the back of one of them. "Ah, where did you learn that?"

She could feel him shrug, her own body trembling, that faint tinkling still in her ears.

"She said, 'They laugh at us.' The Deva I just saw. I knew she meant the elephants and whales. Why would they laugh at us, Arn? We have hunted them, driven the elephants off of all their land, practically exterminated them, hunted the whales and made them into pet food and lipstick. What do they have to laugh at?"

"Maybe they know something we don't," he suggested.

"What, Arnold? What do they know?"

"The Joke?"

She turned under his hands, stared up at him.

Okay, he smiled, then shrugged. Why not?

"Arnold!" she chided him.

"In fact," he said solemnly, "I am serious. About the Joke. Remember the Taoist sage in the painting Monday. It's at the heart of Zen lore—the Buddha's smile."

Later she was still looking for surprises, some new and unexpected insight, a random collation of stimuli to break the stalemate. The world shifted under her feet, turning, vertiginous. Her head was empty.

Belief, she thought. Everything relies on belief—law, custom, social grace, and discord. More nukes, less kooks. Jihad and crusade, traffic lights and Inquisitions.

She saw herself seated at the dressing table, and her stepfather approaching, in the mirror. She was trying to curl her hair under her ear. She'd said, "Damn!" She remembered running, a nightmare paralysis dragging at her feet, the light falling in shards.

In her office there was double exposure as she swiveled in her chair, light flaring off the edges of things, her desk, the CRT, the window. She stood, and her body felt itself standing before her dressing table, a kinesthetic déjà vu, turning to run, as her mirror shattered. She took a step, and that eighteen-year-old self took the same step, away, toward the door. She moved through it, tranced, thralled, into the hallway, where this awful spell was broken, gone as if it had never happened.

The status wall was a flare of colors. She watched graphs swoop and fall and rise again, watched alphanumeric data swim upward across the tiny screens, the network news via satellite, switching automatically, searching for that random concatenation.

She typed in some cues for the computer search: UFO, whales, DLF. Across the bottom of the status wall the six screens began tracking.

There was violence on the second screen, the camera unsteady in the midst of it. A demonstration, placards waved aimlessly, a group of tense, angry faces wading among them, swinging. The readout stated it was Atlanta, Georgia, 5:47 P.M., March 28. She typed in a request for text on number one.

UPI described a Friends of the Sea demonstration in Atlanta. As she watched, an inflated humpback whale broke loose and drifted into the sky, a vast gray shadow over the tumult. She saw placards with "whale bait," "animal lover," "traitors." The camera bobbed, trying to take in everything, the drifted whale balloon, the placards, the scuffles breaking out here and there; suddenly the picture tilted sideways, picked up an out-of-focus face clenched white as a fist.

"Someone was killed yesterday. In Houston." L.R. pointed at the screen with the stem of his pipe. "Damnedest thing."

"I've been missing something," Cassie told him. "What is going on?"

"Antiwhale groups, all over the place. Demonstrations in Houston, Atlanta, Kansas City, Chicago. All inland. Violent clashes with the Friends of the Sea, Sierra Club, Greenpeace."

"What are the issues? Why be antiwhale?"

L.R. sighed, raised his bushy eyebrows expressively. It was, he fancied, one of his better facial gestures; it always made Cassie smile. Not this time, though.

"Resources," he told her. "Nuclear power on the ocean floor."

"I saw that group, at the La Jolla airport."

"Mmm. Mariculture, mineral deposits on the continental shelf, tidal turbines, fish herding. Pollution, on the other side. Mainly, though, it seems to be protein. Whales are both useless and filled with protein. It would be better to take the protein before it gets turned into whale—more economical."

"But whales are intelligent!"

L.R. shrugged. "Never stopped humans before, has it?"

"No," she admitted, saw a montage of armies clashing in dust.

He tapped the screen. "A bunch of crackpots, perhaps. But someone was killed in Houston yesterday. Not funny."

"No, not funny. Is there any connection here with the DLF, do you think? Between PEST's failure and Millet's reticence, we are stuck. I thought the status wall might jog something. 'A judicious increase in turbulence' it was called once."

"Put in an hour on it," L.R. said. "Then come up with something. We don't have much time." He turned away.

Cassie curled her lip after him. Then she went into the library.

There were books, journals, a DataNet terminal. She ran a fast literature search on interest groups. An article in the *Michigan State Bulletin of Psycho-Sociology* caught her eye: "Scarcity Scares and the Irrational: An Inquiry into Millennial Belief."

Since the late sixties, belief in the irrational had increased. Books on astrology commanded some of the highest paperback advances in the history of publishing. Ancient astronauts, the Bermuda Triangle, psychic archaeology, Indian magicians, and Tibetan fakirs all captured a large share of the public attention, paralleled by swiftly increasing membership in a broad range of religious cults, from the Visitors' Disciples to Reverend Moon. There were American Sikhs (called "diaperheads") in Lansing, Michigan, and Hindus in Duluth. In the late seventies a journal had been founded for the express purpose of combating this increase in the irrational: *The Skeptical Inquirer.*

It was energy-scarcity, inflation and millennial thinking among other factors, which might be causing this increase in irrationality. But the results were an abundance of opportunities for cynical manipulation of belief. Friends of the Sea, for example, and affiliated or sympathetic groups, were seen by many people to be the equivalent of Communists in the 1950s, softheaded, misdirected do-gooders, fellow travelers who would betray the human race for some slimy fish.

Despite *The Skeptical Inquirer,* the experiences of many believers appeared to be "real."

It was the job of the Society for Psycho-Sociology to remain impartial, to investigate belief, and the experiences that led to it, and the manner in which it could be manipulated.

This was, however, the final issue of the *Bulletin.* Lack of funds was closing both the society and its publication.

Cassie slapped the computer console. The whole article had turned out to be a complaint.

"There is no magic," she said aloud. "No free lunch . . . You can't get something for nothing."

She went in search of her partner in the DLF project. "Arnold, there is no free lunch."

"Are you hungry?"

"I am not joking. There is no such thing as magic. People are unhappy and will not accept that. People want the Visitors to arrive and solve all our problems for us. They are not going to do it."

"They aren't?"

"You're being sarcastic. Of course I don't believe in *them*. The question is, is there such a thing as psychic talent? That seems to imply something for nothing. No energy to carry the information—no photons or molecular vibrations, nothing. Something for nothing. See? It can't exist, but this morning I saw Millet's clothes. Accurately."

"There has been research, quite a bit in the last fifteen years or so, in support of psychic abilities, though no adequate explanations as yet; a hypothesis or two revising our notions of time and causality, mostly from high-energy physics, look promising though."

"What about *The Zetetic*, the *Skeptical Inquirer?* The Committee for the Scientific Investigation of Claims of the Paranormal?"

Arnold shrugged. "The world is a busy place," he observed.

"Okay. I want to try something. All this busy work, these literature searches, even the status wall—we're getting nowhere. I want to get a room, hook up to the feedback machine, try a little *mushin no shin* . . ."

"A little what?"

"It's Zen. Something like 'A mind of no-mind.' "

"Ah. A discrete altered state of consciousness. What Charles Tart called a d-ASC. You've already been doing that."

"I know. What I want to do now is try magic."

"Oh."

It wasn't working, that much was obvious.

Rich sandalwood odor filled the room. A twist of smoke coiled upward, found the ceiling, flattened against it. She watched it absently, and her thoughts coiled in her mind, twisted upward, spread. She tried to let her thoughts go, and her thoughts became trying to let thoughts go.

It made her angry. If there was no magic, what had Joanne seen?

But this wasn't magic, this was meditation, and she wasn't good at it. It wasn't working.

She had tried a spell. The hypnotic effect of words. Calling up the spirits.

Now it was lychnoscopy.

Three candles were burning, special candles, purchased at an occult paraphernalia shop in Palo Alto. Candles of very fine wax, with sandalwood aroma; they were arranged in a small triangle on the bare floor, and the smoke rose, coiled, flattened.

If the flame wavered from left to right, an early change of surroundings.

When L.R. stuck his head in the door by mistake, the flame had wavered from left to right. A change of surroundings.

It wasn't working. There was so such thing as magic. No free lunch.

If it turned in a spiral then there are maneuvers by secret enemies. And of course it was turning in a spiral. The goddamn smoke was coiling like rope. No, like a double helix. This was DNA she was watching, a twisted ladder of life.

Just three sweet-smelling candles.

Long ago she had given up on the alpha-theta machine. Somewhat later she had given up zazen, *mushin no shin*.

If the flame alternately rose and fell, perilous vicissitudes. With every beat of her heart, the flame rose and fell, lub-dub, lub-dub. So perilous vicissitudes. Perilous vicissitudes.

Was there a very fine point of brilliant light forming just at the end of the wick of one of the candles? A spark of white among the blues and dirty oranges? Successes will come in ever-increasing numbers. She could not be sure there was a bright point of light in there, for smoke coiled and writhed before her, touched the ceiling and spread. The room itself was quite ordinary, one of the smaller conference rooms at IF, windowless and fitfully lit by these three very special and quite expensive candles, manufactured in a dungeon somewhere by a coven of twentieth-century witches.

She knew that if one of the candles burned more brightly than the others then she would have unforseen good fortune, but if the flames threw off sparks, then it was a warning of reverses or disappointments and an appeal to her prudence. And if, God forbid, one or more of the candles went out suddenly, that was an extremely tragic augury.

It definitely was not working. Cassie closed her eyes.

For a moment she was seated at her dressing table, the image of her stepfather's face printed against the inside of her eyelids as she closed her eyes.

Then she was holding a jar in which a milky crystal coiled, smoky and lunar. She heard it clink faintly against the thick glass.

She watched a vast elephant lift his trunk and wave.

An orca's mouth open, showing teeth.

Her mother's prim and bitter mouth.

Her own face, aging before her horrified look, sagging, wrinkled into decay, hair graying, turning white, twisting like smoke.

She opened her eyes, then, sharp fear searing through her. And was Wesley Millet, driving through glittering March sunshine toward the freeway, humming a tuneless and ragged song.

She fretted, uncrossed her feet. Arnold dozed against the opposite wall, his face wavering in the candlelight. There was a dry ache high in her nasal passages, an uneasiness in her stomach as of motion sickness.

"Motion," Wesley Millet said, "is life. Keep things moving and you've got it made."

"What about the planets?" Wesley Millet asked himself in a snide, sarcastic voice. "They move, and they aren't alive. Ha!" he slapped his palm against the top of his dashboard. "Where would we be without this one?" As if that answered the question.

Cassie sighed. It wasn't working. She watched the smoke from the candles twisting in a spiral, braiding, twining, climbing the helix. Maneuvers by secret enemies. New green wild oats stirred by the roadside as Wesley Millet's car sailed past. The towers of the city rose on the horizon. Wesley Millet was a stew of ideas, plans, ambitions, random deceptions. At times the clown, at times the king.

It grew dark as his car threaded between the city walls, the skyscraper canyons. He parked under the freeway south of Market and walked with a jaunty stride to his office, an antique oddity among the glistening towers, a three-story brown brick building with the streaked patina of too many seasons, passed over in the urban renewal rush. All windows on the second floor were boarded up, a graying plywood row of dirty eyepatches. Under the intricate chipped cornices of the roof all the windows had white X's painted across the glass.

Cassie knew this was the former world headquarters of the DLF, now moved to Embarcadero Center, those tall, cement gray monuments to dead space. A heavy chain was draped across the doorway, and Wesley Millet pulled a key from his pocket and opened the padlock. The chain fell to the sidewalk with a heavy sound, metallic and harsh.

She opened her eyes gain, and saw, in the watery light of the candles, the gypsy caravan clattering toward her with faint metallic sounds. Hot sun in a pale sky, heat waves over asphalt. A dry and brittle land, much like California.

She was a tired crone of a building, didn't even dye her hair blue like the elegant Victorians across town; just an old widow with muzzy light filtered through dust on the ground-floor windows hatched with chicken wire.

Wesley climbed the frayed stairs to the third floor, unlocked a door, and entered his office with a bang.

She stifled a sneeze, and a stab of pain shot through her sinuses. It was the sound of the door hitting the wall, that sneeze, her own eyes squeezed shut. And then, perhaps, the sound of a telephone ringing, though she could not be sure it was not a telephone in a nearby office, ringing distantly, alone in an empty room.

"Hmm?" said Wesley Millet's voice into the receiver.

"How much?" he said. The office was plain, clean, bare. A cheap wooden desk, a swivel chair, a metal filing cabinet that contained, she somehow knew, a bottle of Scotch and two glasses.

"Since Houston," Wesley Millet was saying, "we have to be careful . . . Our own people. We have very little time left, now." He drummed his fingers on the wooden surface before him. "This is big, Tom. A big campaign. IF is just a tiny part of it. There is nothing to worry about there, only if Brockhurst . . . Yes . . . Yes, Okay." Wesley Millet stared thoughtfully at the inside of the white painted X on his window. "The girl?" he asked softly. "No, I don't think so." A naked light bulb hung down from the ceiling, throwing a hard light over his desk, his knuckles. "Stay clear . . . she will lead us there."

The old-fashioned filament of the bulb flared brightly inside the clear glass. That brightness appeared to twist sinuously, to undulate.

Lead us there, Cassie thought. A thick-veined hand reached out. "Lead me." A face without eyes, the voice low and commanding, yet pleading. A distant light, where the others waited, she took the hand, felt power and life in the ropy muscle and tendon of the hand.

"Don't worry about that," Wesley Millet said. "I'll let them stew this afternoon, call later with their instructions. That is what we are paying them for."

Wesley Millet hung up. The light bulb flared violently, and Cassie sneezed, her head snapping back against the wall behind her.

"Look," Arnold said. He was pointing.

One of the candles had gone out; the wick glowed with a dying red ember.

"You sneezed," he said.

She nodded. An extremely tragic augury. But for whom?

She stared out her window at the thick bed of daffodils in the foreground. Her eyes rested on the rich yellow blooms as they bobbed before an errant breeze. The weather outside continued fair, but this wind meant clouds, cold, rain. There was a front off the coast, and although they often broke before reaching shore, a few made it through the natural high pressure there this time of year.

The daffodils were almost finished. She could see that now, looking closer, the droop to their heads, the curl of petals; she could imagine the thick, cloying scent of their decay. Yet the leaves were dark, rich green, and the tulips in the next bed were showing promising streaks of color through the sepals.

She felt a gloom in spite of the clear, windswept skies, the hard, brilliant sunshine. A chill, although she was inside and the temperature was mild. Not just the cold building in her head, but a greater, vaster chill.

She stared at a slit of crimson tulip that tossed intermittently into view behind the daffodils. Was fog curling just out of sight over the mountains, waiting to bring its cold touch? Pah.

The world was filled with strangeness: the dead walking at night, flying saucers, meetings with little people, virgin births, mud rains and lights in the skies and toads falling. Inexplicable paralysis, mechanical failures, dwarfs in metal suits.

Yet the scene before her was ordinary, solid, pleasant. March sun, daffodils and tulips, the green hillsides. The oleander hedge was in bloom across the driveway.

She remembered that oleander was extremely poisonous.

Her head drooped; the pounding in her temples grew. She thought the word *temple*. The time of year. It was March, of course, springtime.

The time of year for the festival of Apollo Delphinios, just now, when the winter storms were almost over and the sea would become tranquil once more. She thought about the festival, as she had studied it once, long ago. A festival of expiation.

What murders, what bloody memory or contaminations did it seek to amend? Some thin line haunted this climate, some thread of evil carried down from a time when there was no such a thing as memory at all, when smoky fires lit the low-ceilinged rooms, when smoky light leaped and scattered and the night closed in. When the bright sun was remote and dim, and the sea a cold, violent, and hostile place, though the birthplace of all life.

Dolphins swam through that sea, cold and salt and harsh, smooth gray bodies at home in its evil dark. They had talked with me before, long ago. In Crete, they told her. An island in the Aegean Sea, where Minos ruled from the labyrinth, until his kingdom was destroyed by volcano at Thera. But in Crete they spoke Greek, Linear B, a syllabic writing system. And then there was Linear A, undeciphered till this day, though the same script. Was Linear A a written form of Delphinese, now lost? It answered questions for her, many questions. Why was it lost, though? Only the memory of that time, preserved in the festival of expiation, the Delphinia. Expiation: Whatever crimes had brought on the winter storms must be atoned for in the spring.

A crime that had to do with dolphins. A crime against the dolphins. Hunting them, not honoring them, man turned his back on the sea. Minos destroyed.

She took an olive branch in her left hand, and carefully wound fillets of white wool around the gray and green leaves, the seamy bark. She would be one of the chosen, one of the seven maidens, sixteen years old, a virgin still (Buddy was later, when she was eighteen). She was the leader of the line of seven maidens who would walk to the Delphinian Temple just southeast of the Olympeion, the odd conical peak of Mount Lykabettos off to the north. The procession, seven maidens and seven youths, would thread around the base of the Acropolis through the dusty streets of the old city to that small temple where the ceremony would save them all once more, preserve the city and its fleet.

It was exciting to be chosen, of course, an honor to her and her family. She jittered as her mother dressed her. She looked in the bronze mirror and brushed back her hair, an errant curl beside her ear exasperating her; she stamped her foot impatiently.

Now she wound the fillet of wool, mouth tight with concentration. All things sacred to Apollo. She held the branch before her and looked at it critically.

"Oh," she stamped her foot once more, adjusted the wool again around the lower twigs. "Better," she murmured.

"Come *on.*" Outside the gate a boy was waiting for her. He too held an olive branch. He was the leader of the seven youths.

"All right, all *right!*" She ran out breathless, her mother hovering at the door, hand braced against the lintel. She did not hear her mother sigh. How big she was then!

The day was clear, the air filled with the dry smell of dust and wild flowers down from Hymettus, where the bees even now would be working to make the sweet honey, taking advantage of the brief spring season just beginning.

She ran a few paces, forced herself to slow down, more dignified, to adopt the solemn pace as she had been taught. It was difficult, very difficult, to contain her excitement. She tried not to glance over at the boy at her side, finally lowered her lashes and quickly looked. He was staring straight ahead as he walked, holding his branch upright before him carefully. Quickly she looked at her own, which had tilted, and straightened it.

The others fell in behind them, and citizens paused to watch them go past. She could hear them tell one another what was happening, this was the time for the Delphinia, to protect the fleet, sacred to the Dolphin Apollo. Propitiation, amends.

She hadn't thought in all the months since she had been chosen about the real purpose of the festival. It had been an honor, naturally, to be chosen, but that was all. Until now, the day was here, she was marching through the streets, and the awed whispers of the older people along her path reminded her of that purpose. Expiate; make amends.

As they wound their way around the base of the Acropolis, which rose sheer on this side over them, hiding the great Temple of Athena from view, a cold breeze caught at the hem of her skirt, tugged at it, begging attention. She tried to ignore it, but the chill seeped underneath, her legs felt cold. It might rain again, though there were no clouds in the sky.

They entered the shadow of the Acropolis, and the temperature, already cold, dropped further. The sun was low, it was late afternoon already. Soon the dazzling violet tops of Mount Hymettus would show sunset colors. By then the ceremony would be over.

They came once more into sunshine, out of the shade, and the unfinished foundation of the Temple of Olympian Zeus was just a few hundred yards away. Beyond that was the stadium, where the boy next to her would compete next week. They passed the stream of Kallirhoe, the pure waters.

It was dark in the temple after the sunlight, and as the two lines filed down the sides of the small building toward the altar, she had to watch carefully where she put her feet. The rough-cut slabs of the floor were too new for the seams to have been worn down smooth. Apollo Delphinios liked natural materials, cut rough.

Standing before the altar, she realized the crime, the solemnity of the occasion, although she could not name that crime, could not say for what this expiation was being performed. Only the terror of this moment, as she stared at the inhuman god, the dolphin-form. Her father was a sailor, her brother had been a sailor before he was drowned at sea. This was her family's god before her. She felt the otherness of it, the alien quality, the impossibility of communication with it, though what she was doing now was an attempt at it. She was trying to get this god's attention, to ask, as others had asked before her, year upon year, in other temples, for forgiveness for whatever crime had been committed, so that the god would help her father, and the fathers of all the others here, to navigate safely through the remaining spring storms, and through next winter's as well.

Surely it must have been a great crime. Surely this sleek phallic shape leaping on the altar would hear them. Automatically she fell in with the chanting, the begging, the promises the fourteen of them were making. Her mouth moved, her throat made sounds, her lungs filled and emptied, but she understood little of what she was saying, felt only the awe and terror.

Once, in the Golden Age, men had been able to talk to the dolphin-form of Apollo directly, but had lost that ability, that equality. The loss was punishment for the crime that could no longer be spoken. The crime too was lost.

Cassie opened her eyes. She was back in her office, the intense vision of the ceremony fading rapidly. There was something just out of reach, some knowledge vital and elusive. She looked out her window again and saw that the sun was low, the vague purple light gathering evening. The peak of Mount Hamilton and the eastern foothills across the bay would be tipped with that violet light, so similar to the light on Mount Hymettus as she remembered it.

There was a knock on the door, and Arnold stuck his head in. "Hi," he said. "Millet called. You might be glad to know that there is life after death. But no consciousness. A mixed blessing for most folks, I suspect. Proof of that will cause something of a stir—organized religion, hospitals. All the hopes and fears. Tomorrow we start on the plan."

She stared out the window again. The hills out there were green, but the air was growing colder.

THURSDAY

MCTAGGART'S PARADOX

6:7 *And when he had opened the
fourth seal*

This was dream. It had the texture, the flag of dream. Yet it was not dream at all, filled as it was with chimes, brassy and small, an underwater sound. Who was it Cassie saw, turning cards one by one, bracelets chinking softly as her wrists turned?

The cards were visible, with a hazy oval around them: a movie trick, to show this was a dream. The cards turned upward one at a time, Minor Arcana reversed, Wands, Swords, Cups, and Pentacles. An impression of Jupiter elevated, Mars squared. Outward form reveals inward meaning, hidden motives, secret desires, and future patterns.

Burgundy cloth covered the table. The hands, all Cassie could see, were clasped for the moment, now, with a deck just beyond, neatly stacked. The Major Arcana. Then they reached to shuffle, and Cassie could hear the spangles, the chiming sound, the bracelets and earrings and rings and hoops that clicked on her skirt, her collar. Precious metals all: titanium, platinum, gold, silver, molybdenum-chromium alloys, special alloys even in her teeth.

The nails too, Cassie could see, were burgundy, flickering as the cards turned over. Deep red, the color behind the eyes squeezed tightly shut. Metal and the color red.

The faint impression of a horoscope returned, Jupiter elevated, Mars squared: powerful protection of the great, a rise of fortune. That was good. But also Mars elevated could lead to mistakes, a compromise of future chances, and the creation of frequent dangers.

Cassie heard a low laugh, a chuckle. A voice, "No need to think of that. Today is the day." Then the silver bells again.

The Church of Latter Day Saints in Cincinnati had bells. When she was twelve her stepfather, Anthony Malatesta, would walk with her, kicking through piles of brilliant October leaves. The bells would ring Sunday mornings as they scuffed through the leaves. She felt no fear, but she did not like him. He always brought his face close to hers, so the pattern of exploded veins in the fleshy bulb of his nose loomed large. She did not like the way he looked at her, at her newly awkward body, small breasts and odd changes.

Cassie's eyelids fluttered. She could feel, transient as the dream she was in, the rough kiss of pillowcase against her cheek. Her fingers fluttered, and she rolled heavily in sleep; light struck her eyes. Her body was stiff, lethargic. Her lids drooped again, closed. She saw the cards, turning up one by one: the Hermit, silent council, wisdom from above; Lovers, inner and outer harmony; the Magician, power through desire to manifestation; Death, transformation; the Tower, upheaval; the Devil, sensation divorced from understanding.

They were laid out in the ancient Celtic method, significator in the center, face up, covered by the first card, crossed by the second, the others in a cross around these three, then four more in a line beside them. Agitated tinkling sounds ebbed and flowed, metallic, shrill. The tenth card was ambiguous, doubtful. She could not recognize it. Start again, using the tenth card as significator.

"Hey, Cass," she heard, very far away. She ignored it. The cross was almost complete. It was important to see that tenth card. This time would tell.

"Cass. Come on, Cassie."

"Mmm," she mumbled sleepily, dream and waking mingled, inseparable. The hands were thin-fingered, burgundy-nailed, covered in rings, bracelets on the wrists. Cassie knew who she was: Madame Glabro, prophetess of the CoreLight Mission. Today.

The end of the world.

The tenth card came up. It was a face: the man at the airport, heavy-lidded and ominous.

"Cassie!"

"Shh," she hissed, but her eyes opened to see Arnold's face close to hers. He kissed her cheek.

"Wake up," he said. She rolled sleepy, pulled him down, sprawled on the bed, a tangle, and hugged him tight, a tightness between her brows.

"Something wrong?" he asked, later.

"Not really. I feel better. Today is the end of the world, you know."

"Yeah?"

"Mm-hmm. What'sa time?"

"Nine-twenty. We're late."

114

" 'S okay. I have a cold. Take a pill."

"Sure. I made some breakfast."

"I can't smell." She sat up, sneezed violently. "Hey!"

He turned at the door. "Yeah?"

"I love you."

He smiled, gray face wrinkled a thousand ways. "Yeah?" He held up his thumb. "You."

Later she shuffled into the kitchen, wrapped in a thick imitation-brocade robe. She sniffled.

"Cold pills over there. I found them in your bathroom," he said. "I love you too. Anyway."

"Yeah?"

They ate in silence. The pill went to work, timed, slow-release, day-long relief from the common cold. Common, but not unexpected. The orca had known.

Her head was full of oceanic pressures, fluids, currents. She pushed away her plate. "Well, what do you think?"

He looked up: ceiling. "The weather has turned bad. That could be an omen. The world is going to end in rain. Doubtful, though. It could also be good news, depending on whether you depend on the weather . . ."

"I was dreaming," Cassie said. "About a woman, with a large blue neon palm. She has dark red nails, doing the Tarot. The last card was the man at the airport."

"Ah. What do you think?"

"I think it was a bad dream. She also turned up the Lovers."

He raised his eyebrow. "A bad dream. And how is the world going to end today?" He played with the saltshaker, tilted it back and forth.

"The usual. Fire and ice, earthquake, cataclysm, flood and loss of faith, bangs and whimpers. We'll never see 2000, for we have sinned, and the Whatchamacallits up there are mightily disappointed in us. Except the Bibbles of course, who will be carried away in saucers to planets appropriate to their spiritual development. I'm a Bibble because my aura is white, balanced, and pure. It is made of synchrotron radiation, coherent white light. Only it is invisible because the light is spiritual. It doesn't matter that I have a cold."

"Ha ha. And what is our Madame Glabro going to do if the world fails to end today?"

"Well, you see, it isn't going to end all at once, today. It is going to *start* today. We may not even notice, you know, it will be the little things. Could take years. Or maybe the galactic Whoosis will change their minds. They've done it before. What if it *does* end?"

"Then we won't have to worry about our report to the DLF. We won't have to worry about Friends of the Sea or Brockhurst or anomie and alienation or life after death . . ."

"That card came up too. You know, I'm not . . . promiscuous. You know that."

He set the saltshaker on the table carefully, aligning the milky beveled edges of the glass with the edge of the place mat. The salt settled down till it was level again. "Neither am I." His voice was sober.

Silence gathered, gray and woolly, in the corners. Outside, the clouds were low and gray.

"Well," Arnold lifted the saltshaker once and set it down. He stood. "I guess we'd better get going."

Cassie nodded. The cold pill was working, but left her dry-eyed and light-headed. "I guess," she said.

It was a weary morning, a thick gray soup of a morning, through which she had to drag herself, slow and mute. A headache developed at midmorning that nothing could shake, not even the news coming in over the status wall, where her mother's face, blurred and small, informed the world of a new DLF press conference, set for the following Monday.

"Christ," Cassie muttered.

From time to time it occurred to her that what she was feeling had something to do with what had happened last night between herself and Arnold, a vague dissatisfaction that had left her nervous and restless. But those thoughts sank again, and she found herself staring sightlessly at a wall, the surface of her desk, the mesh curtains, all the time her fingers twined and clenched.

"The end of the world got you down?" Arnold asked. She didn't answer except for a weak smile.

"I know," he said. "I know."

"This is silly season."

"It seems."

"The end of the world. Life after death. PEST has given up. I'm getting psychic flashes that don't make sense, aren't reliable, and scare the shit out of me, Arnold. I feel like taking the rest of the day off."

"Why don't you?"

"Because the DLF report is due Monday and I have a Puritan upbringing through all that feeble parenting I got. Maybe it's the Midwest in me."

"You were born in New Jersey," he pointed out.

"Just as bad." She almost laughed. Almost. "Something is going to happen."

"What makes you think so?"

She laughed then. "Because it's got to. The world can't go on like this, flying saucers everywhere stealing statues' arms, cults springing up predicting the end of the world, the millennium coming. Everything is up—unemployment, inflation, the stock market, production, tension, cancer. Everything is up and keeps going up and nothing seems to happen at all; nothing changes. People get sick, people die. The air is foul, there are strikes everywhere. We've done projects on all this stuff, you know it as well as I do. We have charts drawn on paper, stored in the computer, published in reports; they all say the same thing: Something has to happen. Joanne's still home with the saucer jitters."

"Would the end of the world qualify?"

"Arnold, I'm serious."

"So am I."

That stopped her. "You are, aren't you?" She spoke softly, pressing a knuckle (so frail) against her eyeball. There was no relief from the pressure there. "The Oslo Conference. Did you see the Japanese proposals?"

"No."

"They have a new method for harvesting krill. Factory ships would sweep it from the seas, treat it, extract energy from it. Krill is a source of protein. Protein for whales, Arn."

"Baleen whales. Whalebone whales, grazers. Not your friends."

"Not my friends," she agreed. "Did you see the animal mutilation reports? Whales among them. A killer whale on the coast of British Columbia mysteriously eviscerated, its brain removed without damaging the skull. The brain *and spinal cord*. Seemingly impossible. On soft ground. There were no tracks. No sign of anything but the mutilation. The tongue was gone, and the sexual organs, though that didn't get noticed for a while since even the males' are concealed in the body."

"When was this?"

"Last week. You missed it. Yesterday I was running a computer check on whales on the status wall and that little gem turned up, along with all those riots. It was a small whale, so they took it by helicopter to Vancouver where some marine zoologists looked it over. There was evidence of heat, though not very high heat, and it wasn't responsible for the nervous tissue, as they called it, being gone. They can't explain it. Flying saucers, of course."

"That does seem a weird thing for a flying saucer to do."

"Ahh. It's standard. There have been rashes of this kind of thing before."

"Sick people, pranksters."

"That's what we want to believe, isn't it? I don't believe in flying saucers, Arnold, and I don't believe in the end of the world. But then, I don't believe in psychic abilities, precognitive dreams, conspiracy theories, ESP, astrology, angels, or Mickey Mouse. I believe in rational science, don't I? And PEST has collapsed into a rational hole and vanished. I have dreams and visions and memories that aren't mine. Look, it's starting to rain."

The first drops splashed against the glass and stopped.

Cassie saw an old woman hunched over an iron pot. Slack, furrowed lips worked at toothless gums as she stirred its contents. She was seated Japanese style on her feet in a rude hut made of twisted sticks. Dense fog mixed with a light rain adrift in wintry woods. A small fire billowed smoke around the pot.

Cassie was walking urgently toward the woman; she felt fearful and uncertain. She held out her hands, palms up, ritual begging.

The old woman's voice was cracked.

"Something must happen." Again the old woman inclined her head.

Cassie couldn't see her eyes, hooded, looking down. "Someone is following me," Cassie said.

The old woman lifted her head, looked into Cassie's face. She had no eyes. "Lead me," she croaked.

"No!" Cassie cried, and Arnold turned from the window.

"Christ, are you all right?"

She sobbed silently, fighting down the hard stone of fear in her throat.

He touched her shoulder. His hand lingered there, but she did not feel it.

"Are you all right?" he asked again.

Now she nodded, struggle almost over. "I'm going crazy," she said. "Crazy, mad. What time is it?"

"Eleven."

Her intercom buzzed.

"Cassie. Line four, a Mr. Rodgers, from DOD."

"Can you take a message? I don't feel good. Arnold, I'm going to aikido practice. Even with a cold some exercise might help. It'll take my mind off this, anyway ."

"Okay. Mind if I tag along and watch? I'd like to see what it's like."

"Sure."

"Mr. Rodgers says he's from the Department of Defense. He wants to talk to you. Now, he says. Urgent. He says."

"Urgent, he says," Cassie repeated. "Urgent. Tell him I'll call him this afternoon." She turned back to Arnold. "Never heard of him."

The brief rain had stopped, for the moment, but cloud still lowered over the bay. "Well, it looks like a perfect day for the end of the world, anyway."

"Right," Cassie said. "A perfect day."

Cassie slumped in Arnold's car, armrest digging unnoticed into her back. "Stop," she ordered.

The hill fell away before them, toward bay water, the urban map lolled out there, thread-roads and shrubbery faintly green and budded. "It reminds me," she said, voice a silvery thread needled through a veil, a tapestry of dense memory and clogged head. "I don't feel well enough to go to practice, really. And I want to tell you something. In case the world ends."

He made a listening noise, switched off the engine. A quiet ticking from the hood. Low cloud close enough to touch, and behind their backs hilltops cloaked in mist.

"It's why I do this, think about the future. And why last night . . ." She shook her head, no. "I was eighteen," she began once more. "His name was Thomas Rapaport, but everyone called him Buddy. We were taking the train to college, an archaic thing to do in 1970, but it seemed romantic."

Buddy was her first lover, there on the train as she looked out the window at the horseshoe turn near Altoona, Pennsylvania. The front of the train, engine and baggage car, around the turn, across a deep, narrow valley, close enough to shout at the engineer, names, insults, rage or joy, and her car here, on the back side of the turn, directly opposite, a moment of balance, precarious as that moment before a child's top loses its spinning momentum and begins to topple: frozen in memory. Her car was number 4156, second from last on that long train.

It was also the second from the last run of that train. The jets had taken over, but the jets did not have sleeping cars, beds that tilted down, and it was on that bed that she had donated her virginity.

She hadn't lost it. You couldn't lose a thing like that, abandon it on the lunch table, absentminded. She donated it: Buddy was nonprofit, tax-free, and she could depreciate it the rest of her life.

"Buddy?"

"Hah?" Buddy coiled and thrust, breath loud in her ear. His skin was smooth, acne scars hidden over her shoulder, opposite their pale reflections in the compartment window, faint against the dazzling evergreen and cinder slopes. Engine coming round the bend.

"Buddy?" Again.

He pushed up to look at her.

"This is my virginity, Buddy. Does that mean anything to you? This is supposed to mean something."

"Oh." He frowned, pursed lips, and his eyes cleared. "Oh, of course it does, Cass. I love you." It wasn't easy to say that, he was only eighteen too, and the catch was there, the hesitation, an expansion gap in the rails, a brief click. "Why?"

"It tickles, is why." It didn't tickle. Not at all. It didn't hurt either. It didn't seem to do anything much.

"Tickles?" His brows knit puzzles. Then, "Well, son of a bitch." He thrust harder.

Cassie sighed. "Oh, Buddy."

He misunderstood, took it for encouragement. Tax-free orgasm for Bud.

She saw the engine, around the bend, going the other way. They would be there soon enough, that was her future, hers and Buddy's, and she knew as time stopped the engine directly opposite that that was so, that one precarious moment, and then on they went.

"Did you come?" Buddy asked.

She patted his shoulder, "Sure. Sure. It was good." An old dishonesty as the train straightened out, on the track again, into the future.

It would be better the second time, so lulling were the wheel clacks, the soft compartment bed, the rosy sun that dappled Buddy's back, her own fair smooth thighs, broad hips. Most likely her belly flushed its rosy rash and she cried out, but she never remembered. What she did remember was Buddy's back etched against the green, and the black cinders beneath the track across the perfect horseshoe valley.

"Cards?" he asked, fumbled a deck from his jeans, seated cross-legged on the rumpled bedding. They glistened still. He was uneasy.

"I don't think so, Buddy. Not right now." She smiled to soften it, but he didn't see, had shrugged his white athletic shoulders and slumped, dealing solitaire. The horseshoe turn was gone, fallen behind them westward as sure as virginity now in the geographical past. He lifted the tenth card, a diamond four, and put it on a heart five, illegal of course, and she started to say so when the train abruptly plunged into a tunnel and darkness fell absolute, clacking.

It forced her mind back to that night on the Jersey Turnpike, first the looping skid in the rain, then the Holland Tunnel, light inside, and her father's face, blanched and drawn, staring over Cassie's head at Martha crying out in pain. There was the same throat-stopping fear, uncomprehension, inside Cassie, staring up at her father's dry, myopic face, blank as Buddy's look now.

"Hey," he said. "Want to do it again?" His voice came out of the dark, hand on her calf.

"You can't put red on red," she said it then, pulling the hand up to her belly, her dimpled navel. Yes, there was a second time, not tax-free; she got her share. She must have.

"I don't mind cheating," he said, putting the diamond four on the heart five. "Not if it means I can win." So that was Buddy Rapaport.

"What do you want to be when you grow up?" she asked him later, in another tunnel.

"A weatherman." He did not mean a meteorologist. "Or a cop."

"You must yearn for adventure."

Red tunnel light flared past them. She saw his eyes glint red, felt a sharp fear, adrenalin and deep cold. He was not smiling.

Then the light was gone and he was saying, "I do, I do. Adventure." They rushed into warm green and sunlight of the mountains. Her brown hair fell across her face and across the white bunching of his deltoid muscles where she had rested her cheek against his arm.

"Don't you have any ideals?" she murmured against the brachialis-triceps groove.

"Sure." Nonchalant. "You're my ideal." He patted her naked side, stroked her wide hips.

"Come on, I mean it. Aren't you against the war?" It was so far from the Midwest, that war, even in 1970. They hadn't once discussed it.

"Sure I'm against it. I don't want to go."

"Oh. I thought you liked adventure," she teased him.

"On my terms. These aren't my terms. It'll be over by the time we graduate, anyway."

That made Cassie laugh.

"You don't think so?"

"No," she said, and that was that.

On the hillside in California the car stopped ticking as the metal cooled. Far below they could see, Cassie and Arnold, the straight line of the Stanford Linear Accelerator, below the freeway, and at the other end, the circles of the storage rings. Electrons and positrons circling near light speed, and the white glare of synchrotron radiation.

"They're doing some new experiments down there," she said, pointing. "Gigavolts of energy, antiparticles annihilating each other. Damnedest thing."

"This is about where Joanne saw her funny lights in the sky," Arnold told her. "A by-product? Artifact? Whatever happened to Buddy?"

His adventures started in college: He grew interested in bombs. He was a good athlete, a high-school track star, so when he blew up a storage closet at the ROTC building and destroyed five hundred pairs of faultlessly spit-shined officers' dress shoes, he ran like hell and got away. She'd been moderately proud to have known him, then. No one was killed, and it rained laces for days. She'd learned a new word: *aglet,* the metal or plastic tip at the end of the shoelace.

Those years became smoke, tear gas and tears, tunnels and light, confusion. Older brothers joined the hippies or the marines, came back delimbed, stoned, dismayed. They put on beads and shells and meditated, levitated, depreciated, invested, and worried about their portfolios, and the future was almost the same as the past again, the same old train.

Buddy had fallen away, joined a strange religious group that wanted to colonize space for Jesus, get away from messy earthbound responsibilities. He lived for the day when NASA would lift him out of this complicated environment, where the skies filled with UFOs, radar picked up a steady stream of uncorrelated targets, psychics predicted everything from the weather to babies' sex, where Christians and Hare Krishnas rioted in the streets, and the Galactic Brotherhood wanted to abolish money and breed pure blond star children.

Or bring the world to an absolute end. Today.

The millennium was getting close. Her mother had joined the Dead Liberation Front, and Cassie had always wanted to believe in science and truth and the triumph of reason. So she studied the future for a living, and found it unreasonable. Most people yearned for and feared the end of the universe. Madame Glabro had a following.

"I don't know where Buddy is now," she said, and rubbed her gritty eyes. "Maybe he became an astronaut. Or a suicide. You know, those clouds look like the surface of the sea, from below, silvery and opaque."

"I wouldn't know," Arnold said. "I don't go underwater."

The rain had stopped, started, stopped again. The foothills across the bay were lost in cloud, fog, mist, a turgidity of the atmosphere. She closed her eyes, hearing only the raspy whisper of tires on gravel, a soft squeal of brakes.

A car had stopped behind them. Arnold made a quiet grunting sound, deep in his throat, looking back. There was a dim outline in the driver's seat. "Cass."

She looked too. "Don't know him," she said. The door opened, a man stepped out. An ordinary man, in a dark suit. And sunglasses.

"He must have weak eyes," Cassie said. The man stood there, staring out over the valley. "Arnold," she said, turning back to him. "I feel shitty."

"Cold." He nodded.

"Maybe it is the end of the world."

The man knocked on Cassie's window. His mouth moved. "Excuse me." She could hear his voice, muffled by her window glass.

She rolled it down a little, felt the cold gust of air, the damp promise of more rain. "Yes?"

"Ms. St. Clair. Sorry to bother you up here, but I'm Phil Rodgers, Department of Defense. I wonder if I might have a few words with you."

"A few words?" Stupidly. "Oh. You called."

He nodded. His glasses were dark, dark. He might have been blind. Then he leaned down, spoke to Arnold through the open window. "Would you excuse us for a few minutes, Dr. Deleuw. This won't take long."

"Do I have a choice?"

The man smiled without humor. "Not really, no." He had opened her door before Cassie had a chance to react. "Please." He ushered her out, led her down the road a few yards.

124

It occurred to her to ask. "Do you have identification?"

"Oh, of course. Sorry." He pulled a black folder from his jacket, flipped it open. His picture, DOD stamped, official insignia, all flashed. Her eyes were runny, vision blurred, and she blinked back her cold, the dry ache. The picture had disappeared, back into his pocket.

"Ms. St. Clair, you have been contacted by a group. Monday morning, to be exact. Called the CoreLight Mission, or the Visitors' Disciples, I believe."

"Yes. What's this about?" She pushed her hands into her own jacket pockets, bunched into fists. Her shoulders were hunched against cold, rain.

He held up his hand. "Please." He pulled a magazine from his pocket. A scrap of paper was clipped to a page. He read. "A Ronald Zsylk spoke to you in front of your house early Monday morning. He gave you some information."

"Have you been watching me? Following me?"

"Please," he repeated, holding his hand up. "We want your help, that's all."

"Christ, the 'information,' as you call it, consisted of a badly reproduced page of automatic writing from Madame Glabro, the leader of this group. It is fertile ground for a psychoanalyst, I suspect, but of very little interest to the Department of Defense. Drivel. It doesn't make sense. And I resent this. He was a harmless boy, Ronald Zsylk, a nut, sure, but harmless."

"Have you seen this week's *Time?*" Phil Rodgers asked. He spread the magazine.

The picture caught her eye first. Madame Glabro seated at a table covered with burgundy cloth. Cards spread out, her hands clasped. Dark-red nails glowed in the color reproduction. Behind her, a little to the left, stood Ronald Zsylk, his face turned to one side, features burned out by a glow from behind, a strange light shot through with violet lightning-jags, fitful fires.

"Don't tell me," Cassie said softly. "A flying saucer has landed and taken these two away, and you suspect they are enemy agents."

He laughed then, though she was sure the laughter had not touched the eyes behind the dark glass. "Not exactly. We are, however, concerned about these groups. The end-of-the-world phenomenon is growing; more and more people in this country seem to believe."

"Today."

"What's that?"

"Today. The world is going to end today, according to her." Cassie tapped the photograph. She could almost hear the bracelets, the earrings and hoops, the precious metals that winked highlights in the picture.

Rodgers nodded. "We have our doubts about that. But we would like your help. They're going to get in touch with you again. Quite soon. You've already . . ." he stopped. "No, of course, you haven't. Well," he took her arm, guiding her back to Arnold's car. She shook it off, stopped, and turned to him.

"Haven't what?"

"Never mind. Tell me, does the phrase 'Wretches, why sit ye here? Fly, fly to the ends of creation' mean anything to you?"

She stared. "Did you send that note?"

"Note?" All bland innocence, no secrets.

She stared without belief. "It's a phrase from the Delphic oracle," she said. "To the Athenians. A prediction of disaster, perhaps. Someone sent me a note the other day, when I was in La Jolla."

"Ah, yes. Talking to the whales; interesting experience, I'm sure. We would like you to go along with them, that's all. Believe it or not, this is a Defense matter. Doomsday cults are increasingly . . . influential, this one particularly. *Time* magazine gives them serious attention, and not in the Religion section either."

"I didn't read it. She's a fake psychic with a pipeline to her unconscious that gives her messages about the end of the world, from the Visitors, handsome blond giants from the flying saucers. She has a following. *Time* takes her seriously. You take her seriously. Why?"

"Because this is a Defense matter. Take my word for it."

"Why?"

"What do you mean?"

"Why should I take your word for it? This woman is a nut. She does numerology, astrology, space-logic. She's not an enemy agent. She's not a bomb."

"That's where you are wrong, Ms. St. Clair. That is precisely where you are wrong. She *is* a bomb."

"Well, she's going to be defused when the world fails to end today. So, if you don't mind." She tilted her head, a half-nod good-bye, turned back to the car.

When she got to the door he called to her. "Ms. St. Clair."

Hand on the door latch. "What?"

"Just play along with them. *Someone* sent you that message."

She got in, slammed the door, and locked it. Arnold watched as she slumped in her seat, stared dry-eyed and gritty at the dashboard. Phil Rodgers walked past her window without glancing in. Behind them, they could hear his door open, close, the engine start up. His car swung around them, vanished down the road.

"Well?" Arnold asked.

"Shit." Her voice was flat, stripped of meaning, overtone, feeling. A dull little syllable in that closed space.

Arnold waited. Then, "Want to go?"

She looked up. "No, wait. Wait." She stared out her window at the flat valley floor. A mist was gathering there, rising to meet the low cloud as the temperature dropped closer to the dew point, when all the moisture in the air would condense into a suspended mist. She could see Hoover Tower on the Stanford campus, pale cream with a red tile roof. She could see the card from her dream, turned up, the Tower of the Major Arcana: conflict, unforeseen catastrophe. Jagged lightning to strike the tower, as in the *Time* photo, and two figures falling from it, headlong to the ground. Herself and Arnold? It could also mean selfish ambition about to fail, a disruption that might bring enlightenment.

That was the trouble with prophecy. Too many contradictory meanings. Anything could happen. The tower down there on the flats was swallowed in the mist, a gray hazy miasma closing in. Water began to condense on the windshield, a light spattering of tiny drops.

And then, surprisingly, real lightning. It crackled around the rim of the bay, shot down aslant the campus below, exploded in a fireball above the Linear Accelerator. Moments later the sound came, the din of rolling thunder, deep bass rumble like an elephant talking; it drowned all thought. Thunder and lightning seldom happened in this place.

Lightning cracked again, close this time, too close, and an oak thirty yards down the road split with a sound like the world ending, shot wood pulp and splinters against the glass before her, simultaneous with the sound now. Then the rain came, dumped heavily from the sky on top of the little car, drumming on the metal roof. She thought, it's the end of the world, it is, and I have not been carried away to safety.

Outside was turmoil, noise, crashes that shook the thin metal egg of the car, over and over again; the deluge against the glass streaked down her windows, the rear window, the windshield, gray, dirty water, tinged weirdly red from time to time, carrying away the wood pulp and oak splinters. The city was gone, swallowed up in that ocean of gray as winds slammed against the car, threw water at them, caught the heavy rains before they hit the ground and swirled them sideways, upward, all directions.

The red color intensified, splashed across their vision, streaked. The drumming increased on the hood, a harsh music, and behind it faint whistling as of reedy flutes, high in the air. The whale song, her duet, but thinner, as the air was thinner even drenched with condensed water now; it was more dangerous than the ocean even. There were fingers drumming out there, taut drumskins, the stops of reed flutes, and a thick chant that told of the creation of the universe, of the earth and seas from the vast swirling waters of chaos; the heaving moistness of Tiamat herself, primordial mother, the great water of the world, slow, heavy, lethargic, a soup of pure energy without form or structure, total death drowned in red-shot formless entropy, and cold, cold.

Slowly the waters parted, timeless, heaving and oily; divided in two, heaven from earth, a subtle distinction of shades of gray only, flickering with red, blood-color. Tiamat divided, became water that was bitter and water that was sweet, and where the waters mingled there was not union, not fusion, but conflict, strife, discord, deception, and new death. Fission: explosive, destructive energy. The flutes in the wind modulated into discord, and rain was the drumming of battle, the ragged march of warriors, the clash of metal weapons.

Darkness swept over them, over the waters, a darkness that differed from earlier dark, a malevolent, tattered dark punctuated by harsh red flickers, there momentarily then gone, the darkness of fear, of terror

128

without mind. The children of Tiamat moved across the waters, vast monstrosities without form, ravening desire, hunger blindly followed. Apsu hated the children, their striving and conflict, and sought to kill them. A thousand mythologies told of these gods, who ate their children, destroyed them, locked them away in the abyss, and who in turn were killed.

Tiamat created more monsters, there on the hillside in the midst of deluge; fearful dragons, half man half beast, and sent them forth. Hot winds swept over the turbulent waters, poisons ran lavalike, clouds were shot through now with sulfurous yellows as well as blood-crimson and whirled violently over the seas. Salt polluted the sweet waters, rivers poured down slopes away from the fragile car, carrying everything with them, huge boulders crashed across the boundaries dividing one thing from another, obliterating both.

The wind-flutes, whistling around the angles of door-gutters, window edges, handles, cut from the reed that grew at the waters' edge, in brackish marshes thick with salt-crust, high penetrating sounds, wavering and harsh, come nearer, filled with whine. The drum-rhythm of rain settled some, found a base, form, shape, emerged from chaos, carrying melody. A plaintive plainsong, liturgical and incense-heavy, wordless, without overt meaning, growing in clarity and desire, telling as direct as experience the story of this creation, the separation of the bottomless abyss, the void between stars, the infernal bowels of the earth, the structures of life, molecular protein chains, the knowable, tangible world.

Whales moved through that water, she saw, through the abyss men feared as they huddled on the dry surface. She saw the orca's face, immobile and alien, his ancient expression of detachment. The music was Brockhurst singing to the whale from the bow of his ship, the *Dreambridge* adrift on the flat and solemn sea. He was breathing order into the void and was answered by the orca in the sea: a fragile, tenuous moment of contact and understanding.

Leviathan, Tiamat's spawn, ancient and dreadful, became known, his face more familiar, friendly and closely related, the dolphin-form so close to man, who moves upon the surface as his cousin moves beneath. And beyond them, out of sight in the depth-murk, vast shapes move, indefinite, gray, slow-moving, deep drums and gongs, gone.

Cassie squeezed her palms between her knees, huddled against the terrible buffeting of wind and rain, her eyes too squeezed shut, as smooth shapes moved through the waters, with speed and control, a swift humming.

She could hear the humming now, as the rain abruptly stopped and in an instant dried on the windshield, inexplicable and impossible. There was no other sound now, no thunder, no drumming rain, no awful din of falling timber, wind-howl, reed flute. Only that hum growing louder, a *thrumthrum* that shook her bones, filled her with terror and panic.

With it came the glow.

It appeared to creep across the bay, now visible with the rain gone, and Cassie's eyes wide open, stretched open, staring. It was white, this new light, the reddish glare gone, the sulfur yellow gone, and it crawled across the water from the east, toward them, approaching with the humming sound. She pushed herself back in her seat, staring.

The white light coalesced, flew together, fused, became not a glow, but a shape, long, white, solid, moving slowly a few hundred feet above the ground, with the hum, a swarm of bees, and under that, the *thrumthrum* that moved through her long bones. She forced herself to look over at Arnold, reaching at the same time with her hand for his.

He was unconscious, his head lolled back against the headrest, mouth slightly open, breathing deeply. His eyes were closed, and a dreamy, peaceful look had settled on his face. Cassie almost forgot her fear in that expression, it was so absurd, so inappropriate at this moment.

"Arnold!" she shouted, but her voice felt pale, thin, a ghostly sound under that intense buzz. He did not stir, head back, eyes closed. His hands were folded in his lap, under the steering wheel, as if in prayer.

"My god," she breathed. The light, radiation, glow, whatever it was had come closer, level with the car, which seemed to be tilted on the slope of the hill, facing more toward the valley floor, as if it had been turned, instead of parked parallel to the road, was now at right angles, facing downward dangerously. She could see treetops below, spears of fir; it resembled the track to Machu Picchu somehow. She briefly saw the faces of the old Chinese couple, narrow eyes twinkling good humor and an odd serenity. Then another sound joined the first, a whine, grating and intermittent.

Far beyond the first light another was coming, this one dome-shaped and faintly violet, with long streamers of white threadlike material trailing behind it, drifting down, separating from time to time to vanish into the gray, dark waters below. The shape made no sense to her, belonged to nothing in her memory or experience. A jellyfish, perhaps, for it seemed to have no substance, no solidity, just a transparent dome of violet light adrift in the murky heavens, trailing gossamer.

The first object had stopped a hundred feet away, hovered above the treetops, shot an intense white light out the bottom which moved over the dark green fir, bleaching it, so intense she could only see vague outlines under there, as if a white mist had obscured details.

This is *not* a flying saucer, she told herself. This is a helicopter of some kind, with a searchlight mounted underneath, probably from the power company, looking for storm damage.

The light moved across the trees, up the slope toward her. She could feel the substance of the car vibrating with the humming sound, could hear the high whine of the other object, more distant, but there. The light moved impossibly swift up the slope. She started to cry out, to Arnold, "Wake up," but the words stopped in her mouth, her throat, as the air stopped in her lungs. A curious lethargy came over her, almost a paralysis, like waking up at the wrong part of the sleep cycle with that powerful inability to move a muscle.

The light was in her face, and she felt a rush of sensation into her head, her mind, a most intense feeling of *repetition,* of experience tagged as memory. Déjà vu.

She knew, just out of reach, what this was, and, released, she opened the door, stepped out without fear onto the gravel shoulder of the road, beside the precipitous drop to the valley below. She walked around the car, down the hill toward the shattered oak, and the vast glowing shape, long, blunt cylinder, moved down the hill in pace with her. At the upthrust jagged stump, still smoking faintly, she stopped, put her hand on the charred spear of wood, and looked out. The light was gone from her face, but the shape hovered there, near her, as though watching.

South, at the bottom of the bay, a group of lights appeared. These were yellow, but bright, gaily-colored, a small erratic trio of yellow shapes that darted through the air, this way and that, without apparent goal, but in pefect formation, perfect harmony. They moved generally northward, spun for a moment, lined up, shot ahead, reversed, raced upward, stopped fast, slanted down toward the drifting dome, raced one two three around it and upward again, toward her position on the mountainside, altered direction abruptly southward again toward San Jose and shot through the pass toward Santa Cruz to vanish.

The dome seemed to be rotating slowly, so the streamers drifted back in a gentle spiral below it, as though about to braid themselves. A long dark shape came out of the north, then, lights out and incredibly swift, more than the pretty yellow shapes darting, raced, blanked the hills opposite as it moved, rose swiftly toward the rotating dome, shot through the white trail of streamers, cutting them; they drifted slowly toward the water. She watched as they began to drape the shoreline, a misty veil of white, barely visible at this distance.

The dark shape, long as an airliner, streaked south, rose precipitously to the very bottom of the cloud layer, then moved east. The yellow lights appeared over Mount Hamilton, down through the cloud, and the dark shape raced toward them, collided with the first, the second, and the third, leaving behind them nothing. Not a flicker of light, not a fragment of debris; nothing but empty air where they had been, as though the dark shape had swallowed them.

Now it began to glow very faintly, a deep red like heat from a furnace inside a cloud of smoke, and moved slowly north again, toward the head of the bay. It drifted over the San Mateo Bridge, still with that inner fire, and on, out of sight around a bend of the hill she stood on. She looked back at the presence in the air before her, the white light dimmed somewhat, but with a watchful air about it still as it hovered thirty yards away, a shape bigger than a house in the air, but with no clear edges, no definable shape to it, just a vast white blur in the air. Under her hand the shards of blackened green oak began to glow with a light of its own, a very pale aura of violet, Saint Elmo's fire, and still that feeling of having been here before, of having lived through this very experience before at some unknown, unremembered time, an echo infinitely repeated.

The violet light shimmered up and down the fractured spears of hardwood, and she watched, bemused, faintly curious, as though pleased with this little trick of light. She felt, without being particularly aware, the deep *thrumthrum* of vibration, heard, without acknowledging, the buzzing whine. Only when the sound and vibration grew louder did she look up again, away from the play of violet around the stump. The white shape was moving closer to her. Beneath it a faint mist seemed to congeal, gather into itself.

She watched as this shape came toward her, approached closer and closer. She felt no fear, now, nothing but a faint thrill of excitement, anticipation. A memory, a real memory, she was sure, appeared, uncritically, unjudged. She had been standing, just like this. At the zoo.

Buddy was behind her, it was summer, his hand was on her bare thigh below her shorts. She leaned on a cement parapet and looked down at the elephants, watched them sway back and forth or move with lumbering slowness across the naked concrete toward the hay. Big beasts, friendly for the most part, easy to train, fun in circuses, sociable and smart.

There was a moat in front of her, overlayed on the green hillside in memory, between herself and the elephants; a trickle of water ran through it, an imaginary river, though the electrified wire strung along the sides, wire that hummed in a slow but regular rhythm, spoiled the illusion, and was also the sound of this white shape approaching her.

She'd had no thoughts then, looking across the moat at a huge male African elephant standing broadside to her, trunk slithering across the ground before him, through the detritus of straw and hay, feeling for edibles, picking with amazing delicacy the tasty stalks and kernels. She had no questions then. They were gray. They were big. They made trumpeting sounds, and huffing sounds, could be startled or soothed. They had sex and size and babies.

Buddy was behind her, and his hand ran down her hip, along her thigh, palm on her smooth adolescent skin; his palm, lightly dewed on this hot day, and slightly shaken, lust light and falsely casual.

Her body was not responding to Buddy just then. At that very moment the male elephant lifted his trunk into the air, waved it aimlessly for a moment and then, very deliberately, turned toward her and stared into her eyes, his trunk lofted, asniff on the currents of air. As Buddy stroked her naked flesh, Cassie looked into the elephant's eye, and he waved. To her. A clear, meaningful dip of his trunk.

Then he turned away, back to his snuffling probe of the straw on the ground, gray broad back toward her once more.

She had not thought of that moment since, not once. As that memory went through her now, facing the vast and growing white glow, she could not judge whether that had been a moment of true communication, as she had not acknowledged the gesture, did not know, in fact, whether *this,* this moment now, oddly echoed with that other moment, overlapped, merged, blended as these two were, and growing more so, elephant and hovering object out of any experience of hers, this unidentified *thing* in the air before her, drawing closer yet, whether this was a moment of communication either, or whether she was slipping into an obvious delusion, a dream that might or might not be waking.

Yet that memory of the elephant in the zoo, the summer before she and Buddy took the train to college, that brief eye contact was so reminiscent of this, and of the other day, when the orca had approached her, had slowly and deliberately *winked* at her, that she felt an almost intolerable pressure of significance, meaning, of absolute indefinable presence.

Then the mist swept over her and she drowned in it, saw in vivid dream-detail her own hair swirled around her drowned and staring eyes, her slack mouth, empty expression, as though from outside, yet perceiving it herself from within. Her feet, so apparently solid on the earth, lifted under her, drifted upward as though in heavy water, salt water, floated even with her head as her drowned and weightless body rose, drawn into that yawning white starcore, a window on creation, and she drifted on, through the opening, pulled down hallways that flickered with white light, darkness, the violet fire of the tree stump, and in the pale mists of the light, the vast gray shapes moved without sense, without meaning at all, just the mottled alternation of light and shade, arhythmic, confused, and mindless.

She was in a circular room, very familiar and never seen before. She was naked on a table, in warm, rather damp air, humid, steamy even, but pleasant. The fear that had come with that vision of her drowned face shredded away like the white gossamer from that dome shape above the bay, vanished in a sense of awe, wonder, a weirdly pleasant lethargy. She moved her eyes slowly around the circle, the walls that flickered with points, shimmers, ovals, indefinite showers of multicolored lights. She saw the people there, men and women dressed in white coveralls with brilliant blue piping, faintly absurd. There was no door, but over by the wall she saw Phil Rodgers from the Department of Defense talking in a low whisper to a man dressed in what appeared to be black leather. She was not in the least surprised to see Rodgers here, in this circular room, nor did her nakedness and vulnerability bother her.

"What time is it?" someone asked beside her ear, and she turned.

"Are you asking me?" she said.

It was an old man, completely bald and small, almost a dwarf, seated beside her head.

"What time is it?" he repeated, almost petulantly. "Time." There was a peculiar emphasis in his voice. "Time."

"I don't understand," Cassie said. She was trying, too, really trying. It was urgent that she understand, that she answer this question correctly, give accurate information.

"Ah," the old man said, lifting a bent, gnarled finger. His tone was exasperation. He thrust the finger outward, toward her. "What time is *it?*"

She looked at her watch, but didn't have it on. "I don't know."

134

The old man turned partially away, and she saw he had no eyes. "She doesn't know," the old voice croaked out, though there was no one in front of him to whom he could be speaking. He sounded regretful, impatient. "She's a Bibble and she doesn't know." He turned back to her. "What time?"

"Oh, no," she said. "No, no." She began to laugh. "This is too much, oh my.". Her eyes closed up in this mirth that swept over her, Bibble, my gosh, carried away in a UFO, saved from the absolute end of the world.

When she opened her eyes again she saw the old man smiling at her, nodding. "Right," he said. "The time is right."

"You're not . . ." she began, but another wave of merriment rose through her and she convulsed on the metal table, eyes filled with tears of mirth and all the multicolored lights blurred, fragmented, shattered prismatic and lovely. "Oh, lovely," she said as the laughter died away. She looked at him again.

He smiled on and on. "No," he said.

"You're not going to kidnap me?" she finished her sentence, though aware he had answered her question before she had asked it.

He reached out toward her with a peremptory gesture, a command. "Lead me," he said, though he was still smiling, and she couldn't tell whether he was serious or not.

"I don't know where I am," she said.

"Ah," he said, and it was the same tone he'd used before, a frustrated regret. Suddenly he held up a clock in front of her face, too close for her to focus. "Time," he said, and tapped the instrument. She had an impression that it had too many numbers on it, and that they were in an alien script, nothing she had ever seen before, and the fear returned.

With fear came the darkness, a sense of vast pressure, infinite depth, space, and suffocation. Forces pulled at her, in different directions, so her head wanted to fly one way, her arms and body another. Falling, pushed, flipped over, drawn out, compressed, tossed to and fro, then sinking through a dim, silty mire.

There was a sound of the sea, washing without pause over loose gravel, a continuous susurration, white noise. She could look down into that darkness and see nothing, only oily depths without content, but she knew there were shapes in there, hard-shelled, with pincers and claws, ready to tear at her flesh, to bite, rend and render.

She was young, then. Five years old, perhaps. Or younger. Later she'd learned it was somewhere on the Atlantic Coast, Toms River,

New Jersey, but for now it was a vast deep gray dish of obscure waters filled with shapes that glided without sound, deep and malevolent.

Her father called to her from up the beach. "Go on, Cassie. Put your feet in."

The water rushed toward her, the white leading edge nearly touching her bare toes, creaming violently, reversing. It suckered fiercely at the stones, and they tumbled down, some of them vanishing into the dark.

"Cassie! Go on."

She took a step, felt rounded stones pressing into the soles of her feet, water hissing, filled with shapes. It changed direction once more, rushed toward her swiftly and she sprang backward, twisted her ankle awkwardly, and fell. The water roared in, over her legs, her knees, her waist, cold, dragging at her, sucking her back into the ocean where the shapes scuttled and crawled. White water curled over her chin, wet her lips, hurled her under, and she was screaming as it broke around and over her.

"Good girl!" her father applauded. George St. Clair, seated on a dune up the beach, among the pickleweed, clapped his hands, but Cassie didn't see. Salt gagged her, hair was clammy, plastered to her forehead and neck. Her ears were ringing with the deep gong-sound of that blast of water. Dimly, through the ringing, she could hear her father say "Good girl."

And then she felt against her leg a slimy touch, an electric shock, the clack and scuttle of those creatures of the depths that smelled of rot and salt. Her leg jerked back as though touched by a wire, and the water drained away with a hiss, leaving a strand of drying kelp across her foot. Her father had turned away, now, and was plodding clumsily up the beach, his broad soft back toward her. She looked after him, one hand raised, reaching. He vanished around a dune, where her mother was seated under a beach umbrella although the day was cloudy.

"She got wet, by God," she heard him say.

She stood slowly, watching the water impassively this time as it rose rapidly up the gravel and swirled around her legs, tumbling stones over her feet like crabs biting her, and she didn't flinch. She watched as the water fell away again, twisted underneath itself, folded over. The sound of it was faint, now, remote and indifferent. Over her head the clouds were as oily and featureless as the water, flat-bottomed, infinite, a ceiling of dirty gray. She shivered and turned, walked slowly up the beach, away from the incoming tide, as small breakers rolled in and out.

Her flannel bathing suit hung heavily around her waist; runnels of salt water ran down her legs, prickled her arms and shoulders.

From the darkness of that memory/dream a milky light suffused gently upward, gathered into itself, coalesced, took on shape and durability, and with it, a sense of time passing, of *event,* beaded onto a string in sequence.

The light became a multi-faceted, coiled crystal of some mineral substance, vaguely serpentine in a geometric way, heavy head lifted slightly, with a feeling of coiled power just under control.

She reached out with her hand to take that crystal, aware with absolute clarity of the importance of this small object. Her hand came into view, elongated as though through the wrong end of a telescope, her fingers curled slowly, the crystal disappeared bit by bit from view, and she could feel the hard edges of it pressed against her palm.

At the same time there was a sense of release, and she disappeared herself, as abruptly as a film shut off, there and then not there.

And she was walking down the road toward Arnold's car under thinning clouds on an ordinary afternoon in March.

Cassie walked down the road. Cassie walked, was walking, down the road toward Arnold's car, toward his car, toward him. The clouds overhead were thin, mere cotton shreds stretched out, with blue above. Sunlight caught in the dew on the shattered oak tree spread prismatic color over her shoulder.

Her feet whispered on the pebbled surface. As she walked toward his car, she wondered: would he be sleeping still, head back against the rest, mouth open? The sun dimmed away from the oak stump. She could see Arnold's silhouette against the glass. She tapped on the window; he blinked and rolled it down, said, "That was it, then?"

"That was what, then?" She smiled. The clouds were skim milk in heaven, and sun was warm on her back.

"A brief storm. A little rain. It's clearing up. Did I fall asleep?"

"I think you did." She was smiling, smiling. "Yes. What time is it?"

He looked, blinked owlishly, as though time were an unexpected bright light. "Two-thirty."

"Ah." She nodded. Through the thin soles of her shoes she felt the knobby surface of the road. No cars passed, no wind stirred the fir branches, oak leaves, hair tendrils at her nape. Sun warm on her neck, March afternoon.

"That's impossible," Arnold said, frowning.

"It's impossible?"

"We came up here at noon. Then, let's see, that man, what was his name? came by and talked to you, couldn't have been more than fifteen minutes. We've lost more than two hours."

"Yes," she said, smiling.

"Where were you?"

"You didn't see a thing, did you?"

"Mm. I saw lightning strike that oak down there. I saw that. Scared the bejeepers out of me." He climbed painfully out of the car, cramped from his nap. He looked down the hill, where the fallen tree sprawled downslope, the blackened stump jutted into the freshening air with a painful clarity, as though etched against the bank of the road's turning.

He shook his head. "I can't believe I fell asleep. Two hours! It doesn't make sense, Cass. Why are you smiling?"

"Arnold. You know something? I feel terrific. My cold is gone."

"Hm?" He shaded his eyes, looked downhill, across the valley floor, the city mapped in roads and barely greening trees. Hoover Tower was there, red Spanish tile roof, cream walls, an odd intrusion in the washed air. The clouds grew thinner.

"My cold, Arn. It's gone."

"Your cold is gone?"

She smiled, took his arm, and they strolled down to the oak without speaking. "Shall I tell you what I remember?" she asked him, her hand on the blackened spear of green wood.

He nodded.

"I stood here. It came toward me, white, glowing, just like all the reports, humming, whistling, throbbing. It had a searchlight underneath, or something that looked like a light, and it pointed it at me. So many things happened then, a dream, all jumbled up, pieces, fragments, hunks of memory, feelings, ideas, all kinds of stuff." She shook her head, still smiling. "I don't know. I feel so *good.*"

"Ha. So that *was* it, then?" he repeated the words.

"Was what?"

"The end of the world. Flying saucers came and carried you away. This is your new planet." He swept in the hills, the city, trees, cars, people.

"Yes. Isn't it fantastic? Here it is, the new world, and it is *exactly* the same as the old one."

They both laughed, not knowing who was putting on whom.

"Okay, okay," Arnold said. "I'll believe you. Something happened, that's for sure. I've lost two hours. I guess you have, too."

"Two hours." She watched the ground. Small, armored gray bugs, pill bugs, sow bugs, crawled from the humus around the stump of the oak. A busy little world down there. They were all sizes, those bugs, adults, adolescents, babies, all busy being born, growing up, eating and dying. A garden pest to some.

"Two hours," she repeated. "No. Not two little slices of the eternal cake, Arnold. Something else altogether. We think about time all wrong. It isn't one after the other at all. It isn't only *now,* either, although it can be experienced that way, like when we're meditating. Remember McTaggart?"

"Sure. John McTaggart Ellis McTaggart, his famous argument for the unreality of time, 1908. Time is either one, static, structured, relational, either *before* or *after* in a static way; what he called B-series time. Or two, dynamic, in flux, moving from past to present to future— A-series time. The problem is one of logic, since approached from different angles makes A subsume into B, or B subsume into A, and so forth. If you can prove that A-series time is inconsistent, you can prove there is no such thing as time, and A-series *is* inconsistent because any event, any *moment* has all three mutually incompatable A determinations. Etcetera. It's all based on a logical fallacy."

"No it isn't. He's right, in a way. There is no such thing as time, no linear time, no causal time. It is a function of consciousness. That's why saying we've lost two hours doesn't make any sense, not to me. I gained a hundred years."

"Oh."

"Oh, come on." She took his arm again, and they climbed slowly up the hill to the car. "I can't explain it," she said at the door. "But my cold is gone. And something important happened. I'm going to know what it was. And very soon."

"Okay," he said. "Trust yourself, Cassie. It's a weird world."

"Sure. Look." She traced the hood of the car with her fingernail, rust-red streaks splayed across the shiny blue paint, as though dried rapidly by intense heat. "Did you see the red rain?"

"What the hell is that stuff?" He poked at it with his finger, the slightly tacky feel of it took his fingerprint. "Looks like some kind of sap or something."

"Blood?"

"You're not serious. Blood? No. Looks like someone threw it at the car. I don't remember seeing it here before."

"Arn. It came down in the rain. Red rain, Arnold. A fall of toads, mudballs, ice out of a clear sky. These things have happened before, they say, odd aerial phenomena. UFO traces, physical evidence. Arnold, I've been on the UFO. I'm a contactee."

"Ha ha. A Bibble."

"Not ha ha. Not a Bibble; God I hope not."

"Was it a spaceship, Cassie? Little green men?"

"I don't know. I don't think so. Sometimes it seemed like metal, that's the memory of it, or plastic. Some material stuff. Other times it was more . . . intangible. Just energy or something. And it has messed up my head, as we used to say."

"Right. It cured your cold."

"Yes. And that man was there, Phil Rodgers, from the Department of Defense. With his dark glasses. You did see him?"

"Oh, yes, I saw him. Looked just like a human person. Do you feel like going back to work? It's almost three, and the DLF report is due Monday, you have that elephant project going; I think Brockhurst sent you down to the whales for a reason we don't know yet . . ."

"And Phil Rodgers knew a hell of a lot about me, now that I think about it. A hell of a lot. Including the contents of that note someone sent me when I was down in La Jolla. Frankly, I don't feel like going back to work at all. It seems irrelevant. Still, there are one or two things I would like to know, and the answers just might be at IF."

There was consternation at IF; turmoil, confusion, hubbub, tumult, and bobbery.

For one thing, the power was out. The print-outs lay flaccid, gutless. Ditto the status wall. The screens were dark. Nothing was happening in the world.

"You mean," Cassie gasped in mock horror, "we are going to have to rely on our *brains?*"

"Not amusing, Cassie," L.R. puffed, pipe full of imaginary shag. "All the typewriters are electric, the dictating equipment is electric, even the goddamn *toilets* are electric. Fortunately Reggie had a flashlight, and Jamie had some candles left from Geoffrey's birthday party, or we'd all be in the dark."

"In the dark," she repeated. "Wow."

"Where have you two been, anyhow? Stuck in the storm?"

Almost everyone else was jabbering away, huddled around the only battery-powered radio in the building, or staring out at the fresh green lawn, the daffodils and camelias, the crimson tulips.

"Stuck in the storm," Arnold nodded.

"Did the world end, L.R.?" asked Cassie.

"You haven't heard? Didn't you listen to your car radio?" L.R. was incredulous.

"Heard what?"

"Skies full of UFOs again. Hundreds of witnesses this time. Strange white threadlike stuff fell all over the San Mateo Bridge, the shore, the airport, half the damned county. Teams from every research institute on the peninsula are called out, investigating. It's a zoo out there already, even though we have just passed through the worst storm of the century, or was it the third worst? Your friend Madame Glabro has been on the radio, too, announcing the total success of her prediction."

"L.R.! You can't be serious. We had some unexplained phenomena, perhaps, but the world certainly hasn't ended."

L.R. bit his pipestem, puffed the whistle of empty air. "Don't look at me," he insisted. "The media are full of it."

"You can say that again," Cassie muttered as she left.

"Not funny," L.R. called after her.

The phones did not work either. "Not funny, he says," Cassie mumbled, slamming the receiver down again. She had gotten the 120-cycle-per-second-circuits-are-busy signal. Switchboards would be flooded with calls, of course. Police, radio and television stations, emergency numbers, politicians, the weather bureau, family and relations, schools, business deals. The satellites would be overloaded with transmissions, relays would be giving out all over the country. The highways would be littered with bad drivers made worse by the weather, the freak electrical storm.

"How are you?" Arnold asked. He seemed to ask her that often these days.

"Hell, how are *you*?" She felt good.

"Me? You could say I'm just fine. You could say that."

"I could say it. Could you say it?"

"No. I couldn't say it. For one thing, it bothers me to have lost two hours out of my life without getting anything for it. And for another thing, I don't quite understand why you haven't said anything about what happened up there today. You were closer than anyone, it appears. So I ask how you are, hoping you'll say something illuminating to me."

She bobbed her head, seeing. "Sure. Number one, a few things are nudging around in my mind—DLF, for instance. Do you know they are going to change their name? Or is it its name? Not the initials, just the name."

"How do you know?"

"Oh, they have to. It's going to be in our report. The Dead Liberation Front just doesn't make it anymore. Too old-fashioned, too political."

"Aha. And what do you see them changing it to, O wise one?"

"I've been thinking about that. How about the Death-Life Foundation? Catchy?"

"Good."

"It is going to give them just the necessary amount of credibility to put over this 'evidence' for life after death they have."

"But no consciousness," Arnold put it.

142

"Yes. But then, it depends what they mean by consciousness, doesn't it? Awareness? Sense of identity? Sense of time? Space, location? Proprioception? Haptic? Blah blah blah. The fact is, Arnold, they are shucking us. They have something else up their—its—sleeve. Something bigger, and probably a hell of a lot more sinister, to use a corny old word. Something that has to do with whales, the Department of Defense, UFOs, the end of the world."

He laughed. "Stuff like that." He pointed at the wall over her desk and the red-inked words: *Flaming Music.*

"Yup. Flaming music. Coincidence or important fact? Hell, I don't know. There's a connection of some kind between all these things, though. When we get power back I want to do a linguistic search on Linear A, the ancient Cretan script. I'd bet it's Delphinese. I have this feeling I know what's going on in the world now, and I just can't quite get it, you know? Tip-of-the-tongue."

He stuck his out, gave her a grin, thumbs up, and left. Or turned to leave, one foot out the door, off-balance, when the telephone, oddly, rang. Busy circuits or no busy circuits, someone got through; he turned back, startled at the sound.

"Hello, Mr. Brockhurst," Cassie said into the phone, taking a chance.

"Hello, my dear," the deep voice answered her without surprise. "A Mr. Rodgers is trying to reach you. Has he succeeded?"

"Yes."

"Ah. I feared so. What did he say?"

"He wanted me to play along with the CoreLight Mission people. I told him it was silly. They're cranks. See, Monday this . . ."

"I know." There was silence. The time passed. She thought he was gone, dozed off into reverie, senile. She thought of speaking, felt her throat tighten, the words form in her mind, then fade away. She knew she too should keep silent.

He was thinking, weighing alternatives, testing the evidence. He knew everything before she did, had anticipated everything. Almost everything. He didn't know she had already talked to Rodgers. But he commanded resources she couldn't guess, intellect that dwarfed hers, power beyond her imagination.

Nonsense. He was a man, an old man at that. Smart, of course, and wealthy. He had foresight, intelligence, power, sure, but nothing supernatural. Just a man, her boss.

"I'm just a man, my dear," he said, and she jumped, glanced at Arnold, standing in the doorway. "You must do what you feel is right. But beware of Rodgers. He isn't what he seems. And we will meet soon, you and I. And Dr. Deleuw, I think. I see him there as well."

Silence again. She said nothing.

"Very soon. Tomorrow, perhaps. Get some rest. Cassie." The last word was so soft, so deep in the near-subsonic range she could barely hear. It was the first time he had used her first name that way.

Before she could answer, the busy-circuit signal came onto the line, the rapid *beep-beep-beep* of an inoperable telephone.

"It seems," she said to Arnold, "that we are to meet with Mr. Brockhurst tomorrow."

"Yup."

She stared out the window. A perfectly ordinary day was out there, with afternoon, then sunset coming up. Dimly she could hear tumult behind her, in the building.

"You're kidding," someone said.

"No. Rock salt, that white stuff is rock salt, spun out in filaments. All over the place. Here, taste it."

She watched a hummingbird hover near a fuchsia bush, the dark purple blossoms hanging down. The bird darted to the flower, penetrated. Feathers iridescent green and black, wings a blur. She thought for a moment she could hear it out there, through the double-insulated glass. There it was, a quiet turbine-throb. Wings. Goring and Goring, wings of green neon lifting aslant the rainy night, into the dark. Rain, water, death by drowning, dolphin-torn, gong-tormented sea. Astraddle on the dolphin's mire and blood. Yeats, it was Yeats, the song, the song, the golden codgers. Millet, the golden codger. And to copulate in the foam, she was naked on that metal table, the blind, eyeless dwarf-man or shape held before her an alien clock. Time, time. *Time is the evil.*

No that was Pound, the *Pisan Cantos,* her favorites once. Time the evil, copulate in the foam, foul goatherd, brutal arm. The Innocents. Relive their death. Their wounds open again. Carried off, her sister's bloody birth in the New York hospital, mother screaming through the tunnel, why couldn't she think about it?

It had happened. She could remember the shape approaching her on the hillside, the *anticipation* of it approaching and it was . . . sexual?

She shied away from that, thought about her cold, instead. The orca had known, she was coming down with a cold, head throbbing, stuffed, dripping. Spirit after spirit! No. Yeats again, the song. She'd been dreaming, the waves, drifting, lifting, falling, crest and trough, tide-pull, invisible powers, visions, the future, what will be. Will be. And the radio had that song, twice and only yesterday. Wednesday. Woden's day. God of wisdom, art, war, culture. And the dead. Don't forget the dead, they shall be free. Liberated. Without consciousness, dreaming only in the dark damp ground. Drowned. Belly, shoulder, bum flash fishlike. Fish! That white glowing shape, fish shape, and the dark one darting upward, through the white gossamer spiderweb tangles. Rock salt, it doesn't make sense, rock salt. Nothing makes sense, it is all void, the space between stars, fusion, fire of creation, and empty cold, 2.7 degrees Kelvin, blackbody background radiation, all that's left of the beginnings of the universe, and cold, cold. The damp touch of salt water, kelp drying on her foot.

She jerked her leg back, No! White water washed over her foot, her leg, foaming; the rocks tumbled, violent, haphazard, unpredictable, random. It felt like dying. This is what it's like, dying? This is what I think it must be like. Carried off by the white light, pulled in. My feet lifted up, as though in water, without fear, adrift, pulled gently by invisible power, felt only in the position of joints, tendons, balance, internal senses, kinesthetic. Through tunnels, then, endless tunnels, without light, just an impression of vast gray shapes moving beyond vision, incomprehensible business, purposes; meaningless.

She stared out the window. There was grass. There were trees. They had names. Laurel. Oak. Camphor. Sycamore. Small, hard names you could touch. The hummingbird was gone. Had it been there? The fuchsia was still there, thick, miry purple blossoms, disgusting color, dried blood, mire, death. Wesley Millet, golden codger.

She heard the tinkling again, faint, distant, and the hum. Hoops of metal, Madame Glabro. The end of the world. It was her world that was ending, ending in death, dried blood, drowning, congealing into crystal, coiled, smoke-white, milky. Milky, like galaxies spun across vast heaven. Was she breast-fed? No milk.

Cassie stood up, staring out the window. I stood up. Why did I stand up? I am staring out the window. Why am I staring out the window. Why am I? Am I? Through the window, onto the green world, green world. Green world and yellow lights in the sky, flying formation. They were there, I saw them, why am I standing up, looking out?

Cassie turned away from the window, away. She turned. What was there, behind her? Fear was there, dark shapes, formless and dreadful, behind her. Devil shapes, in red smoke, monstrous, shambling, dragging useless limbs, thick-bodied shapes, squinting eyes, small and red, piggish eyes, the evil, all the childish shapes that evil took, that vague uneasy word. Was that time, that grotesque shape? She turned away from the window, to see what was behind her.

There was nothing behind her. Nothing at all. Nothing. Not a door. Not a desk. Not a wall, nothing, nothing. There was a corner. The corner, where two walls meet. That corner drew her, drew her, pulled at her. She must approach that corner, it was there, some secret, something she must know, not the dreadful shapes, not the monstrous shambling *things* that she must face, but some terrific corner-secret, some illumination, that all-suffusing white light that would tell her everything, all the necessary things. Fear would fall away in that corner. Worry would vanish. Cares would be dissolved. The corner-light would take her in, rock her gently; she could sleep after great effort then, tired, so tired.

Cassie walked to the corner there, where the white walls grew together, moved in a fluid stream together, flowed upward, downward at the joining, the flow of walls together. She stood and faced the corner, watching the streaming, on and on, flow, stream, event after event, as the light came on and on, flowing through the corner, upward, downward, pulling her. Carried away, saved. Saved. She stared.

She stared.

And the lights came on. Power came back. She didn't notice. Her shoulders shook. She pressed herself into the corner, formed herself to its hard, tangible shape, the V-shape of it, pressed inward, her hands in front of her, pressed together too, into that corner. Shaking, staring. She shook. Her shoulders shook. Her hands shook. Her eyes danced, shaking. Her knees quivered, thighs tired and shaking with fatigue. Her feet were numb and shaking too.

146

She shivered. Her teeth clashed together in her mouth, loud, so loud, the chattering, the hard clatter. Her eyes, staring, saw only a dance in the air, in the wall, the random dance of particles. They jiggled, danced, vibrated, moved, flowed, grew and shrank, lived and died, came into existence and disappeared. She stared at them, within her eyes, the gelid humor of her eyes, the floaters there, detached cells that danced in there, dead cells, floating in her eyes. She saw them, the careful circles of them, outlined against the walls she pressed herself against. She became the corner.

Her mouth was wet, filled, and open, pressed to the wall. Her cheeks against the wall, a pebbly feel against her face, and the wet against her chin, blind tongue, chattered teeth, clackety. She pushed her shoulders against the two walls, pushed hard, harder. She must push harder, she must be this corner. It was her corner, no one could take it. No one. No one. Nothing.

Phones were ringing, the quiet chatter of the print-outs filled the empty air. The status wall flickered into life, its pictures turbulent, confused, a world in minor millennial chaos. The reports came in. It was the world series, out there, as everyone gathered around to laugh at the reports.

"Silly season," L.R. was saying. "Omens streaming in the firmament." His head was shaking, wag. "But Madame Glabro has not been carried off in a flying saucer, yet. That's one thing, anyway."

It was only a local disturbance, this fall of white streamers on the bay, rock salt. A minor ripple in the stream of the world. In Houston things went on. The death of a rioter the other day was lost in more recent news. In Atlanta the Friends of the Sea were holding a news conference to protest the Japanese program for harvesting krill. In Washington the president would not talk about seeing a flying saucer, but said he was sending a special commission to investigate the afternoon's events in San Francisco. A disk jockey in Peoria played "Death of the Large Mammals" and got several appreciative calls. The song was catching on. It was being played in New York, too, and Bakersfield, Sarasota, St. Louis, Seattle. The elephant herds drifted across open savanna, were gunned down, wept for their dead, trumpeted. Moved on, pushed further and further. Small intelligent eyes filmed over, poisoned by radiation, flesh decayed. Anxiety, masochism, fear, and hatred.

The world was normal, absolutely normal.

Cassie settled in her corner, knees bending. She shrank into her corner, now with another dimension. Floor. Three walls came together, there, and she must mold herself to it, triangle, pyramid shape. Her head lowered, shaking, chattering.

She stared at the focus of three walls, the floor-wall-wall corner. It was dark there. She brought her head closer, stared. They all came together there, a point. A point in space. A point in time. No dimension at all. A point.

Sounds faded away. She couldn't hear them talking outside her door, couldn't hear anything. Nothing. No flaming music. No forecasts, no prophecies, no songs, no poems, no idle conversation, polite greetings, threats, or loving words.

She saw only the point.

She was only the point. Without dimension.

"Cassie."

She had no name, for she was nothing. Just a corner, a point.

"Cassie. Where are you?"

"Drink this."

She shook her head; a feeble gesture, but a gesture. His hand took the back of her head and tilted it back. Something hot touched her lips, ran down her chin, thrashed the back of her throat. She gagged, spit it out.

"It's okay. Try again, come on."

"No. No." Her voice was a rasp, a whisper, dry and frail.

"Cassie!" Arnold's voice snapped, and she opened her eyes.

"No."

Eyes closed once more. Her chin touched her chest, hair covered her face; soft, auburn hair.

"Come on. Drink."

She shook her head, but it was too late, of course. "Too tired. So ... tired. Don't want."

148

The hot liquid touched her again. This time she swallowed. It went down. A flavor entered her mind: chicken.

"No!" she shouted. "Not chicken soup." Her head was up, now, and she looked straight into him.

So he nodded. "Chicken soup. The Universal Panacea. Combats viruses and bacteria, broken legs and broken hearts."

"And absolute freak-out victims? All right, never mind. I'll be okay. I won't ask what happened, but I will ask where am I?"

"My place. Sorry about that, but I had to take you somewhere. L.R. was going to send you to the hospital. Can you talk about it?"

She shook her head not yet, started to stand, fell back. She was on the floor, in front of a couch, her back to the cushions Arnold had tipped off onto the carpet. Cross-legged, wrapped in a blanket. Otherwise naked.

She didn't seem to mind. The soup was good, clear, rich, warm. The room as well was clear, rich, and warm. Something vaguely Spanish about it, tile over the fireplace, dark polished wood floors where there was no carpet. An arch led into another room, filled with books.

A fire on the grate, small flames leaping, red and smokeless. Oak, split, dried; hard, hot-burning wood. Smoke smell faint in the otherwise darkened room. Outside the windows an evening collected, pooled in the shadows, filled the yard, where a cedar tree threw ponds of dark beneath itself. Juniper bushes bordered the walk. Even from here, near the floor, she could see their fronded tops against the house across the street, the window was that big, that low.

"Your place," she mused aloud, looking back to him.

"Mine. A small house."

"A shady street, with sycamore trees that fall in autumn, swirl around your ankles when darkness starts coming early?"

"Yup. All that. Almost like Connecticut. College towns have a lot in common, don't they? Those quiet, comfortable middle-class residential faintly intellectual streets. You know the name of this street? Wilmot. I checked it out once; he was a seventeenth-century English poet, who wrote scandalously dirty poems, some of them. A shocker, I'll tell you. An aristocrat, too, the Earl of Rochester."

"An aristocrat. Homemade soup?" Conversation swerved.

"Actually, it is. I would have opened a can, but the fact is, I like to cook, and soup's kind of a specialty. Whole chicken is the secret, long, low fire, and secret ingredients I may someday reveal to you."

149

She sipped. "It's very good. You do like to cook."

"Self-defense. You have aikido, I have cooking. It's important for someone with a perfect sense of direction to be able to cook. You never know when you're out on the trail and have to rustle up some grub for the hands."

"I thought you never went anywhere."

"Don't. Stay home and cook. My wife knew a hundred ways to make potatoes taste terrible, so I had to learn. Now it's a hobby. Want some more?"

She handed him the cup with a nod. "You collect books? You cook. What else do you do?"

"I do indulge in a new form of divination: gonatoscopy, the art of reading the future by means of the configuration of knees. Yours, for example, tell me a great deal."

She pulled the blanket over the jutting knee he was ogling. "That won't do any good," he said. "I've seen them. Both of them. Broad, square patellae mean wisdom and courage. Rounded at the top, the rest smoothly vertical: indicates noble and well-balanced faculties.

He was in the kitchen then, pouring more soup. From there he said: "Faint lines underneath are ruled by the planets. Saturn rules the top line, for instance. Yours is very faint, and broken, a compromised future, I fear. Then there's Mars."

She peeked under the blanket, knew they were avoiding the subject of what had happened to her up there. Didn't care, not just then. "Come on," she said. "I don't have any lines under my knees."

He handed down her cup again. "Sure you do. In back."

"In back?"

"Indeed. A letter C on the line of Venus. That, of course, is danger arising out of amorous encounters."

"Amorous encounters?"

He nodded, abruptly sober. "Very dangerous for you, amorous encounters."

She too sobered, looked into her cup of soup, felt beneath her hand the impress of stylized bamboo; he had the same cups she did. Was that odd? "Encounters are dangerous, Arnold. I had one up there, didn't I? A close encounter, as the people who investigate phenomena like that call it. I must have acted pretty strange afterward. I mean, I was in shock. It was . . . not describable. Shattering. When it got to me it was upsetting, to say the least. I wanted to die, thought I was going mad. I mean, really stark insane, out of touch, no hold on reality anymore. Like

I fell into a dream and couldn't get out. But Arnold, whatever those things are, there is really an overwhelming impression of *intelligence*. Incomprehensible wisdom, even, watching. It was studying me, trying to tell me something. But it got all mixed up with my fathers, childhood, and childhood fears."

He didn't say anything. She sipped at her soup. Finally she said, "My cold is gone. That part is true. I fixed on that, sort of. Physical evidence, an artifact, a by-product of the . . . experience. One thing they ain't, though, and that's spaceships come to save us from Armageddon, carry us off to Saturn or Alpha Centauri or whatever."

She hadn't said the word. Not *flying saucer*, not *UFO*.

Still he said nothing. She finished her second cup of soup, put the cup aside. He got up and stirred the fire, put on another precious foot-long split of oak.

"And I'm still so tired, so god-awful tired."

The fire burned, small red flame-tongues leaping. The fire-runes of a forgotten tongue.

He hunkered down beside her, and she leaned against him, staring into the heat-dance in the dark fireplace. Outside, darkness settled on the house.

She dozed, on and off; he sat, once, got comfortable, and she stirred, lifted her head, made a questioning sound, dozed once more. The fire sank in the grate; stars appeared in the clear skies; traffic moved occasionally on the street.

The log broke with a soft fall of ashes, and the embers flared sparks up the chimney, glowed red, sank beneath the white ash again.

"Arnold?" she murmured.

"Mmm?"

"What kind of books do you like to read? You have a whole roomful in there."

"Promise you won't laugh."

"I promise."

"Guidebooks."

She laughed.

"You promised." Rueful tone.

"No, I know. Guidebooks?" She straightened her face, collapsed, straightened again.

"Sure. To the United States. Where to eat in Dayton, what to do on a Saturday night in Omaha, what sights to take in when visiting Joplin, Missouri. What to do in Arkansas. That sort of thing."

"What is there to do in Arkansas?"

"Well," he began. "There are the folklore workshops in Batesville, for instance, held in conjunction with the Ozark Folk Center. Spinning, quilting, shucking, weaving."

"My God."

"Oh, well, I never go to them, but it relaxes me to read about it. Goes with this infallible sense of direction I've got. I have something to tell you." He eased into the change in subject.

"What?"

"Rodgers called again. He wanted you. I talked to him. I didn't like his tone, Cass; that's really why I brought you here, instead of your place. He was . . . threatening. Belligerent anyway. I thought you ought to know, in case you wanted to, you know, go home."

"Thanks, Arnold, for taking care of me. I must have been a problem."

"Yes," he agreed. "A small problem. You're all right now."

"I'm all right now. It is all going to be fine, now. I'm going to figure it out, Arn. Soon. All of it—DLF, my mother, my sister, elephants and whales and Brockhurst. Unidentified Flying Objects."

She had said it. Not so bad.

He was smiling in the dark. Yes.

"You," she said.

"Me," he echoed.

"You know what the Zen master says? He says the wood does not become ash; wood is wood and ash is ash. Now you are wood, now you are ash."

He didn't answer. His hand on her shoulder. Her head against his. She fell asleep. Deep, dark, filled, dreamless.

FRIDAY

LUST
IN
CINCINNATI

6:9 *And when he had opened the fifth seal*

Cassie, lying on the couch in the filtered gray of early morning, slept, one arm thrown across her body toward the back of the sofa. The arm twitched in sleep; it was hurling her hairbrush at a mirror, glass shattering into a cascade of brilliant fragments, each reflecting her face, the face of her stepfather, Anthony Malatesta, her arm bent awkwardly as she threw the plastic object, threw it at the mirror, opened her eyes, throwing it, seeing the sharp-edged light reflected in her eyes as the mirror broke, seven years bad luck, bad luck to plague her, her eyes opened.

Cassie rolled her head away from the back, toward the window, wondering briefly, without curiosity, where she was. The curtains were drawn, a white material barely seen, backlit with gray. The living room was filled with indefinite shapes. It must be early, early. The day after the end of the world. She remembered again her stepfather, his fleshy nose, slightly alcoholic network of veins in its bulbous end. The way he leaned forward toward her, from behind, that night, when she was eighteen. The summer before college, before Buddy Rapaport, the train to New Jersey.

Cycles to her life, motifs appeared, vanished, reappeared. Faces she'd known once, gone, returned. Smells, tastes, body postures, the feel of grass, pavement, forest floor, sand, mud underfoot. Music she had heard and forgotten. Voices that spoke to her out of the silence of night, voices that were heard but were not there: her father's voice, calling her name: Cassie! Hot asphalt, the smell of it, the sensation of its heat rising around her bare calves, shimmers of the heat from a road in Greece, near Eleusis, the sound of small bells, dangled from the sides of the gypsy caravan, hauled painfully along by a donkey. She had been taking a separate vacation in Greece, after years of marriage, had been to the necessary places, to Delphi; to Patmos where Saint John had revelations, saw blood in the firmament; to the Cape at Sounion.

This moment it was Eleusis of the mysteries. There was the faintly sulfurous smell of asphalt, esters of petroleum, in August heat. No breeze turned the olive leaves. She had stood there in the heat, tried to imagine the mysteries, the sacred mime, the fasting and initiation: Demeter returned to the earth where her daughter Kore lived with the god of Hades.

Only a part of Lycurgus' wall still stood, and the Sacred Way, steps cut into the rock, and the dust broken by pale scrub and a few trees.

August, and the earth had died. From far away, there would be chanting as the procession from Athens brought back the sacred symbols, the ear of corn, Demeter's corn. Dead earth, dead as her marriage, dead as her father, both her fathers. She stood in full sun, a slab of rock underfoot, listening for the chant, the first dust-cloud of the procession from the East. Around her she conjured up the Telesterion, the darkness of it, the heady wine, thick in her throat and head to give her visions. Waiting for the sun to crash through the opening in the roof, the poised moment when light would flood the room after all the hell-darkness Persephone had lived through half the year before her release into the upper world again, the autumn green, when rains returned after summer drought.

Her hand held the curtain material slightly aside, and an empty street curved away from her. Out there, the buds on the sycamore trees, the grasses on the hills green after all the winter rains. She turned away from the window.

She had slept a long time, felt the slow rhythms of it in her body still, receding, giving way before the more urgent needs of day. The bathroom, for one.

She didn't turn on the light, but felt her way along the walls, through an archway. Found herself in the room filled with books, his books. Beyond that, a bathroom. She sat in the darkness there, and still felt good, being now. Alive. Expectant.

The floor was cold under her feet, it crackled with the chill of it, sent shivers up her legs: delight. She was alive. Walking back through the library, she paused there at a window and looked out on a dim courtyard. She could sense a garden there, and a fountain, perhaps. Yes, a faint lightness to the air, the predawn hint: now. The color of ash.

Her dress was draped over a chair opposite the couch, and she slipped into it, folded the blanket, and placed it square on the sofa. Waves of sensation sighed through her body, memory, texture, fragments of her dance with the dolphins, her conjured vision of Eleusis, the *clopclop* of the donkey's feet on the road, the feel of her hairbrush in

156

her hand. She walked back to the library, found a small table there, with a lamp and a comfortable chair.

The shelves were lined with books, and she ran her fingers over them, the spines hard on the older ones, soft on the newer. Some were thick, took in vast territories: Soviet Union, China, the Middle East. Others thinner: Nepal, Alaska, the Caribbean, Japan. The thinnest ones were extremely specific, taking in a single island, a walking tour of Baton Rouge, trails on a small mountain in New Hampshire. There was one called *Sacred Places*. She knew about sacred places; she put that one on the table, went back to the shelves.

The dark window glass reflected her image. She looked at it curiously for a moment, thinking that *now* her hair was shorter, she didn't need to worry that curl anymore. Tilting her head forward, she watched the hair fall around her face. Well, not that short, but the curl was gone. Had it ever been there?

Her face in the window grinned back to her, winked when she did. She looked around the room. There were tiles set into the plaster of the walls here and there, blue ones with ornamental designs glazed onto them in white: a bird, or a simple flower. Nothing symmetrical about it, just a tile where fancy had dictated. Houses were not made like that anymore, and it told her something more about Arnold: soup, guidebooks, chalk, an old Spanish house, a damp and slightly sour smell to him. Wood, tile, plaster. A Japanese health club. Divorce. Systems analysis.

Leafing through *Sacred Places* she found many familiar ones. Places she had been. Eleusis, stone drenched in sun, pale earth tones under that aching blue sky. She stared at the page, the color photograph of the flagged marble floor of the Stoa of Philon, and briefly remembered standing there. A node, the orca called it.

Later, when Arnold shuffled into the room with a sleepy look, he found her leaning back in the chair, a guidebook to the United States open on her lap. He leaned over her and saw it was open to Cincinnati, one of his older books.

Her eyes, when he looked at them, seemed to be filled with tears.

"Been up long?" he asked, a flannel robe clutched around his waist, his pale sparse-haired legs.

"Hm?" No tears in her voice. "No. Yes. I don't know. An hour. Thanks."

He chopped the air, sure. "Whatcha reading?"

Then he noticed. The tears, not crying. Laughter. She was laughing, laughing. "Oh, Arnold," she wailed. Her finger on a sentence.

He leaned over and read it. A guidebook, listing sins in various towns. Gluttony was Cincinnati's primary sin: lust, the most difficult sin to indulge there.

"Lust in Cincinnati is something of a problem," he read.

"You're laughing," he told her. "This is funny, this lust in Cincinnati? Something of a problem?"

She shook her head, looked at the dark window. Her own reflection was faded now as the day came out. Somewhere invisible to her the planet was turning, the sun was rising, the light was growing.

"I've been thinking ... remembering. An incident when I was eighteen. My stepfather, you see." She shook her head again.

"He did something?"

"No. Not really. Do you know how he died? A grotesque accident. His golf cart swerved on a bridge over the water hazard just before the sixteenth hole. He drowned in three feet of water. See, he had his golf bag draped over his shoulder and apparently it pinned him to the bottom. His electric golf cart fizzed in the water there for several minutes before it shorted out. He was still seated, hand on the steering lever, his head inches from the surface, a leather bag of Sam Sneads or something caught in the silt on the bottom, pressed down by the side of the cart."

She watched, and her face in the window faded, replaced by shrubs in his courtyard. There was a fountain there, a broad, shallow cement bowl fluted like a shell. The water was not flowing, and new water lilies spread their deep green pads on the water below. "There had been a fair amount of untimely death in my family," she said softly. "Father, stepfather. Accidents." She looked at him. "I get images of my own face like that, drowned. Hair swirling around, eyes open, staring. Or my hair plastered to my head when they haul me out, my eyes still staring."

He touched her shoulder awkwardly, leaning slightly off-balance. "How do you feel?"

"It's still a crazy world. I feel wonderful. This has been a busy week, hasn't it?"

"Yes," he said. "The future has been a busy place this week." He rubbed her neck lightly with his thumb over and over, up the delicate spinal groove, down the muscle, as she gazed out the window.

"Look," she said.

Outside the sky had come down to the ground. Tendrils of morning fog drifted into the courtyard from above, wisps, veils, shapes; semitransparent wraiths settled on the fountain shell, floated over the lilies. The wall opposite faded in the fog, grew dim and indefinite, vanished. The fountain disappeared into the mist as well, and outside the window was nothing. Dimensionless gray, depthless and infinitely deep.

They watched the transformation of the dawn, from the clarity of growing light to the disappearance of the world. There were only the two of them now, inside the house, enfolded, enclosed, suspended.

"Fog stops time, doesn't it?"

He murmured something vaguely comforting. She stood, leaned against him, watching the mist begin to collect on the glass, minute droplets that defined the limits of their world. Beyond this glass is nothing, void, infinite unstructured space.

"It stops time," he agreed. "For a while."

"For a while . . . all right." She caught the joke, his grin, and laughed. "My turn to cook."

He leafed through *Sacred Places* while she sliced onions, stirred eggs, toasted muffins.

"You've been some of these places, hm?"

"A few. You like your eggs soft?"

"But not runny. You've been to Machu Picchu. And Greece, of course, Delphi and such. Tien Shan? No, of course not. Pretty mountain, though, isn't it?"

"Beautiful. A sacred place. Have you been to any of them?"

He laughed. "One, Fajada." Flipped pages to the photograph, sun behind the outline of an irregular hill. The facing page showed pale tan

sandstone, a spiral carved into it, and a dagger shape of sunlight pointing down, through the heart.

"Where is that?"

"New Mexico. This is a solar instrument that marks the divisions
of the year: solstices, equinoxes. At noon. Very precise. But you
wouldn't know it was there; it's in a cave shielded by three slabs of
sandstone tilted against one another. They look completely natural, as if
they fell that way."

She was laughing. "I thought you never went anywhere; just stayed
home and read the books." She slid the eggs into a hot frying pan.

"Except this once. I was driving across the country, coming out
here, and I'd read about it . . . There was something spooky about the
place. The silence, and a kind of . . . emptiness. Very old."

She was watching him, with occasional glances at the eggs firming
up in the pan. "I know," she said; she quoted: " 'Places, in the sea . . .
land as well, that made themselves during the dream time.' The orca
mentioned them. These places in the book. He called them power
nodes."

"Well." He laughed uncertainly. "It was a strange experience. Like
being around high-tension wires. Makes the hair on the back of your
head stand up, but there doesn't seem to be anything there."

The fog lasted, a thick, featureless, and insubstantial mist, through
which traffic groped blindly. It took them half an hour to get the few
miles to IF. Arnold peered intently through the windshield, wipers
clacking back and forth from time to time, wiping away the dew without clearing vision.

He began to fret.

"Calm down, Arn. There's nothing we can do about it. Relax.
Enjoy."

"Ha ha," though he threw her a wolfish grin, sideways, Bogart style. "In fact, I'm concerned about the DLF thing. L.R. is crazy, all the holdups, Joanne out, you out yesterday afternoon, and sent away on Tuesday like that, it's all got him nervous. Our report has to be in Monday."

"Yeah. L.R. won't like it if we don't collect a fee from Wesley Millet. Don't worry."

They crept on, through gray clouds. The temperature outside was neither warm nor cold; it neither rose nor fell. They saw no one else, no other signs of life, though they were in the center of one of the largest urban areas in the world.

"What direction are we going?" she asked, later.

"North-northwest. Soon we turn more westerly. Why?"

"Just checking. I'm amazed. Are you sure?"

"Yup." Wolf-grin again.

"Why the grin?"

He pointed at the dash. A compass built in. "I don't need it, honest, but it's nice to have the feedback."

And again, later. "How do you know this is even the parking lot? I can't see a thing."

"We walk that way." He pointed and his fingers faded in the mist.

"Okay. I'm hanging on to you."

"I like that."

The door was there, the lights were on inside, and up close the yellow glow through the glass was a beacon. Up very close.

"Joanne!" Cassie exclaimed. "You're back."

Joanne was at her desk inside the door, where she had always been before this week. She waved but did not smile.

"Are you okay? You look pale." Cassie was still holding on to Arnold's hand.

"Yes. You know the world is ending?"

"Pardon?"

"Today. The world is ending. Madame Glabro has told us. It started yesterday. Did you see them? Of course. You are a Bibble, you must have seen. And now, just as they foretold, the world is ending."

"In fog? The world is going to end in fog?"

Joanne shrugged. "Don't worry. You'll be saved. The Visitors have told us, and they do not lie, ever."

"You're a member of the CoreLight Mission, Joanne? A Visitors' Disciple? Since when?"

"Since it happened to me." The telephone rang, and she turned away to answer it. Cassie chewed her lip and frowned for a moment. Joanne transferred the call and turned back. "This is the last day, Cassie. I nearly didn't come in today, since this is the last, but Ronald said I should."

"Ronald?"

Joanne gave Cassie a penetrating look from under her thick brows. "You know him, Cassie."

"So I do. And where are the floods, Joanne?" she asked sarcastically. "The fire and smoke? The black waters and ineffable music?" She felt cruel, but some knot of anger tightened in her belly, and she wanted to strike.

"There is the smoke," Joanne was saying. "And the waters. Outside, thick smoke, water everywhere, drowning the world."

Arnold pulled at Cassie's hand, and she let him lead her away.

"Did you know she was like this?"

He shook his head. "No. She had called in that she was getting help. No one told me it was Madame Glabro who was giving out the help."

L.R. Hubletz was leaning forward, one hand braced against the side of his precious status wall, glaring at the screens, tiny blazes of color. He had a gloomy expression.

"Where have you two been?" he demanded. "Never mind. You see what's going on? The whole damn place is falling apart. Joanne's gone to cloud-cuckooland, the fog has tied up traffic in the city, the telephone never stops ringing even this early. The only good news, if you want to call it that, is that they now have a definite analysis of that white stuff that fell all over the San Mateo Bridge and the shore yesterday."

"What was it?" Cassie asked, suppressing malice.

"Salt and dust. Plain, ordinary, air pollution dust. Held together by a freak electrostatic effect, because of the lightning, apparently. The stuff fell apart in the lab, but they got careful samples, and that's what it was. Nothing."

"Oh."

"That's right. All that to-do yesterday. A storm, fireballs and dust. The air force and the weather bureau have announced jointly that although the weather was unusual yesterday, it was nothing to get excited about. But of course, everybody's excited anyway. Phone's ringing all the time." He turned back to the status wall, glared from screen to screen, as if an answer were spelled out in color-code there if only he knew the key.

There was a muffled sensation at IF that morning, an intangibility, a hush. Cassie didn't feel like working any more than anyone else. She was waiting for something. Arnold felt it too: He didn't say anything, but his fretful manner had returned, and he paced impatiently, in silence. From time to time he muttered to himself with an air of intense problem-solving. Finally he said, "I'm restless. There are too many parts, and no system, so what's a systems analyst to do?"

She looked over the messages on the bulletin board. There was a new crop since last she had read them. Some were jokes, of course, factitious announcements. Others were provocative, cartoons or sayings. There was also the usual assortment of new and not-so-new therapies, self-actualization programs, spiritual counseling services (although Madame Glabro did not have a place there), Post-New-Age churches.

She read about Mineral Therapies; Feldspar Alignment; Mineral Chakra Regulation. Transsexual Cosmic Joy. Universal Jungian Infant Massage. The Intuitive Self Clearinghouse for Pan-Cosmic Metempsychosis and Body Restructuring.

The Vegetarian Extraterrestrial Society; "They don't want us, they want our vegetables." Arnold had told her the first governor of California was a zucchini. She thought of him carried off by a UFO to the Vegetable Plane where spirit became carbohydrate. Later he would be canonized as the State Vegetable. This was the kind of silliness the CoreLight Mission might indulge. She considered sending them the message.

Joanne handed her a message chit, left without a word. Cassie stared after her, wondering what the look had meant, that flash of animosity, envy, awe.

Phil Rodgers had called. Would call again at eleven. And Izzy St. Clair had called from Ohio.

Isabel. She had toddled after Cassie through the humid heat of all those river valley summers. Izzy's pudgy fingers were splayed around a glass jar, as she peered intently at the winking firefly dance inside, you could see her face in the blinking from the jar.

Watching her Cassie could not suppress the impulse to seize the jar away from her little sister. Her mouth tightened in the dark. She tightened her leg muscles and reached. Just as she touched the punctured lid of the jar, felt the sharp little metal nail holes against her palm, something *prevented* her from finishing the gesture: She had been staring off into the trees, where the fireflies winked and swooped, and had a sensation that she was stepping through a doorway, or between two walls, or trees, and was holding in *her* hand a glass jar.

As she stared at the pink slip of paper she did not know *where* she was, holding that glass jar, or *when* that strange overlapping of event, that déjà vu, had stayed her hand.

But she did see what was in the jar. There was, coiled at the bottom, an irregular lump of mineral, a curved hook of polygonal gypsum crystal, off-white and faintly luminescent. It lay, a geometric worm, at the bottom of the jar, resting against the side, wedged firmly there. She did not know, then, and did not know *now,* what made this jar valuable, what gave it intensity, focus.

When L.R. walked by, she touched him on the elbow and asked. "Do you know anything about a bit of gypsum crystal, four or five inches long, coiled in the bottom of a jar?"

"No." He said it quickly, pulled his elbow free, and walked briskly to his office.

Puzzled, she went into her office once more.

Flaming music.

Mineral Chakra Regulation.

Gypsum. Used to make plaster of Paris, an ordinary mineral.

Sacred places.

Power nodes. Dream, theta, UFO, ESP. The ocean.

Outside her window the fog was plastered to the glass, featureless and empty. She could not see the daffodils, the tulips, the camellias. There was nothing outside; she had arrived with Arnold through a zone of emptiness.

She was in a diving bell, a tiny submersible, peering through a thick porthole at the dark depths. Vision penetrated only inches down here, at the very bottom of the fog. Surely there should be things out there, lantern fish, jeweled and grotesque? Things that scuttled, crabwise, waggling fronds and feelers, eyestalks and segmented legs? Things with bizarre colors, distorted bodies, ravening hungers? Things made of stomach, mouth, and jaw alone? Blind things?

"Thick, isn't it?"

She turned. "Oh. Hi, Reggie. Yeah, it's thick."

"It'll burn off by noon, I expect. L.R. wanted me to bring this to you. He's on a conference call, but he said that Brockhurst just called, told him to pass this along, and a message. You're going up there this afternoon. To Brockhurst's. Lucky you. Arnold, too, he said. Here."

He held it out to her. A jar.

A coiled, geometric worm of crystal: gypsum.

"It's called selenite." Reggie prattled on. "Because of the pearly luster of the cleavage; people think it looks like moonlight." He had the grace to blush. "I used to be something of a rock hound when I was a kid. Collected stuff like this."

"I see. Where did this come from?"

"L.R.'s office. Why?"

"No, I mean where. In the world."

"Oh, right, right. Utah, I'd say, or Kentucky, though that's less likely. I think Utah. A hunch if you will. And look, the monoclinic plate structure, the way it fractures; and it's soft. You can scratch it with your fingernail, really. I don't know why anyone would want you to have this. Worthless, really. Used to make plaster of Paris, but you probably already know that. Well." He bobbed his head, springy curls all tightly coiled, like the crystal. She took the jar.

An ordinary jar, nothing unique, individual about it. Clumsy raised letters on the bottom, flaws in the glass. A cheap industrial artifact. Mass produced. Nothing special.

"What chakra is it associated with?" she asked softly.

"Hah?" Reggie was about to leave. "Chakra?"

"Seven psychic energy centers, ascending the spinal cord. Start at the genitals. Is gypsum a genital mineral?"

"I don't get it."

"Never mind. Is there anything else you can tell me? About this stuff, what it might be for?"

"Uh, well, its chemical composition is $CaSO_4 \cdot 2H_2O$. It is soluble in warm hydrochloric acid." He shrugged.

"Probably stomach chakra, then."

"Oh, right. Stomach, hydrochloric acid, ha ha." Reggie vanished from the doorway.

She put it on her desk. It meant something, but what?

It just sat there.

"Come on, glow, or something."

She turned on her computer terminal, called up DataNet, and asked some questions.

The answers weren't particularly helpful. Gypsum fluoresced after firing. It was a sulfate. It was phosphorescent in long-wave ultraviolet light. It grew in caves.

She tried entries under magic, but DataNet was not stocked with information on that subject, so she left her office and went to the IF library.

Paul Christian's *The History and Practice of Magic*, vol. 2, was a bit more helpful. "Brings the wearer the good will and friendship of all." Great.

She stared at the jar. It sat in the exact center of her otherwise empty desk and did nothing. Not until she picked it up and looked at the bottom closely. It was carved, lightly, with the crude image of a bird. A swallow? And the crystal was coiled, the fatter end lifted slightly in the air, where it curled over its own back. If she squinted her eyes it could be a snake.

Or perhaps not.

"To hell with it." She dialed her sister in Ohio.

"How long has it been?"

"Eight years." Izzy sounded the same, a brisk, efficient, sensible person, competent with small children, well-adjusted and well-socialized. Cassie had not, after all, taken the jar away from her.

"How have you been?"

Izzy had been fine, just fine. The children were growing, in school, Little League, accomplished musicians. It was a relief that spring was on its way, already the forsythia was putting out yellow buds, the dogwood blossoms were gaudy this year. But she was coming to see her sister, to see Cassie.

"What? Why?"

"I'd . . . rather not talk about it. On the phone. I need to see you. Some things have happened. I have a feeling."

"What kind of feeling?" Izzy didn't have feelings, not those kind, that vague supernatural itch. Izzy had only sensible, sturdy, intelligent feelings.

Cassie realized she wasn't being fair when Izzy said, "Someone is watching me. And I got a visit yesterday, right after Mel went to work. Right after he left. As though they were waiting for him to leave."

"They?"

"Two men. They said they were from the Department of Defense. I guess they were, Cassie, because they had identification, but there was something strange about them. And they asked a lot of questions about you."

"Me?"

The questions were harmless at first: Have you seen your sister recently? How did she seem when you did see her? Where did you go to school? Izzy thought they were doing a routine security check on Cassie. "Are you doing government work, something that would need a clearance of some kind?"

"No. We don't do classified studies, Iz. What else did they ask?"

"They wanted to know if I thought you were psychic."

"What?"

"Yeah. Did you have odd visions, premonitions, or unusual experiences. Did you talk to people who weren't there. Cassie, they . . . scared me a little."

"Yes. This was yesterday?"

"I tried to call last night, but your phone, well, it didn't go through. I don't know whether it rang or not, the sounds were funny. Were you home?"

"No. When can you get here?" Out there, in the fog, there were shapes, moving through the dark, in silence, purposeful and malign.

"Tonight."

"I'll have someone pick you up, somehow. I'm going out of town, but I'll arrange it."

"You're worried, too."

"Yes, Iz. I'll talk to you later."

A silence for a time, then. "There's one other thing."

Cassie knew what it was. "Mom."

"What are those people after, Cassie? The Dead Liberation Front? She's gotten very secretive lately, always smiling to herself in that sullen way of hers, you know?"

"I remember the look. I don't know for sure what they want, Iz. But I'm finding out. They are going to make an announcement soon, an important one. They say. But there is something going on that I don't understand yet, either. Don't worry. Later."

Cassie played the conversation back through her mind, listening to Izzy's tone, her voice. There was something different in it, not quite a perfect match to her memories of it. A strain in the vocal cords, an overtone of fear. A catch that betrayed her usual briskness, her sense of fulfillment and power.

Something had shaken her. Two men from Defense? Phil Rodgers was from Defense. Or was he?

Thinking that, the telephone frightened her, buzzing then. Joanne: "Mr. Rodgers on three, Cassie."

It was eleven already? There was no sign of lessening in the fog; the glass was dappled with droplets, an atomized mist across her vision. Reggie had thought it would burn off by noon. Cassie held the receiver against her ear, finger poised over the button that would connect her with Phil Rodgers, and watched the featureless landscape of her window, waiting for a glimpse of something there: teeth, a smile. An answer.

"Hello."

"Ah, good. I'm glad you're in. Very glad. We can talk, now that yesterday has happened."

"Now that . . . What are you talking about? And leave my sister alone."

"Misdirection and confusion, Ms. St. Clair. Good tools when used appropriately, but just now they are not going to work. I have had nothing to do with your sister, nor has the department. As for yesterday, you know what I am talking about. You are a contactee, Ms. St. Clair. We have been following you with interest for some time, and now we need you."

"I'm sorry, Mr. Rodgers. I'm not inclined——"

"Please. This line is not secure. Shall we meet? In an hour, say, in front of your office building? We can take a short walk, and I will explain."

"I'm not required——"

He interrupted again. "No, not required. A favor, perhaps. For your country."

"You have a hell of a nerve, Mr. Rodgers."

"Yes."

He hung up. She listened to the silence; after a moment the dial tone returned, an even hum. It reminded her of the sound that came from the air yesterday, up on the hillside, *thrumthrum*.

What did Wesley Millet want?

Life after death, but no consciousness. Somehow it didn't seem enough, even with proof. It sounded important, but explained nothing. It could be that PEST's self-destruct sophistication was completely appropriate after all.

If that was the announcement they were going to make on Monday, there could well be no impact at all on society.

Renata Glabro and her followers would continue to proselytize the end of the world, in spite of its failure to appear (assuming this fog did, in fact, burn off); inflation would increase, cancer would increase, general discontent would increase. As always. In other words, nothing much would change.

Therefore, that was not the announcement they were going to make.

Then why did Wesley Millet hire IF to do a study?

"I have some news," Arnold said. He sat on the edge of her desk and rested his palm on the top of the jar containing that enigmatic gypsum crystal. "What's this?"

"A crystal. Don't change the subject. What news?" He had interrupted her thoughts; the least he could do was deliver.

"Item: The DLF has, as you *predicted,* changed their name. And to exactly what you said they would. The Death-Life Foundation. Same letterhead, you see."

"I didn't predict it. I said we should recommend it."

"Be that as it may"—he waved it aside. "Greater credibility, more serious. Impact on religion and metaphysics blah blah blah. And so on."

"Okay."

"Okay. Item: Wilbur Stapleton Brockhurst has telephoned again. We're leaving."

"That is a tasty bit of news, but I can't. Not for a while. I have a prior engagement."

"Oh, that. You are to miss that, if you mean a confrontation with Phil Rodgers in front of this building, in, let me see, exactly thirty-seven minutes' time. If you mean that, I fear you must miss it."

She stared at him.

"Has someone been listening in on my telephone?"

He held up his hands. "Oh, not I, my dear." He had lowered his voice on the last two words, deep, penetrating rumble of W. S. Brockhurst there, "My dear."

He slid down off the desk. "There's something else you might like to know."

"Yes?"

"There has been a man in front of the building all morning. He has been monitoring the entrance with an infrared scope of some kind. Watching us, as it were."

"How do you know? You can't see anything through this fog. Certainly not a man out there. He'd have to be right up next to the door."

Arnold smiled. "Mr. Brockhurst told me," he said primly. "Shall we go?"

There was no landscape outside the window of the car either; only bleak gray as fog rolled past, a minute tremor in the mist as droplets rolled aslant on the glass. The fog was as thick as ever.

"The trouble with being psychic," Cassie said suddenly, "is the trouble it's always been: No one believes it, not even the person who has the talent."

"Cassandra," Arnold said.

They could have been drifting in limbo; there were no referents; no horizon, neither up nor down. She could see only the back of the driver's head, and his eyes in the rearview mirror, peering out at the road. For a brief moment they were her father's eyes, staring through the rain at the New Jersey Turnpike. She turned away, to Arnold. "Where are we?"

He puzzled the question a moment, mulling the implications. "Friday, a little after noon," he said. "Headed southeast. Somewhere on the road to Brockhurst's place in Calaveras County. We will soon get to the Dumbarton Bridge, cross the bottom of the bay. We have made no progress on the DLF report, which was the big event of the week only last Monday. Yesterday was the end of the world, and the world is still here." He smiled.

Cassie did not smile. "Is it?" she asked.

"Yes," he assured her. "It is. Out there, in the fog. In other places, up a few hundred feet, for instance, the sun shines, the air is clear. There are birds, airplanes, the laws of physics. And I *predict* the fog will begin to lift soon."

She did smile, then. A thin smile.

But he was right. The car swung out onto the bridge, which crossed the bay low to the water, and the fog thinned too, allowing her to glimpse the surface of the water, the low railing at the side of the bridge. The fog took form, then, ragged tufts, curtains, wisps, wraiths, reaching down to the smooth oily surface, stroking it, drifting, lifting, returning. The gray was luminous, a differentiation between up and down: sun. *Brightness falls from the air.*

Then they emerged from the bank of fog, into sunlight, and the world snapped into focus, form, brilliance. Ahead was more fog, in streaks across the road, but it was partial, normal, just low cloud, an accident of moisture content, air pressure, temperature, the laws of physics. Beyond the tatters of condensation there were hills of a startling emerald green.

"See," he said, but he seemed as surprised as she at the success of his prediction.

She laughed. "Yes. Finally. It was Carneades who said the only certainty we have is that we will go on making assertions even in a world of uncertainty."

"He also said some statements are more appropriate than others."

"Such as that the fog will lift, the sun will come out, the world has not ended."

"Not yet."

"Cold comfort," Cassie said. In her lap she cradled a glass jar, and the jar in turn cradled a smoky crystal, worthless but important, it seemed.

"Someone's following us," she said abruptly.

"What makes you think so?" Arnold asked.

"I don't know. I don't know why I said that. But I'm sure."

"Any idea who?"

She frowned, shook her head. "No. Nothing. Not a clue." The sun was behind them now, and for a moment, as the car swung off the bridge, it caught at Arnold's hair, giving him a narrow nimbus against which his ear stood out sharply, a delicate whorled shell-shape. She pulled in her breath, herself caught for that moment.

"It could be," Arnold listed, "Rodgers, for one. He seems most likely to me, since you failed to meet him, and he must have been nearby. Besides, we were being watched, according to Brockhurst, and it might have been one of Rodgers's people. Or someone else, and it could be the someone else following us, though whatever for I can't imagine."

"It could be Wesley Millet," Cassie joined in. "Pursuing us for his report."

"Dubious, but we can put him on the list. Anyone else?"

"Glabro, Zsylk, or someone of that ilk? Sorry. But they assured me they would be in touch, and there was Joanne, a kind of emissary from them, since she's joined the CoreLight Mission."

"Okay, we'll add them, too."

"There's NASA, Friends of the Sea, that band from the Space Academy the other night, sister Izzy. My god, I forgot Izzy ! Arnold, she's coming in tonight, I have to get someone to meet her."

She rapped on the glass that separated them from the driver. The glass rolled down; his head did not turn.

"Yes?"

"My sister is coming in tonight. Will we be back? How far is it, anyhow?"

"Don't worry, Ms. St. Clair. Mr. Brockhurst has arranged for your sister to be picked up. She will meet us tomorrow."

"What?"

The glass rose smoothly again, sealing him off.

"Did you hear that?"

"He thinks of everything, doesn't he?"

"Arnold! He must listen in. How else could he know?"

"Relax. Enjoy," he said, echoing her earlier cautions to him. "Consider a different problem. The Dead Liberation Front."

"The Death-Life Foundation."

"Right. DLF. What are they after, really? What do they do?"

Cassie thought about what they did. She thought about her mother working her way through the graveyards, seeking emanations, residues, psychic debris, ectoplasm, spirits. Is that what they do? To state it seriously, they investigate death. They study, they research. And they have learned something.

Did it really have to do with life after death?

Or something else.

"Arnold, what if they aren't really interested in life after death? What if they are interested only in life?"

"Go on."

"I don't know, really. Some connection between the psychic realm, consciousness, and the physical? Maybe what they say they are going to announce is true, there is life after death but no consciousness? That doesn't sound very startling, does it? But it might be true, and irrelevant. Misdirection and confusion, as Rodgers said. Maybe they want to corner the organ transplant market or something. I don't know."

She slumped back in her seat and stared out at the landscape flowing backward; rapidly now the fog was gone. They had risen into the hills soon after leaving the bridge and now had left houses behind as well, moving down narrow country roads through green-draped canyons studded with live oak. From time to time they passed ancient orchards, pale green buds on bare branches, or plum blossoms, the last of the season, just giving way to the leaves. Graveyards, sprouting grasses.

They passed through a gap in the hills, and looking back could see the bay, a thick carpet of white fog, brilliant in the sunshine, covering the opposite side. IF would be under it still, and she thought briefly with a smile of Reggie's erroneous prediction. It looked as though the bay were filled to the brim with foaming white.

Then they went on, over the top, and began the descent on the other side, headed east. Looking back, she couldn't see any other cars on the road; no one following.

"I don't care," she murmured. "We are being followed. And it's silly."

"What's silly?" Arnold asked. He was gazing out at the empty, twisted hills around them.

"Being followed. It's silly. Probably it's that Rodgers, but what the hell does he want? He seemed to think Glabro was dangerous, and that's stupid. He also knew I was a contactee, as though he understood what that meant. I don't, that's for sure. It was like a dream; but it wasn't a dream. It was something else. Just as talking to that orca, and swimming with the dolphins, they were something outside anything in my experience before. And I'm sure it has to do with the DLF."

"Mmm." He gave her an absent smile, looked back out the window, turned back to her. "Could they be developing a consciousness technology, do you suppose? That was one of the potential future problems in the SRI report a long time ago. An underestimated problem, and therefore more serious than the others we seem to be continually plagued by . . . energy, economics, and so on."

She stared at him, though he didn't notice. She stared hard, for what he had just said meant something to her. Just beyond comprehension, but urgent. Consciousness technology.

That implied some kind of direct, physical control of consciousness.

Which implied behavior control. From outside. Mood altering.

The government was interested.

She shivered, in spite of the increasing warmth of the day. And yet, that had a feel to it, the sense of being there before, the frisson, the shudder, layered time, now, then, then, but *when*. What did it mean?

She thought her hands were growing warm, and looked down.

It looked as though the crystal were glowing more brightly, giving off a heat and light of its own. But that was nonsense, of course. She didn't believe it.

They rolled through hills in silence and the sun shone down. A deceptive warmth, slashed by hill-shade and March chill. Wild oat pushed through last year's tan stubble, and the orchards, this far into the foothills, gave way to occasional stands of live oak, gnarled limbs and rough gray bark, festooned with green-gray moss. They turned off the highway, and the road deteriorated to dirt, then ruts; the car's suspension was tested as they wound slowly along the bottom of a steep, narrow ravine.

Cassie felt a terror of the ordinary as they bumped over the ruts. She reached for Arnold's hand. As far as she could tell, there was no one behind them.

Around a turn was a rusted cyclone fence with peeling wooden signs on it. A sagging wooden gate blocked the path. The weathered wood sign said: U.S. Department of the Interior. Restricted. No Admittance. Project A12.

"This is not Zeno Valley." Cassie said, though she had no clear idea where the valley was.

"No." Arnold seemed excited: "This is where I worked, before. It's an interesting place."

The driver pressed a button, and the ancient gate swung open smoothly. As they drove through, she felt the hair on the back of her neck stand up, a faint prickling, and turned suddenly.

It was there, the anonymous gray sedan, just nosing around the last turn. It stopped, waiting, and the gate swung shut between the two cars. Then it was gone, concealed by the intervening hillside.

The ravine widened into a broad, shallow valley; at the opposite end were the buildings: a round cement tower with vertical slots broken by a series of concrete vanes, like a heat sink or cooling tower of some kind; and a long rectangular building whose blank facade was broken by one door. Both buildings were painted wheat brown and blended with the bare earth of the hillside.

Arnold had seen the car behind them, too, and as they slid to a stop in front of the door, he said, "Do you get any impression of who that was back there?"

"No. I'd have to relax, and I can't."

The driver opened the door. "Mr. Brockhurst is waiting. This way, please."

"You know we were being followed?"

He nodded in silence. The front door opened. Before entering Cassie paused for a moment.

It was the silence.

No cars, no airplanes. None of the urban din to which people became so easily acclimatized. The sky was absolutely empty, not even a contrail. They had stepped outside of their time.

There were the small sounds, of course. Finches, towhees, a jay or two. Slight breeze moving through the dried stalks of last year's grasses. Nothing else.

"It's too quiet," she said.

"This is a restricted zone." the driver told her. "No air traffic is allowed overhead. The buildings are shielded so even infrared satellite coverage won't find anything unusual here; looks like an abandoned Interior Department experimental station, which, of course, it is."

"Surely someone could climb that fence, though?"

"Oh, sure. There are other ways of discouraging visitors. Mr. Brockhurst values his privacy."

"How do you suppose he does it?" Cassie whispered to Arnold.

"He has his own Senator."

"Oh." Their whispers sounded conspiratorial in the darkness of a cool Spanish entryway. Wood paneling, stained dark and ancient with wormholes; tapestries in faded colors depicting medieval hunting scenes or unicorns; carved wooden chest against the wall, a Navaho rug. Subdued lighting, concealed and indirect. Everything was indirect.

They moved down a hallway over uneven tiled floor and scattered rugs. At the end, the driver opened another door, and they came into a broad, thickly carpeted room, very modern, a complete departure from the style of the entry and hall. The walls and carpet were muted earth tones, ochers, dark red brown, tan, yet the room had a very tactile sense to it, as though textures were more important than colors and shapes.

She saw the man in her vision, the blind man, a moment before she saw Brockhurst, and it was with a feeling of utter *familiarity* that she faced him.

He was at the far end of the room, facing them. The light was high, bright and flat, without shadows, and for a moment she was distracted by it. She noticed the thick, dark glasses he wore.

As they approached him, he murmured in his deep, resonant voice, very slow: "Come in, my dear. Welcome. And Dr. Deleuw. I trust your drive was pleasant."

Cassie said something pleasant, fascinated by the lenses of his glasses, which, as she drew nearer, seemed to ripple, a prismatic shimmer, like snakeskin or scales.

He was blind. And yet he wasn't.

She had never seen him before, but she knew him, as he held out his thick-veined hands to her. "Lead me," he had commanded. "Lead me."

"We were followed," she said. It seemed inappropriate, but the words were out there and could not be retracted.

"Yes." He acknowledged. "Your Mr. Rodgers, unhappy you failed to connect this noon. Please do not fret about him just now. A number of events are coming to a . . . cusp, shall I say? And I'm sure you have questions." He walked forward, hands clasped.

She had a number of impressions of him all at once: serenity, flowing, unhurried. Yet fragility, concealed disease, even; a weakness. He was small, his hands folded across his stomach. His forearms were bare and thickly furred with gray. His face was deeply lined, and whatever

176

hair he might have had on his head was concealed beneath a black skullcap of some woven fabric that shone, like nylon.

And he was old. Although there was that odd balance between vigor and wasting disease, he gave off an overwhelming impression of age.

"I'm ninety-six, my dear. I've been around a long time."

"You can see," she said.

"After a fashion." He reached up to touch the glasses, the cap. "It is rough, I fear. Very rough. Just outlines, really, shapes, an impression of what is light and what is dark. A crude device still, though someday ... Well. Electrodes implanted in my visual cortex." He touched the back of his head. "Charged-couple devices in the lenses, several thousand in each lens. They send impulses to my brain. It is sufficient for now, for present purposes. Not so precise in space as hearing, but more amenable to a proper sense of time, eh? I listen more, and I hear impatience in your voice. You must wait a bit more, I fear." There was a finicky, almost prissy undertone to his voice.

"Why——"

He interrupted her, raising his hand, palm out. It was a dark hand, she saw, swollen-knuckled, and gnarled. "Please. All in good time, as they say. In good time. We are going somewhere, today. To the valley. I want you to meet someone; I need your help, you see." He smiled, revealing age-yellowed teeth, like old ivory; the smile told her nothing, no more than his eyes did.

"Do you want this now?" she asked, holding out the jar.

"You are referring to the crystal. No, I do not want it. You must keep it. It has a history, and you will need it." He turned away. "I am being a bad host. Some refreshment? I have nothing alcoholic, I'm afraid, but Fritz can bring you juice."

"That would be fine," Arnold said.

"This has been one hell of a week," Cassie said. She stared at Brockhurst.

He held out his hands, and she recognized the gesture as a beseeching, a subtle pleading. Lead me. He said, "I have seen things become manifest in unexpected ways, my dear." He seemed to be blinking behind those dark faceted lenses. "Patience."

"Become manifest?"

"I say it deliberately, my dear. Soon, tomorrow, you will understand. Become manifest. Imagine there are only two tenses to our language. They might be, those tenses, *being* and being *manifest*. Becoming. Not past, present, or future. But what is, and what might be, what is becoming to be."

On impulse, she said, "Dreaming?"

He smiled again. "Precisely," he said. "Dreaming."

Fritz came back with juice, and they drank, waiting for something to become manifest.

She faced a mirror again, in Brockhurst's home. Her face stared back in the harsh light. She noticed lines, gray in her hair.

She was pulling a brush through the hair, stroke after stroke, and as she did, a core of anger flickered into life: lust in Cincinnati. Anthony Malatesta approaching her from behind as she brushed her hair. His lips were dark and perpetually wet, his thick nose through which his breath seemed to snort continually in some animal whinny and her mother's face crossed through her mind then, thin, drawn, bitter. The two of them together. Cassie had been convinced that Anthony was interested only in the hefty insurance policy left by George St. Clair. Yet he had that look, what Cassie sometimes imagined to be a comic-opera lust, and her mother's unpredictable anger.

She leaned forward, examined her skin closely. Pores on her nose, the faint lines around her eyes, a subtle coarseness in her skin she had never noticed before; they reminded her of Martha, her own skin thickening, hair streaked with gray and white among the auburn. Time. The evil. *Beauty is but a flower / Which wrinkles will devour.*

Suddenly she felt depressed, a cloying lethargy that pulled at her flesh; the anger vanished into that bleak mouth, swallowed by a gravity that pulled everything into it. Regret. Her life wasted. Was this the face that attracted Anthony Malatesta's lusts? Or Buddy Rapaport?

Beside the depression came futility, and that almost made her laugh, for there seemed to be something so *ordinary,* so vulgar about this awareness of time passing, the sense of decay. It lacked destiny. It was simply that she hadn't noticed before these signs of her aging; she had been careless, unthinking, and her life had been a failure. Her marriage had been a failure; she was not particularly intelligent or successful at what she did. She had been lonely and foolish and had waited for something to happen to her.

She barely noticed Arnold behind her in the room, his pale reflection frowning at her as she trailed her finger down the line from the corner of her eye to the corner of her lips (pale and dry, those lips; colorless, lacking in vitality). She barely felt his hand on her shoulder as she considered her thickening thighs, the soft, pebbled texture of the skin on her chin, the stringy tendons in her neck. It was a spell that had seized her, a magic curse, evil and profound; she was enthralled, trapped inside this pathetic and dying form. A long way from light and love. Waste, regret, despair. *Fond are life's lustful joys;/ Death proves them all but toys.*

She heard metallic clattering, distant and diffuse. The gypsy caravan creaked up the road toward her, through the heat. This time she allowed the memory to continiue, had, in fact, no will to stop it. The bells clinked softly as the hoofs clopped on the soft asphalt. The man was seated in front, long reins draped casually over his dark hands, gold flashing in his mouth as he smiled at her. She had turned to see where the sound was coming from, hesitant about approaching the service station ahead, since she had missed the bus and thought she might be able to hitch a ride up there. A Shell station, the gold shell hanging in heat haze.

A gold-filled smile, hard sunlight flashing off the teeth. She had been as frightened when Anthony Malatesta had reached toward her from behind, reflected in her mirror; his damp, plump hand, wet lips, pulpy nose. She had thrown her brush then, and now, as this dark man's smile broke the scowl and stubble, gestured toward her to climb up beside him, he would give her a ride down the hot road through that shimmering heat, the smell of asphalt and bougainvillea; perhaps to the station up ahead. Perhaps beyond. Now she stood rooted to the roadside. She was Daphne turned to a laurel tree rather than submit to Apollo's lust. The gypsy leaned down to her, breath hot, grin filled with sour spices and animal lusts.

Then his wagon passed on, trailing his laughter, a donkey bray that shattered the hot still air, the rank smells. The clattering of small bells moved on, faded, were gone; the creaking of wooden wheels, the clop of

179

hoofs, passed the station, into the haze, vanished. Cassie stood rooted. Her stepfather had reached for that opening in her robe, Apollo turned her to a tree, still quivering from her flight.

She turned in anger, an outraged sense of all that was unfair and mean, and swung, as hard as she could, at Arnold Deleuw's thin belly behind her.

Goddamn you. Goddamn you. The words flared in her mind, intolerable. "You!" she screamed into the critical light, the soft, comfortable room.

His breath exploded, and he sat, abruptly, on the carpet behind her chair.

He had such an expression of pained bewilderment in his eyes, such surprise and betrayal there, that Cassie came to herself and laughed. "Oh, god, I'm sorry." Her hand covered her mouth, stifled laughter. She wasn't sorry any more, she thought, than she was sorry for all the times she *had* taken away from Izzy, Isabel, her baby sister, who had betrayed her that night by leaving her to sit between George and Martha, father and mother, as Martha heaved in agony, contracting to hemorrhage, to Izzy punching her way to the light. She took from Izzy continually, took toys, boys, everything that was untidy and unsafe. Left Izzy only the narrowest of lives. She did not regret it.

"Did I do something?" Arnold asked.

"No. No, you didn't do anything. Ah, God, Arnold." She wailed her laughter now. "My life is a mess."

"What else is new? We're leaving." He shook his head, perplexed still.

"Are we?"

"We're going up to the valley. To meet this elephant. He seems to feel urgent. The son of a bitch doesn't say anything that makes much sense; talks in riddles."

"I noticed that. So did the whale. Either they're all crazy or we have the wrong referents."

He shook his head again, standing. "Oof." He rubbed his stomach. "Aikido?"

"No. Anger. There is no attack in aikido. That's one of the clichés of the art, you see. It is defensive and nonviolent. But, to use another cliché of the New Age, I'm just a beginner. I started it because I thought I didn't do anything, didn't make contact easily, that sort of thing. Oh, hell. It's going to be lively out there, wherever it is: the valley. Lots of folks going to show up. Some of them are after this." She waved at the glass jar.

"Them?"

"Yeah. You know, Them. The universal They. Them. The Bad Guys. The Opposition. Whoever. Are elephants intelligent, do you think? After all, they say he talks to them."

Arnold shrugged. "Are people intelligent? Hey, I have a joke." She rolled her eyes. Her mirth had subsided, but perked under the surface, ready to boil over. Arnold was clearly uneasy.

"Joke?" she asked.

"Brockhurst reminded me of it. You know that Eskimos put people out on the ice when they get old, to die?"

She nodded into the mirror, eyes glistening, squeezed to bring out those corner wrinkles. Old.

"Would you say they go with the floe?"

She groaned. "Arnold, you surprise me. I thought you had a sense of humor." A wave of fatigue swept through her, and her head lowered, exposing the back of her fragile neck.

Arnold slapped his leg, and Cassie looked up again. When she spoke, her voice was frail. "Arnold, I can't even interpret reality correctly. How can I understand what's happening to me?"

He sat facing her from across the room. "Explain," he demanded, voice carefully neutral.

"There have been times ... when I've reacted to things, struck people, taken things from people, my sister, been afraid. And those reactions were *not appropriate*. I've been afraid of myself, Arnold, of what I would do; that I would make a fool of myself. Because what goes on in here has not been related to what goes on outside, and I act on what is happening in my head instead of in the world. Do you see? I was afraid I was crazy. And then I get these flashes, these things happening to me—those UFOs, for instance. If it hadn't been for you, I probably would have left, gone away. Always, before, I would go on a trip, go to Machu Picchu or Greece or Stonehenge, and try to find some contact with what was ancient and holy. Hell, I'm talking nonsense."

There was a long silence before he said, quietly, "No. Not nonsense."

"Thank you. But do you see what's been happening? Brockhurst says go to La Jolla, and I go. You say explore your visions, and I do. Wesley Millet says take the project, and I don't put up much of a fight about it, even though the whole thing makes me uneasy. L.R. says do this, do that. I do. What the hell am I doing here, Arnold?"

"Your job."

"What is my job?" The thin edge of hysteria was back in her voice. But he took the question seriously, did not try to reassure her. "I don't know. But it is important, I'm sure of that. You, and that silly mineral, and everything that has happened."

The hysteria collapsed, replaced by a bitterness. For a moment the shock of sounding like her mother froze her. She said, "Important to whom?"

"What is the most important thing in the universe? What goals are there that need to be achieved? There must be something worth preserving, worth doing."

She thought hard.

"I can't think of anything," she whispered at last. "I feel futile. Healthy and futile. This country doesn't seem worth keeping. My job doesn't seem worth it—second-guessing the future, which is never what we guess. My moods swing around, I'm isolated and unsure, I'm pissed off . . . I'm getting older, like everyone else. There's nothing. I keep thinking of a poem, Nashe's 'Litany in a Time of Plague.' 'Adieu, farewell, earth's bliss; / This world uncertain is . . . a brightness falls from the air.' Is this a time of plague, Arnold?"

"No!"

She didn't hear the controlled anger in his reply. She was staring at the floor. Fragments of memory, the Telesterion at Eleusis; that narrow hole in the earth at Delphi where the priestess sat cross-legged in the dark; Stonehenge at dusk; the final steps to Machu Picchu. She heard the old Chinese woman reciting Li Po, the odd tonal syllables falling through thin Peruvian air.

She thought of ice floes, moving seaward down channels between low walls of ice, in a white and wintry world, with an old person seated there, looking forward to sea, listening to the soft sounds of ocean, the call of whales, creaks and groans and clicks, that eloquent wordless call of sea mammals, who had been on this world for more generations than people had years, and she saw a calm acceptance in those old hooded eyes as the low platform of ice moved out into the open sea, drifted away from shore, dwindled in the currents, under a white-and-gray-streaked sky, over cold gray water. They knew something she did not know, those ancient people.

Zeno was a ghost town.

There was about it that sense of massacre and violent death, of red-eyed greed and the oblivion of whiskey; the ghost of opportunity, of gold fever, of pleasures quickly faded, lost. All these ghosts met in winter, when the streets ran with slick mud, or in summer when they gagged on dust. The boards clung to redwood frames desperately, as if to match the desperate, often fruitless grasp for the real thing, for love, or gold. There was little of the real thing rippling along the bottoms of Zeno Creek, and the leather pouches that thumped softly on the bar of the Nugget Saloon were small, pitiful things compared to what could be had in the more prosperous towns farther up.

The town, riddled with cracks, holes, ghosts, dust-devils, mud slides, was a pretense at best. It had only three buildings, even during its four-month boomlet back in 1855. The three buildings were ill-made, slumped, slouched, corkscrewed, ramshackle, dying from the final nail. Those who remained after the boom fell quickly into despair and ennui.

It was too far off the trade routes, where the traffic in women and whiskey flowed from mountains to city and back; too far north, too cold in winter, too niggling and retentive of its riches, too obscure.

It had as well a sullen, irritable band of Indians who deeply resented the hearty, degenerate prospectors who appeared that afternoon in 1855. The miners stayed, panned for gold, drank, brawled, screwed the one sad, sloppy girl seeking her fortune there, threw up in the street, and finally wandered off, leaving seven or eight too tired to move on any more, and the three buildings to sink into the shadows of their own ghosts, echoes of echoes, the very gasses of futility.

Eventually the Indians left as well, in search of blankets elsewhere, and for a hundred years the town did not move, except to continue its inexorable and glacial descent back into the earth. It did not attract a profitable number of tourists for the mock gun battles so beguiling elsewhere. Once or twice a failed entrepreneur attempted to stage the quick-draw showdowns, fake cattle rustlings, and other trappings of the TV West, in hopes that the ghost might take on flesh once more, and life, and bring the gold back to Zeno. But even the unemployed actors quickly succumbed to the fetid miasma of despair.

Yet it looked oddly beautiful, a virginal simulacrum of authenticity as the sleek helicopter settled onto the main street in the late afternoon sun. Little dust flew up around it as the rotors wound down; recent rains had packed the street without turning it to viscous goo. The hills rising steeply on either side did not hide the setting sun, and the fresh green was tinged with gold. No wind blew, to fill the street with the melancholy sounds of rusted hinges, weather-beaten shutters, or the creak of warped flooring pulling futilely at the nails.

Instead, spring birds flashed and glittered in the town, finches, orioles, a crimson cardinal. A flock of off-white doves rose behind the saloon and settled again with a whirr. Cassie, Arnold, and Brockhurst climbed out, stood under the sagging rotor and looked around.

"I bought this place in 1955," Brockhurst said. His low, rich voice lost some of its resonance in the wide, empty air. "There was a troupe here, doing Wild West shoot-outs, but not too successful, I fear. The final performance had only four spectators, bleary refugees from a halfway house in Shasta, and that was in the days when halfway houses were not even half way. I stood here and watched the four sitting in the dust, drooling onto their flannel shirts, staring blankly at a perfunctory performance by three aging actors, and the fellow who owned the place stood beside me and spat in the street in disgust. 'Didn't even pay,' he said, pointing at the audience. 'I'll pay,' I told him. 'How much?' he said. 'Hundred and twenty thousand, cash,' I told him. 'For the valley and town.' 'Done,' he said."

He moved his head, as though looking around the town, and his dark, faceted glasses caught the afternoon sun, winked it back.

"Can't see much of it, now, of course. But there's twelve thousand acres here, inaccessible from the highway, and the elephant can roam wherever she wants. If I could find her a mate, she might be able to start a kin-group, though this isn't really good country for elephants. Too cold. Still, it's something."

His voice trailed off, wandered down the street, sucked back into the earth by those same forces of age and decay that dragged at the buildings, the flesh, and spirit. Cassie shivered, despite the sun.

She felt the old man slipping away already. Some beast in his mind paced, just outside of rationality, ready to drag him off. She followed slowly, the gypsum crystal hugged into the crook of her elbow, as Brockhurst led them toward the one building that still had a roof.

"This was the hotel," he said. His gnarled hand moved in an arc, taking it in.

"Two rooms," Arnold said. "Including the lobby."

"He he." Brockhurst's laugh was two dry hacks. "Right."

"Do we stay here?" She didn't believe it, since there was no visible furniture behind the broken glass of the windows.

He didn't answer, but walked away without a word or a look. There was nothing to do but follow. Fritz, the pilot and chauffeur, had vanished after the landing.

Brockhurst walked slowly, as though the filaments planted into the back of his skull, under that black silky cap, were failing, the messages losing tone, vigor, coherence; as though the lenses in his dark glasses were clouding over.

They left the town behind, turned up a narrow footpath into the trees, climbing the gentle lower slopes. A few minutes later they came out into a broad meadow, set on a shelf of the hill.

Under the trees at the far side was a cabin of logs chinked with mortar, windows filled with glazed, discolored glass, a stone chimney against one end: it gathered to itself a rustic, abandoned air. The tops of the trees behind it were blazed with late sun, orange against the gloomy green of the mountainside.

As they approached she noticed a new and unfamiliar odor; a warm, heavy odor, enduring: elephant.

That gesture from the zoo elephant so long ago came back to her, that momentary contact, that *intelligence.*

Inside the odor was gone, replaced by leather, cedar, woodsmoke, and pine. She found Brockhurst facing her once more. He had his crooked, yellow-toothed smile, and behind the smile she saw the empty sockets and dry bone.

"Mr. Brockhurst, this can't go on. There isn't any more time."

"What do you want to know, my dear?" His smile seemed foolish and empty.

"For one thing, what the hell is this?" She held up the jar, the coiled crystal.

His lips sagged, almost a frown, and the smile vanished from his

185

face. Absurdly, she remembered the back of his neck, before her in the helicopter on the way up here: furrowed deeply, rough-textured, with faint wisps of gray down that stopped where his hairline should have been. He was completely bald under the cap. Hairless, naked, utterly ancient.

"I could tell you a history," he began, paused, frowned, began again. "The crystal is from Utah, from a cave near Nine Mile Canyon where an extensive series of petroglyphs, Indian rock carvings, were found. The crystal had lain in the cave, which had been sealed for more than a million years, yet it had that carving of a swallow in it. The petroglyphs, of course, date from no later than A.D. 100. How the carving got there, who did it, and how the crystal got into a sealed cave are a mystery. There were, presumably, no people around a million years ago, not in North America. Since it was found, in 1877, the crystal has passed through a number of hands, and there have always been . . . stories. When I acquired it, I did a number of tests, mainly using sound frequencies. It has some peculiar resonance properties, but nothing I could find to be useful."

He paused again, looking at Cassie with those strange glasses. "The real power of the crystal is psychic, though. I'm sure you know that."

"But how? Psychic how? It seems inert to me, just a lump of gypsum."

"Selenite," Brockhurst said. "It has an affinity with the moon, perhaps."

"What am I supposed to do with it?"

"Keep it," he said. "It's yours."

"Shit! What about the others? There are other people coming."

Brockhurst nodded, his round, dry head bobbing on its immensely wrinkled neck. "Tomorrow. Plenty of time." A smile twitched his lips again: a private joke, time. "You two take a walk. Up that way. Dinner when you get back. Plenty of time," he repeated, then he turned abruptly and shuffled through a door beside the fireplace.

Outside they found a path, thick with needles, and walked under the shadow of the firs, winding slowly away from the cabin, upward. Cold air moved down the mountainside onto them with a scent of snow, high pine, bare granite. Mingled with those scents was the faint aroma of the elephant.

Faintly, in the distance, they could hear the sound of falling water. Their feet moved silently on the soft cushioned path; their breath moved deeper into them, and the woodsmoke faded from the air with altitude.

Cassie walked ahead, and from time to time Arnold put his hand on her shoulder. She didn't feel it, conscious instead of the smells, the heavy jar pressed to her side, the sound of water, water, the terror of drowning, eyes staring, hair swirled in it.

The water was picking its way down a moraine, through heaped boulders, runs of soil, tree roots, a complex series of cascades, underground falls, and smooth sheets. At the end of the path, beside an absolutely flat and nearly motionless sheet of falling water, two enormous boulders had fallen together, forming an arched doorway of granite, a narrow entrance to the earth.

She knew instantly why Brockhurst had sent her here.

"Wait," she said quietly, pushing her left hand out behind her without looking back. Arnold stopped. She could hear him sit on a log, stretch out his long legs. She stood at the entrance for a few moments, absorbing terror from the dark and narrow space, breathing the damp earth and moss smells, the dank underground odors, the mire. Death and dissolution. She saw the entrance to a hundred similar caves, a thousand places where the earth made an opening into time, where event doubled and redoubled onto itself: where tenses were simultaneous, being and becoming, manifest and becoming manifest, material and dream, vision and possibility, all one.

It was Delphi, a hut in the winter pine forest near Lake Biwa, a cave in the Zagros or the Atlas Mountains, a hole in the earth in Africa.

She took a step forward.

It was the car, when she was just seven, moving in a skid on the New Jersey Turnpike toward the tunnel, filled with fear, and the wings of the funeral home sign were a neon angel with broad, enveloping wings, tilting into the air, carrying away her soul, some indefinable but absolutely essential part of her; when Isabel tore loose from that blood-dimmed dark, and she fell from innocence into malice, envy, sporadic hatred.

She stepped inside, and the darkness closed around her.

It was a grave, of course, doom-filled, corrupted, slow crumbling, softening flesh wrapped in linen. Time crossed here like the blue crackle of electricity between two metal towers, and the instant lasted and lasted.

She could hear water falling as the rain had fallen on her father's car on the highway, as it had drummed on the roof, as it fell on rock; she could hear the ocean in that water, the crash of a whale-body falling back, flat onto the surface and submerging, the rise and falling away of salt-spray, a gray white flower in the sea, the color of her hair, swirled around her drowned face, and she saw the black body twisting once and flashing downward, into depths where she could not follow.

She sank slowly, cross-legged, deep in the cave, her hands falling naturally onto her knees, cupped, fingers and thumbs circled, the cosmic mudra, and with eyes half-closed she stared into the swarming dark, where the armies clashed, distant shouts rose from the plains before her, the baby thrashed into the light, hooked by life, and with her first breath, ignorant and blessed, inhaled a lifetime of pain.

She was not suppliant this time, not approaching the Pythoness, the Sibyl, the tranced witch in the forest; she was all of them, tranced herself, feeling rise in her the power, the vision, absolutely clear, sharp, fabulous, utterly ambiguous, pregnant with answer, conflict, death, the point of balance where human event could fall one way or the other, poised on the terrible brink between flowering and falling: merging, rising, union, success, unfolding, and isolation, despair, wandering into the desert alone and without sustenance.

The instant.

She was there, she saw it, all the armies, all the tiny death and pain, all the blood, birth, joy, the awful sorrow.

And she knew, absolutely, and with total certainty, what the objects flying in the sky were, and why her life had been what it was, and who she would come to be, and why that was right and necessary, and in her lap, between her cupped hands, the crystal began to glow, and cast its pale silver light upward, against her face, and the low ceiling of this narrow sacred place, and between her hands and that crystal, and through her body, up the spine, through the seven chakras and out the top of her skull, the power flowed, exploded, crashed, filled her ears with din.

She knew why they wanted the crystal, why Rodgers and Renata Glabro and Wesley Millet were converging on this place, and what they had and what they wanted to prevent or take.

It could be hallucination, fragmented imagery from her unconscious, delusion, or delirium. It didn't matter. She had no doubt about it now, as that pale moonlight filled the tiny space, and electricity crackled through her.

The instant.

Lasted forever.

When she came out into the violet dusk, the humid, cool, insect brisk forest floor, she asked him what he saw or heard.

"You moaned," he said. "No words. Just moaning."

His voice was small under the trees, lost in the mountains.

SATURDAY

THE
THREE
WORLDS

6:12 *And I beheld when he had
opened the sixth seal, and, lo, there
was a great earthquake*

Time, now fluid, now static, once temporary, then jumping quantum-like, the moment both particle and wave, laps at the shore of awareness, recedes, tunnels again, advances in its own terms, and awareness follows as on a lead, leashed to those fragments of time and event. Midnight was one moment, paused, passed on. Moment to moment. The sliver of moon shed little light, and Cassie twitched in her sleep. A sylph was speaking to her, as it had hundreds of years before, to another, named Facius Cardan: God creates the world from moment to moment. Should He desist for an instant the world would perish.

Perish.

Arnold Deleuw, awake in this dark room, pulls his arms tighter around Cassie's fragile shoulders, and the twitching in her sleep subsides. Against his thigh he feels her hip, has felt it for immeasurable time as he stared into the dark. He has been watching the shadows in his eyes jump, has heard over and over low moaning from that cavern in the rocks.

Friday, an invention of the calendar, has turned into Saturday, another fiction. It happened, and was not acknowledged. Tomorrows. March was going to become April as larvae become insects, blindly, inevitably, its meaning only a matter of belief.

Her face was pressed against him, and as the sylph's voice faded, her own eyes opened to the night. She could feel his even breathing and tell he was awake too, but she said nothing, closed her eyes once more, and fell back into sleep where dreams waited; out in the forest the ponderous elephant lifted and lowered the thick pads of her feet, felt along the ground, her trunk twisting, then lifting to sniff the night air. She tested the currents of air, heavy pads falling soundlessly on the forest floor, thick with pine needles.

As she fell into being the elephant, Cassie lifted, felt the two thousand muscles in her trunk contract and coil, tested, and memories shot through her, stories, migrations, the making of a world. She feels water glide along her flanks and flukes, tastes salmon in the sea, can hear the whale call race through the warm-cool interface 3,300 feet below the surface, across the Pacific to the Mariana Trench, and the answer return, small and clear. Her body has trunk and fluke, vast lungs, ears, heavy feet and no feet; it can smell and hear the shape of the world. She can hold her breath, rise and blow in a fraction of a second, she can let the air flow through her trunk, in that long tube and out again, a wild movement, wind, not quite a whistle, longer than any breath should take; and shorter, too, as whale. She is both at once.

She screams, shrieks, high-pitched and brief beyond hearing. And she whuffles, a loose-lipped huffing sound. She is three worlds in one, creating the world from moment to moment, and she cannot desist, not for an instant. Or the world will perish.

Over it all the cool silver light, moonlight, faint light, casts ink-shadows and peaks of frost. The crystal rests in its jar across the room, on the dresser. Gypsum, innocent as any stone, curled at the bottom, inert and bathed in that faint light, waiting. The swallow carved into the soft mineral swoops and dives in the milky light. Good will of all.

Dawn, moment by moment, filtered into the room. Cassie opened her eyes and sighed. She was tired still, her night had been long and troubled. Beside her, Arnold curled, hands clenched between his knees, gray hair across his eyes. His breathing, now that he was asleep at last, was irregular, a silence punctuated by occasional sharp intakes, a soft murmur on exhale.

She reached gently and touched his shoulder. As she did this, she heard far away, nearly lost on the dawn hush, an elephant trumpeting.

She tried to read the meaning of the sound: fear, warning, excitement?

It faded away. Silence hovered outside the windows, webbed in the branches of the pines and fir, in the still running of the creek, the light, soft mist that breathed above new grass.

Her hand moved slowly toward the jutting shoulder before her, and the painstaking movement reminded her of Brockhurst, so slow and deliberate. It was the lethargy of sleep on her, all her central nervous system still shut down. Her fingers felt along the skin, felt the fragile bone beneath, where shoulder and arm joined in a complex knot of calcium and life.

Out in the pearly dawn the elephant spoke again. She heard it, a long, sharply rising call.

She listened for echoes, repeats, elaboration, and what she heard was silence that stretched out, tighter and tighter without breaking, as Arnold moved under her hand, reached up and took her fingers in his.

A knock on the door broke that contact. "It's time," she whispered, and felt Arnold nod. She slid from the blankets and wrapped the robe Brockhurst had provided around herself.

He was there, at the door, one hand against the jamb, his glasses probably useless in this faint light. Yet she could see his face, his ears, gnarled and woody looking, and soft wisps of white hair like dandelion floss around the edges of his cap.

"Good morning, my dear." His voice a low rumble in the dark passage outside the room. "I trust you slept well."

It was not a question and she did not answer. "What time is it?" she asked instead, automatically. Fragments of her sleeping life shredded away, and the day itself, this artificial Saturday, this late March, this precise moment defined in calendar and imagination and belief, coalesced around her, came into focus, and she was completely awake, and *knew* who she was, and why, and where she was going.

"I don't really know," Brockhurst was saying, his head tilted impishly to one side; he sang the words with an odd intonation that reminded her of the orca song. She remembered he was the only other person in the world who had sung with a whale. "What time do you think?"

"Cassie?" Arnold called.

"It's all right," she said. "It's time to go to work."

Brockhurst nodded, hand on the doorjamb, as though rooted to the spot, his small body light-boned and avian, poised yet unmoving. Balance, a cusp. Cassie sensed none of that decay, the senility, she had felt in him yesterday. He was completely there, his attention on her. "You are right, my dear," he said. "She has called."

"I heard."

He nodded again. "She wants to tell us a story. Shall we go out to meet her. In ten minutes, say, I will return. Be ready."

She walked around the room, touched log walls, the rough texture of furniture materials, the blanket. She had no thoughts in her head, no anticipations or memories. Wood is wood and ash is ash. Now she is wood, now she is ash. Moment by moment.

Arnold watched, his face a chalky shape in the dimness.

"Cassie," he called softly.

At last she sat on the bed, head tilted forward, hair around her temples; eyes in darkness.

"Cassie. We've got to get ready."

She nodded, stood up, and dressed slowly. The light grew in the room, gray turned milky. She could see his face, pale and drawn, hollows under his eyes, as he too dressed.

"You look terrible. Tense?"

"I don't know," he said slowly. "Are you afraid of elephants?" She did not acknowledge his attempt at humor.

"I think I'm afraid *for* elephants. For all of us."

Brockhurst was waiting by the fireplace. "Good," he said. "I was about to call." He paused, seemed to have lost the thread, forgotten what he was going to say, to have drifted away, and Cassie felt how frail, how tenuous was his hold, the tides of life turning so swiftly in him. He stared moodily through those reptilian lenses at the fireplace, the soft gray mound of ash there.

"Before we go out," he began, "I must know if you . . ." He stopped. "The crystal," he said.

"Yes. I know."

"Ah. That's good. You understand, it has no power of its own. It doesn't *do* anything. This is something well known to Indian medicine men, for instance; and I got that crystal from one. The stone is only a lens, and only for those with the eyes to see. Yet there are those who would have it."

"I know that too."

"Ah, of course. You have the eyes, my dear. You've been up to the cave."

"It's a sacred place. A power node, the orca called it."

"No," he murmured, lost again. He stared once more into the blank, empty fireplace, as though fatigued by the effort of talking.

Arnold started to speak, but Cassie put her hand on his elbow and he fell silent. Here in the shadow of the Sierras the sun did not appear. The light was cold and gray as it filled the room, growing with the tension, the sense of something important slipping away, out of reach.

A sharp crack showered window glass across the room, bright shards spilled across the couch, the carpet, the chairs, fragments of mirror-gloss reflecting a thousand lives in all directions, and the nearly instantaneous leaden sound of a bullet flattening into the log wall across from the front door; time utterly stopped in that after-echo: where Cassie saw that mound of ash in the fireplace collapse silently, minutely in the sudden stillness; and one long wicked spear of glass poise in the air then drift slowly, silently, to the carpet, where it tumbled once and stopped against a chair leg.

No one was hurt; the bullet had flown diagonally across the room. They both heard the old man say, "Ahhh," a long drawn-out sigh, as though the world had changed its shape with that tiny heap of ashes in the fireplace.

Silence and cold flowed in through the broken window, bringing the light, altered by the absence of glass. Birds paused in their singing, the breeze fell off, brook water made no sound. They stood in the room and stared at one another.

Then, through that glutinous silence they could hear, farther away now, a sad distance separating them, the elephant trumpet.

Brockhurst moved first, an uncertain gesture, reaching toward Cassie his twisted dark hand.

"So soon," he said. The words were faint and so low she could barely hear. "We must hurry. Take my hand, Cassie. Lead me."

She took his hand in hers and clutched the jar to her side, and the three of them made their way out the back of the cabin and into the forest.

It was a strange procession, the trio moving through the pearled, half-illuminated air heavy and resinous with pine. The trees brushed first against Arnold, in the lead though he did not know the way, brushed Cassie as she walked, one hand on Brockhurst's forearm. She steered him easily, passing direction to him through her palm, subtle adjustments of pressure, now this way, now that.

The forest floor exhaled to them the scents of moist earth, turpentine and resin, rich and nearly stifling odors of decay and growth.

Webs strung between branches sagged with dew, sparkled when they caught reflected light. There was no sun as yet, though the fingers raced eastward toward them across the valley floor. They made no sound as they walked.

And no sounds came to them. They were alone in the forest; elsewhere the universe rolled on, eddied and swirled, coalesced and collapsed. Elsewhere were people, intent with other purposes, moving through other forests, cities, open prairies, rooms, or mountain paths. Elsewhere dew trembled in the strands of spider webbing, and the thick odors of resin floated upward from footsteps. Elsewhere, not far, and on an intersecting course, the elephant, one of the few remaining, the only free-ranging elephant in North America, moved as a gray vastness through that same scented air, those thick-boled trees, the first link in a long chain of circumstance and event.

For now, she was her own history, the pads of her vast feet falling on the forest floor as silently as all the other steps there, her trunk lofting from time to time, feeling out the currents of pheromone, chemical scent, the esters of friend and foe, human sweat, fear. She was in a dance, a game, evasion and pursuit, a circling, shuffling gavotte, without music except the rhythms of blood and breath.

She was alone, the last matriarch, repository of an endless span of memories, of fabled breeding and feeding grounds, of intricate families, kin-groupings, respect and authority, peace and rage.

So she circled, and Cassie led Brockhurst where he indicated with nods of his impish head, and in the wood others were circling. As the breeze shifted, the elephant tested its threads of current, found out the others, counted and measured.

"Where are we going?" Cassie whispered, as the path they had been following faltered and disappeared, leaving a maze of open spaces beneath the bottom branches. She couldn't see the mountain or the open meadow where the cabin was. .

Arnold pointed with certainty, though. "North," he whispered, leaning close to her ear. Somewhere the rifle that had fired that shot was hunting them. She saw the man in the airport, hard familiar eyes staring at her without guile or evasion—only threat. *Wretches, why sit ye here? Fly, fly to the ends of creation.*

In her left hand the jar grew heavy, the crystal pale and poised, as though ready to strike.

Brockhurst hissed between his teeth, calling for quiet. He tilted his head, as though listening, paused, raised his hand and pointed. "That way. You lead."

"I didn't hear anything," she murmured, and felt her voice die in the distances of the forest. The old man shook his head, loose on his wrinkled neck, wisps of final hair gossamer in the wind of that shaking. "No. But I can." He touched his belly. "Here."

She started out in the direction he indicated, and as she walked, tried testing with her mind for the elephant, aware her senses were too frail. Her own eyes were half-closed in the gloom, and she tried to set aside the apprehension, the confusion, and fear.

The shot had been a warning.

Someone wanted the crystal.

No. She put aside all of it, felt for her theta state sensations, the dream-imagery of the night before, lifted trunk, inhaled the long draft of air, felt the body, the solidity, the mastery of all that bulk. Felt for her own scent on the air, mingled with pine and earth, the ions of water and springtime.

Brockhurst broke her out of it. "Hurry," he urged, his whisper a rasp against her trance. And the elephant sounded again, a deep rumble in the vast lungs, her call.

He answered her, his rumble faint and tiny, his lungs inadequate, but she heard and answered him again; I want to tell a story, she said to him, her message carried in frequencies too low for proper hearing, felt in the gut but not in the ear. There is not much time for stories, and I have one to tell. Overtones of grief and acceptance, resignation and assurance. The last unfettered elephant, deeply wrinkled side shifting to and fro as she ambled through the wood.

In her huge brain, beneath the deeply cleft skull, the thoughts flowed slowly, but with imponderable certainty. Short of a gun—and she knew about guns, had heard the evil crack, the chime of glass, even the faint splat of the lead into ancient wood, heard in her vast ears turned to the sound—short of a gun she was safe. Yet she moved with caution, in silence, speaking across the spaces that separated her from Brockhurst in that low subsonic tone only he could sense.

And Cassie, listening with her mind, felt as if she could almost understand. They approached one another, as magnets, slowly at first but with gathering speed, and her comprehension gained certainty as well, a full understanding flowering in her, what the elephant meant, why she was here, what her place in all the events of this week could be, the lights in the sky, the shapes in the sea, the cave in the earth, all her travels before, the years of her own life, growing to this point, this moment, this meeting.

She could hear water, falling in the distance, flowing over granite, wearing it away, carving with infinite patience new grooves, new shapes, which would not become manifest for thousands of years, beyond all her time.

The sound was infinitely reassuring.

She led the old man through high grass toward the gray shape opposite, indistinct against the trees, and under her feet the green stalks bent and swayed: wild oat. As they approached, she could hear, then see, the elephant, grasping the tall grass in her trunk, scything it neatly off near the ground with her toenails. She lifted a bunch to her mouth, then lifted her trunk and rumbled, deep but audible.

"Ah," Brockhurst said, and made a whuffling sound with dry lips.

She reached forward with her trunk, and this close, Cassie felt fear; she was so big, thirteen feet at the shoulder at least, her powerful trunk stretching toward them through the brightening air. Cassie could see coarse hairs on the trunk, and then the eye, large, liquid, and brown, with long black lashes, just like the whale, and she had to remind herself that the elephant, like the whale, had a gland there to produce the tear, and that it was not emotion that made that look of grief.

The trunk reached straight toward Brockhurst's face, and he did not move. At first Cassie thought he couldn't see, but then he leaned forward and let the moist tip of the trunk touch his face, his lips, and he blew, gently, into the twin holes of the nostrils. Now she could hear the breath going in, through that long tube, an endless echo: wind in a tunnel.

This trunk touch greeting was filled with gentle curiosity and pleasure. The two prehensile lips at the end of the trunk felt with extraordinary delicacy the skin around his lips, nose, cheeks. Cassie forgot for the moment that the trunk could pick him up and throw him across the clearing if she wanted.

He gave no sign that he could see, but reached up with his hand and touched her mouth, under the trunk, which coiled up out of the way. The pointed lower lip dropped, and inside the thick pink tongue, slick and smooth to the touch, licked out once.

Then he scratched the tongue, rough strokes of his hooked fingers, and the elephant grumbled with pleasure, chewed gently on his spotted hand as he scratched, her eyes rolling back.

Then she looked at Cassie, he dropped his hand, and deep in the elephant's mouth she made odd gargling sounds, clacking the flesh of tongue and cheek together.

"She knows you," Brockhurst said. "Let her greet you. Then she will tell us, and we have to try to understand her."

So Cassie stood silently as the trunk reached out to her face. She could see the intense pink of the nostrils inside, surrounded by gray skin, coarse black hair, the two tough fingers.

Then the trunk touched her face, smearing it with moisture, groped around her mouth, a damp, chilly kiss.

A jolt of intense sensuous pleasure went through her, the sensation of concern, nurturing, interest; of connection. She reached up and put her hands around the trunk, felt from the outside the thousands of small muscles that made up the power of this organ, felt its rough texture, wiry sparse hair, its ridges and folds.

The trunk dropped, and the elephant screeched, a brief, high-pitched blast.

"What does that mean?" Arnold asked, behind Cassie.

"She's happy," Brockhurst said.

"How do you talk to her?" Cassie wanted to know. "This is communication, but it isn't talking, not really. How can you understand her stories?"

He looked confused, and she sensed decay, held at bay for the moment, but encroaching. Death coming on. She knew it. He was old, too old, and the fatigue poisons of a lifetime were dragging at him.

"I don't know," he said uncertainly. "She signs with her trunk, of course. And makes sounds, many of them so low they are only felt. I make some sense out of them, but there's more than that, of course. Much more." He lapsed into silence, his lips working, as though talking to himself in an ancient, silent language.

"But she tells stories," he said. "She will tell one now. Listen with your ears, look with your eyes. You will understand."

The trunk reached out again, touched the glass jar in Cassie's hand, the two fingers grasping it for a moment, and then she began to speak, waves of vibration rolling through Cassie's body, one after another, as the thoughts turned into meaning and sound and the story of elephant migration and prophecy unfolded.

"There are three dawns," the elephant said, in the slow deep tones of the old man, seated in trance beneath the swaying trunk, the gleaming ivory tusks, worn smooth on the outer side where she had scraped them in her sleep all the years. "There is the first dawn, the purple dawn, when the outline of an elephant may be seen against the sky. There is the second, when the breath plumes from the trunk, the yellow dawn. And there is the last, the red dawn, when the eye may be seen under a canopy of leaves. It now is the third dawn, the last dawn, and so it is for the elephant."

Cassie heard, without looking up, the *thrumthrum* sound, the beat of rotors, and felt as a chill the shadow of the helicopter streak across the valley, hover over the town somewhere down there in the distance, beyond the trees, settle into the dusty street. She heard, and did not wonder; listened instead to the tenuous deep voice, so frail in this third dawn, enter the elephant story, carry it forward.

"It was foretold, in the stories of the elephants, that when the third dawn of the third world became full, and all the migrations were ended, the first migration over this world, where we are now, and the second migration in Asia, and the third in Africa, and only one mother of one family remained, then the migrations would end, and the lost would be found, and there would be no more families. The three worlds would unite, and the elephant would vanish forever."

She was telling of the end of the world, when the legends would die forever. For numberless years the families had drifted among the trees, come down to the waters to cool themselves and drink, followed by the bulls, who fought great battles in the dust, locked tusks and trunks, screamed and died. The four directions had been covered, the families had always known when it was time to move, and the great migrations had taken place, the herds had moved, family upon family gathered together, in unpredictable migrations man did not understand, but which the families did because it was time.

There were conflicts, of course, times when families collided, arrived at the same feeding grounds together, tried to share and could not, tried to merge families, and fought instead. Times when there were no bulls, or too many, when the families grew too large and split into factions, or grew too small and died out. But always they performed the migrations as required, from the mountains to the ocean, as far, in the years of first dawn, as the snow and ice, the mountains of snow, and the seas of ice. They had trumpeted at the sun circling the horizon, and at the long darkness, and they had lost touch with the others, had forgotten the ancient languages of the mind, when sea and land were joined, when the first dawn was perfect, and all could see shapes against the sky.

That world had ended, as it must. The second dawn came, when the spirit-breath was seen, the plumes of breath, and from time to time, rarely, but enough times to remember, the elephant could stand beside the ocean and see the spray from the shapes in the sea, and the plumes of breath from the trunk could answer, and the first dawn could be remembered. But in that time, it was known that this moment, too, would be gone, and the families would move on, and the second world, the second dawn, would end.

Then would be the third dawn, when man would appear, and the whales and elephants would be dumb, and blinded by light, and man, who had hands, would shape things, and turn himself away from mind, and the spirit, breath would no longer be visible in the yellow light.

This moment, now, was the end of the third dawn, the red dawn, and the world was at a balance, a log held in the trunk, the precise place where it could tip.

"It is man's turn to decide for the third world."

Cassie's eyes closed against the growing dawn. She listened to Brockhurst's voice fade away, tremble on the final syllables and falter, halt. She could feel the faint vibrations in her spine, her gut, also fade, could feel between her palms the jar, warm to the touch, thick with energy.

Light grew in the clearing, and Brockhurst, momentarily silent, reached up and carefully removed his glasses, folded the temples together, and placed them in a pocket. He removed his cap as well, the black silky material collapsing to a small package, which he also put away. The electrodes were built into the cap, placed over the implants in his occipital lobes when the cap was on his head. Cassie glanced at him, noted the furrows of his scalp, the wisps of powdery hair around it. There were no visible scars or marks to show where he had filaments in his brain, but without the glasses and cap, the charge-coupled devices of his lenses, he was sightless.

"It is better," he said quietly. "In the day there is too much light, as she has said."

He was quiet again, seated cross-legged before the great gray form of the elephant, the ancient matriarch who would be the last of her kind, perhaps, the one to pass on to this man, and through him to Cassie, what she could of the old stories. The thick trunk writhed for a moment in the dust and dried grass, last year's grass, delicately cropped the fresh green and curled to the mouth.

While the elephant chewed, Cassie looked at Brockhurst, and saw in the brightening day his sightless eyes, pale and milky, plain blank sclera without iris or pupil, not even a hint of the vision he must once have had. Yet when he turned his own head to stare at her, she felt uncanny, as if he saw her even without eyes, or was hearing her perhaps, her breath, the liquid pressures of tendon and bone moving in sockets, the pulse in her neck; it was a naked feeling. He could hear better than she could see, had developed senses she couldn't guess or understand.

She closed her own eyes, relaxed away from that unspoken scrutiny, forced herself to relax, realized that forcing was not relaxing, and let go.

Just like that.

Theta state. Images, sounds, the vibrations of a universe moved through her. Brockhurst took up the narrative, and she did not notice the transition between what was happening in her mind and outside. They had merged.

The infant is born with a soft spot on top of her head, the voices told her. The pulse beats in that spot with a gentle insistence. That is the mind talking to the creation of everything, of grass, and water, and sun and dark, the ice at the top of the world and the heat at its center. The infant can make that vibration and can understand the answers, for at the poles of the earth are twin white elephants who regulate those vibrations, slow as heartbeat, by which all are bound together, the one Family of families; the twin white elephants speak directly to the infant, through the soft spot on top of his head, the fontanel.

But as the infant stands, and moves, and grows, the bones of his skull grow together, seal, and the door is closed. So it is with the worlds, they grow, become full, complete, and their door, which is the door of memory, closes. The other worlds are forgotten, the old stories are forgotten, the meaning of migrations is forgotten, lost in the conflict and disorder of those locked inside the boned arch of skull.

For many generations now man has been closed off from the vibrations of the pole twins, the soft spot at the top of his head, his doorway into the other universe of vibration locked. He has fought, with himself, among his own kind, as did the elephant. He has fought with others, has killed; and because he has hands, and can shape matter, can put his mind on things, he has been successful, has taken lands from the elephant families, has forced the migration into smaller and smaller circles, into completeness.

Cassie heard Brockhurst, and she heard the elephant, and without trying to comprehend, she merged, through her own doorway, at the top of her own skull, the spot soft again. She felt inside Brockhurst's skin, felt the head lifted, the sightless eyes staring off into a void that filled with swirled shapes, coalesced out of random patterns. Her own breath rose and fell with his blood, the tight swelling of his joints. He was ninety-six, and the dark spaces where he lived were alive with things he had known and thought and remembered.

Briefly she wondered how it could be that the constricting of migration could lead to completeness, how it could be that man's success could lead to fulfillment for these vast beings who had been here before the first men, had made their circuits of the world through the earliest dawn, and the next one, and now this, the third. Then she merely accepted it, as she could accept the overtones of regret and joy, of grief, solitude, and ancient reassuring memory.

Brockhurst spoke on, his voice rising and falling, frail and relentless. He spoke of the feelings that flow through a life, through her life and the lives of her family, her aunts and sisters and her calves, gone now. The fierce, slow anger of adolescence: the gradual coming to fruition of gestation over the course of nearly two years; the sharp joy of birth, and seeing the slow pulse of direct vibration in the baby's skull; the resignation of endings, and the awe at being so privileged. As he spoke, he stared off into the slowly shifting colors inside his own mind, where the images of elephants remembered from sight marched and gathered, threw dust and water across backs in the heat, threatened and protected, nursed and nurtured.

"Soon," he said, lifting his hand to touch the trunk, at rest now beside him, "they will come, and all this calm, this center, will break, shatter. The pivot will move and the third world will end."

The sun moved in silence above the mountain peaks and filled the clearing with light. The tops of last year's oat were tinged with yellow and tan, mingled with the brilliant green of the new shoots. Insects moved in the grass, busied by the growing heat of the day. Her breath no longer misted visibly before her. Rich smells filled the glade, laurel and damp earth, and sounds as air moved through the leaves, bent the grass, and the insects chattered and shrilled and whined, and the vast heart of the elephant beat, and her own heartbeat, and Arnold's and Brockhurst's, and the air moved in and out of them all.

Too much light.

She was outside her own body, looking down on the group, drenched in light, aglow, on fire, with light. A dark violet light around Brockhurst pulsed with his heart, dimmed and brightened. She saw the strength in it, the drive of purpose, and also the swift approach of death.

She stood at her own shoulder and looked at herself. She saw the skull under her own skin, the ancient Sibyl face that peered out, blind as Wilbur Brockhurst, blind as Tiresias; this face saw all the horror hidden by the sun. She saw her own shrunken belly, her barren life, blighted by family curse, fathers dead, her mother shrieking in agony in her sister's bloody birth, and the brush that shattered her mirror, thrown in fear.

There were stories in her life: She was part of migrations too, of vast movements, populations, conflicts and sorrows. Never, in all those changes, shifts, movements, had she understood them, or even been aware. New Jersey to Ohio. Greece to South America. California.

She too had quartered the world, had touched boundaries, had moved and stopped and said, "Now I have seen this; it is time to go on."

She saw a door opening in the top of her matter-skull, the precise point where all the sutures joined, where the plates of her skull had fused so long ago. There was light there, too, vibration, ordered motion, music. And arched upward from it to the poles of the planet, to the others present in this clearing, to the others approaching and to the minds moving in the waters of the world, lines of light, vibration, music. Connections. Voices. Energy, immeasurable, unquantifiable, intangible, but nonetheless real.

She could hear the voice go on, "When a mind comes to its end, and death merges with the time of a life, then the door in the skull opens once more, and the life flows out to join the patterns around the world, the dance. So it must be with worlds, too, as the first grew into the second, and the second into the third. The elephants will be gone, the families will be gone, because the time for it has come, the migrations have completed the world, and it is made. As there is infancy, and childhood, love and birth, age and death, work and play, so there are the dawns and the days and nights that follow."

She saw herself on the hillside, in memory, as the shapes of light played in the air above the bay, the dome-shape drifted trailing white streamers that could be dust held together by electrostatic energy, or could be rock salt or spider web, but were in reality something else, which existed in the mind. She heard, once more, in memory, the deep hum, the power, and saw light increase and overwhelm her. There was music, which could have been choirs, or instruments, or no sound at all, and there was light that could have been sound or taste, or only an orientation to gravity, or the positioning of limbs and joints, a music played directly on the nerves. She saw the dark, evil shape rising out of the depths to consume the darting yellow shapes, and she saw herself seen from above, by someone else, who could have been Brockhurst, or only someone who knew Brockhurst.

She sensed Arnold, the melody of her connections with him, as the light arched from her head to his, her heart to his, and the frequencies were harmonics of each other, a blend that was, as it must be, only partial, but present just the same. In her hands was the song of gypsum crystal, meaningless in itself, tuned to the diffractions of crystal, the leap of quanta, the resonances of the heart of matter.

Beyond all that, beyond the vision, in all the senses she experienced, was regret. In the stories she was hearing, in the decline of those tightly bound families, their care and wonder, their imprisonment and humiliation in zoos and parks, objects of pity or contempt, the elephants were telling their regret, and under that, the fear.

Always, before, through the other worlds, there had been enough, the families large and strong, with young to carry on the lines, to fill the empty spaces; always, before, man and elephant had lived side by side, before planting took all the land.

Now all was changed, different, a manifestation of the new dawn as events became realities. Cassie hovered by her own side and saw, across the few paces between herselves and the elephant, that the shape was moving, nervous, the trunk now twining around itself, twisted, straightened, ruffled along the ground near Brockhurst's knees. The

207

ponderous body, all ten or twelve tons of her, all her thirteen feet of shoulder height, was in motion, the skin crawling over bone and muscle, the bones themselves changing their relationships with one another as joints shifted, and the muscles too tightening and relaxing in constantly altering configurations.

Cassie realized as she perceived that this change was a result of the story being told and the new presence of the sun, its direct heat and light, the visible acknowledgment of the day, the passing of dawn. And that the sun was the medium through which all the power of the stories was focused.

So she felt it too, the warmth of it on her skin, although she stood in some curious and not at all frightening way beside herself; she felt it as a source. She heard the elephant say, through the old man, "We cannot look on the sun," and she saw that Brockhurst was in fact looking at the sun, his sightless eyes turned upward, and the expression on his face was a curious one: rapt.

She heard her own voice. "You worship the sun."

It was a word she would never have used before, *worship*. A word she had never understood, with its implications of subservience and dependence that filled her with a vague anger. Yet now, at this precise moment, in this strange state, suspended in the air outside her own body, it was the most natural word available.

"We greet the sun," the elephant was saying to her. "It is necessary that we do so." As he spoke, Brockhurst was greeting the sun, face toward it. "We do it for the world, for all of us."

"Yes," she heard herself say, and turned her attention to Arnold, who flamed with a silver blue light, concern, beside her. His hand was on her other shoulder, and she could see, without being able to respond, that his features were set and hard, his eyes held in tight by the muscles around them, as if somehow the grief he clearly felt would escape him and only his eyes could hold it in.

She wanted to console him, to reach up and touch his hand there on her shoulder, but her body did not move, could not respond to her wishes, for she was not there inside it.

So she lifted herself instead, into the air, and looked down on the clearing, the grouping of figures foreshortened by perspective, the back of the elephant, the huge ears tilted out, away from the massive, bony head, trunk reaching toward Brockhurst; Arnold cramped in an awkward gesture toward her own physical self with shock on his face. Higher, she could see, walking through morning light, two figures moving through the woods from the direction of the town of Zeno; and recognized, without sensation, her sister and the pilot, Fritz.

She shouted, but the sound echoed only in her head, not in the world, and her perception rose higher still, into the calm, cool air, into the light, and she could see the whole valley laid out beneath her, the rutted dirt track leading up from the highway to the west, winding through forest and meadow, around the curve of the valley; the ghost town itself, foreshortened by distance; and at the entrance to the valley, a cluster of redwood buildings at the edge of another clearing.

There was no time passing, no motion, only the still shapes of trees and buildings and people, the elephant. On the street in the town she could see the helicopter that earlier had scissored overhead, deep *thrumthrum* silent, the rotors hanging slack, waxy. She could see them all at once, her clearing, the meadow with the buildings near the highway, the ghost town. And beyond it, the gathering of events, distant dust on the horizon, armies clashing, smoke twisting over the ritual fires, sacrifice, expiation, and entreaty.

Then time moved again, the elephant took two steps toward Brockhurst's seated body, stood over him, trunk on his shoulder, and he was seated between her front feet. At the same moment, another figure stepped from the edge of trees into the clearing, a stranger; Isabel and Fritz walked toward the clearing too, and Cassie was back in her body, reaching for Arnold's hand.

"Welcome back," he said quietly. She looked at him. The flare of silver blue light around him was gone, but the expression of shock and grief was present, the oddly wooden set to his eyes and mouth.

"I was gone?" she asked, though she knew he knew.

He nodded. "Why is she protecting him?" he asked, with a gesture toward Brockhurst, seated between the stumpy front legs of the elephant, whose trunk was lifted, the twin nostrils flared, flaps grasping at the air, her ears extended threateningly. The old man reached up then, touched the trunk, which curled under to his hand, took it to her mouth with a deep rumble in her chest.

"Someone's coming," she said, and then the someone was there, watching them across the open space.

Brockhurst paid no attention, his hand in the elephant's mouth, scratching her pink tongue and cheeks, a rumble in his chest too.

"So the old man talks to animals, too?"

The face was familiar, the man in the airport, the same heavy lids, the same thick jaw. Only Tuesday he had sent her the Delphic oracle.

Now, though, hearing his voice, she made a peculiar sound, a sharp nasal twitch: a laugh stifled. "Still putting red on red, Buddy? Diamond four on a heart five. It's too much."

"Hi, Cass. Did I do that?"

"Anything to win, you said. Remember?"

"I was young then, Cassie. Not anymore. Things have gotten real."

"Real," she said softly, almost to herself. "Yes, they have. Real, and complicated. You sent me that message, didn't you? 'Fly, fly ye wretches.' That was poignant. A cheap shot, but poignant; I should have known."

He smiled. "Now you do."

"Yes. Now I know. And you know Mr. Brockhurst, of course."

"By reputation. The genius of sonar. Good morning, sir," he called in a louder voice.

"I have good hearing, Mr. Rapaport," Brockhurst said slowly. "There is no need to shout."

"Was that your gun, Buddy? The shot through the window this morning?" Cassie asked.

"Oh." He looked genuinely chagrined. "I am sorry about that, really. And it wasn't me; my assistant, actually. He's overeager and not very bright. We are not violent people, Cassie. Believe me. We only want to convince. This is an important time, just now, in the world. We need you, Cassie." He spoke earnestly, in a rush. "We need you, and Mr. Brockhurst, and your friend Dr. Deleuw as well."

"Who's 'we'?" Arnold asked.

The question surprised him. "You don't know? No, I see you don't. Didn't Rodgers talk to you?"

"The Department of Defense? That's who you work for? Come on." Cassie stared open mouthed, almost amused.

"Did he say that? As I say, stupid and overeager. No, not Defense. Of course not, although it is plausible, don't you think? And it does involve defense, in a manner of speaking."

"Buddy, you're talking in riddles. What do you have to do with all this, with whales and elephants and the DLF proposal?"

He sighed, still smiling, and she felt all his old charm, the warmth of his smile, his adventurousness. "I better start at the beginning. What you and I do is not all that dissimilar, Cass. I do work for the government, and we do monitor social trends. You have no doubt noticed over the past decade or so an increase in fundamentalist religions, very moralistic and authoritarian. And in magical thinking, wish fulfillment—astrology and such. Looking to the stars for guidance, for salvation."

"Flying saucers," she said, and her tone was so strange that Buddy stared at her hard for a moment before he nodded.

"Flying saucers," he agreed. "The budgets for space research and exploration have been dwindling for years, but NASA still has a job to do. So we have looked into these things, UFOs, astrology. Magic. We've been doing research on psychic phenomena for years, Cassie. You know that. It doesn't cost as much as hardware, for one thing, and if there is anything to it, there are possibilities for doing what the NASA charter calls for, research. We can look at Jupiter by remote viewing, Cassie. We've done it, and had the findings confirmed by orbiters."

"So you work for NASA? Okay. Why are you interested in me, in us?" She took in Arnold, the elephant, and Brockhurst. The gesture continued and took in the two new people at the edge of the clearing: Isabel and Fritz, the chauffeur and pilot, who moved over to Brockhurst and murmured something quietly to him. The old man made a reassuring gesture back, his small head tilted, listening to Cassie's conversation. Isabel waited at the edge of the clearing, responding with a small wave to Cassie's greeting.

"We monitor the literature, Cassie. All the think-tank stuff, all the material about the future. It's part of our job. At the same time, we have so-called psychics on our staff, or as consultants. Part of their job is to search for others with talents. I'm not completely convinced myself that it isn't all a waste of time. They sit in a dark room and smoke pipes, or throw the I Ching or do nothing, and from time to time they tell us something. We have to check it out."

"They told you about me? Who was it? Someone thinks I'm psychic, right?"

He nodded. "Madame Glabro told us . . ."

Cassie was laughing then. "Oh, no. But of course, it all makes sense, now. She would. Did you know I was a Bibble?"

Buddy was smiling, too. He put up his hand. "I know what you think. She's gone round the bend. She started getting this outer-space stuff a year ago. Flying saucers, the end of the world. It's very difficult to sort the wheat from the chaff, Cassie. So much of this consciousness research turns out to be completely nutty."

"Buddy, don't you understand? That's the point of it. That's why it's all so useless. The things you learn are either irrelevant, or useless, or so unbelievable that nobody would act on them. The Cassandra syndrome. It's like PEST, our damn computer model. Useless."

He shrugged, a wry downturn to his mouth. "Not entirely. We do need you, Cassie. Now. There have been UFO sightings recently, and she's been using them, as others have, to gain a following. The world is in a very volatile state. Millennial thinking, Cassie. The year 2000 is coming up. That's a magic number for an awful lot of people, even those who think of themselves as rational, intelligent, educated. We are all swayed by it. Books are written about it. Apocalypse, catastrophe. What will the world be like in the year 2000? Millennium. It goes along with religion and reaction, with fear and magic. There are cynical people, too, Cassie, who use the fear, the hunger for reassurance. Who manipulate belief."

"And what are you doing?"

"Ah. The same thing, I suppose."

Now that was surprising candor, and it gave Cassie pause.

She watched the elephant, standing over Brockhurst, watched the trunk quest at the air, her strong, thick legs spread protectively on either side of him, the pads planted firmly in the earth. Her ears were still distended from her head, huge flaps of skin that gave her an immense threatening dignity. From time to time her rumbles could be heard, faint, as from a great distance, and Brockhurst's responses. He had his hand now against one leg, touching the thick folds of flesh under there, the furrows and flaps of it, reassuring.

It was with shock then that she looked at him, at the milky eyes, downcast now, shoulders slumped in weariness, and realized that his own dark seamy cheeks were wet with tears, that those blind eyes were weeping silently.

She forgot her conversation with Buddy for a time, tried instead to regain channels of empathy, to be completely aware of what flowed between Brockhurst and the elephant. She wanted to understand his grief, what had moved him so to tears, which flowed without pause down his cheeks, unashamed.

And she knew, in that rapidly fading contact, that the loss was on him, and felt herself moved too, her own eyes fill for that vanishing species, that great, slow intelligence across from her, the last elephant calf dying somewhere in the world, all the migrations finished. Barren as she was, she felt it, and for the first time in her life, she turned toward Izzy, mother of three, and felt a powerful kinship with her, as aunt to her children, sister to her, a constellation of relatedness among them all, constantly shifting and eternal.

Suddenly it wasn't fair, people wanted too much from their world, and she felt a wave of such powerful hatred and anger toward Buddy, and the thinking he seemed to represent, that she turned her back on him and gazed down at the crystal coiled in its jar, as if the atomic structure of that inert object, the dance of particles held in place by forces she couldn't comprehend, could help her now, could focus her power.

"Cassie!" It was Brockhurst's voice, cutting through her preoccupation. She looked up. He was pushing himself to his feet, his dark, twisted hand pressed against the side of the elephant, who seemed to lean into him, to support him, as he struggled upright. He paused, breathing heavily.

She looked at him, through her own tears, and the light was fragmented and prismatic, as it had been up on the hillside when the objects had cavorted over the bay and come for her, as it was inside whatever it was that had taken her in; she was reminded of a childish fear, of crying and staring through tears at the colors it made, distracted momentarily from what had grieved her.

"Don't," Brockhurst said.

How had he known? Those awful empty eyes were turned toward her, and once again he had known what she was feeling, what she was thinking.

"There is a time for grief," he said. "There is a time."

Very softly the very tip of the elephant's trunk rested on Brockhurst's shoulder, the most tender touch, light as the tassels on the ripening oat grass.

"Our friend here is right, in one way. This is a very important time," Brockhurst spoke with effort now, as if all the years were pressing on him, pushing him down, back into the earth beneath the great gray shape that loomed so protectively. "You are the lever that can move the world, Cassie."

"No!" She shouted it.

Even as the word died in echoes around the granite cliffs, in the gloom beneath the trees, the distance of the open valley, she knew that it could not hold back what was coming. That it had no power to change things.

"I know what they are," she said finally. "The UFOs. I know where they come from and why they are here. I know why we have never been able to understand them before, why they have always been so capricious and fey, why what they have done to people has been so strange and inexplicable. I know how they are connected with everything happening in the world."

Brockhurst nodded, satisfied.

Cassie ignored Buddy, she ignored Arnold, puzzled at her side, and reached for Izzy, who approached tentatively, then embraced.

"Yes, you do," Brockhurst said. "You know that if the world does not change, now, there will be a great and irrevocable tragedy. Fortunately, perhaps, we may never know it has happened." He clung to the heavy leg, weariness clawing at him as he spoke; this was a monumental effort, this coming together. Slowly, though, his voice gained strength. "We will be alone," he said, after a long pause. "Completely, absolutely alone."

Cassie was crying again as she nodded. She did know.

It made no difference. Nothing happened. The clearing filled with silence and warmth, sap moved in the trees, obeying the laws of physics and capillary action, the imperatives of growth and life. Dust sifted through the air, propelled by vague currents, random breaths of the planet. Pollen fell, gathered in the cups of cones, blended, joined, fertilized. Ground water moved through the earth itself, through limestone and shale and sand, between layers of granite. Snow melt fell down the narrow tip of the canyon, tumbled over stones also tumbled, scored by ancient glaciers, ground beneath their implacable motion at a time when elephants and mammoths migrated over this part of the world.

Time was many things. It was the rhythms of glacier and melt, the minute, imperceptible perturbations of the planet's orientation toward the sun: rhythms that extended over millions of years. It was grander than that, the rhythms of orogeny, the rise and fall of mountains, thrust upward by molten magma from the earth's heart, worn away grain by grain under the sun and wind and rain. It was in the life of the mayfly, the fission of single cells, the birth and decay of particles whose fleeting lives were measured in units so brief they might not have happened at all.

Time was invisible; the rhythms of it were everywhere but unseen, unsensed. Herds grazed on open plains, and the heads of all the animals rose and fell in an undulation, a rhythm outside time. Birth took place, and in the vulnerability of that moment, death too, predators and prey, the quick kill, the slow agony. Scavengers floated on the currents of air, the heat rising from the ground, and fell with a cry on the dead. There would be no one there to see or hear, no awareness to say, this is the world. But the rhythms would continue; as the breath came in, the breath would go out. As the hush fell over the world, it would be broken.

Cassie held Isabel and allowed the unseen motion to flow through her, allowed the pressure and release of mountain building and continent subsidence, the advance and retreat of ice and jungle, the birth, and feeding, and death of herds, the fierce explosion of blood in the mouth after hard running, the satiation, all to flow through her without naming any of them.

Only this way could she escape time: letting go.

It was enough. She didn't care that Fritz had drifted away, back into the woods, back to his helicopter. She didn't care that Buddy frowned, puzzled at the conversation just ended, unsure what had happened, or what it meant. Nor was she concerned that nothing was resolved, the tension remained.

She was outside of time for that one long moment, holding her sister, and the opening in her mind was broad and clear, the light, the hun-

215

ger for consciousness, flaring between them, related, nearly, for a moment, twins.

"I couldn't find it," a voice said, and the rhythms of that sentence fell into harmony with all the other rhythms in the world. The voice was very far away, as important as the push of grass toward the sun or war or ethics or dream.

Buddy said. "It's all right, Phil. She brought it with her."

"Oh, great. I've been wasting my time grubbing around that place and it was here the whole time."

She kept her arm around Izzy's waist as she turned, the flow of invisible time through her no longer perceptible, the spell broken. Event took over, and the world created itself moment by moment.

"You were looking for this?" She held up the jar, could faintly hear the crystal clink against the glass.

"Yes." Rodgers reached for it. "We need it."

"No," she said. "It's useless for you. Just a chunk of gypsum. They make plaster of Paris out of it. Common as dirt."

His hand was out, reaching. He ignored her words. She noticed his chin was narrow and receded slightly: a weak chin, she thought. No guide to character. His hair was slightly curly beside faintly bulging temples; handsome in an anonymous way. Buddy's assistant. Overeager. He likes sports, goes hunting, keeps up his skills on the rifle range. Not really aggressive, or malicious, as he reached for the jar in her hand, just single-minded and not too bright.

It was automatic, her assessment of his intent, her gauging of distance and direction. Deep in her cerebellum motions were programmed, available without thought or consideration, just as routine motions like buttoning a shirt were programmed, did not require deliberation. She had spent thousands of hours training herself to do certain things, things she had always thought of as exercise, discipline for the body, but not as *useful* particularly. Not something she would ever have to employ.

Still, the movements were there, and she did them. As simple as that. Neurons fired in sequence, messages went to her muscles, and she felt an exultation in her timing, as a musician or an athlete would feel it. The jar was just out of his reach, and he strained toward it, put more energy, a bit of anger, into his grasp, his intent. She felt it, held the jar in her right hand, starting to turn slightly toward him with her left side, so the hand holding the jar crossed her, and he followed, crossing in front of her, reaching. As he passed in front of her, she pivoted slightly on her left foot, stepped in with her right, extended the jar before her. He was forced to pivot as well, slightly off-balance, caught in a turn.

She reached up with her left hand as she was stepping in, rested her palm on his left shoulder, his back nearly to her, and helped him over backward, extending the jar at the same time. It was a dance they did together, a subtle tango; but he fell, and she continued her pivot, away from him, but facing him too. She kept the jar.

"Bravo!" Buddy was clapping his hands. "That was lovely, really it was. Aikido, right? I didn't know you were that good. What's it called, anyway?"

Cassie stared at Rodgers, sprawled awkwardly on the ground. "I didn't know I was that good either," she murmured. "We call it 'down the drain.' A variation of *kokyu-nage.*" She shook her head. "I'll be damned."

Phil climbed to his feet, brushing himself off.

"Phil," Buddy said, laughing. "You are an idiot. That is no way to deal with this situation. Do you think we should kidnap her? Steal her precious crystal?"

Phil glared at him. He would not like to be rebuked in public. Not at all.

"Yes," he said. He started toward her again, but this time the elephant, now cropping grass again, moved toward him slightly, ears flapping a little, not threatening exactly, but watching him as she ate, her trunk moving over the ground with a sliding sound. She was only a few feet away, and Phil thought better of it.

"Dammit, Tom," he said. "We have to do something. This is ridiculous. I won't be made a fool of."

"Easy, Phil. I apologize. Cassie, there are other things at stake here, of course. The DLF, for example. They are going to release certain information. Monday. That's another reason we need you. We know you've been working on it for them."

"Wait a minute," Arnold broke in. "Wait just a minute. There was somebody named Tom working for the DLF, or so it seemed." He turned to Cassie. "Remember Millet? He telephoned someone named Tom. I just thought of that. You don't work for the DLF by any chance, do you, Mr. Rapaport?"

He shook his head. "It might seem that way, but it's not what you think," Buddy said.

217

"You were following me," Cassie reminded him. "I can't believe I didn't recognize you, but it has been a long time. Are you working for Millet?"

He shook his head again. "No. I've been in contact with him. The fact is, there have been close ties in some quarters between NASA and some people in the DLF. Yes, Millet, for one. Don't think this hasn't been a matter of concern for some of us; there's a public relations problem here, for one thing. The DLF is not completely credible, you know. Not with everybody. But they have influence, and they do significant research, much of it in cooperation with the medical people at NASA."

"Tom, I don't think we should——"

Buddy cut him off. "It's okay, Phil. We aren't going to get Cassie's cooperation any other way. She's got to trust us. Look, Cassie. The DLF is doing something, but they have not been entirely candid with us. They are on to something important, and we need to know what it is. I've tried dealing with Millet, to see if I could find out. He won't say, even though he thinks I'm working with him." He held out his hands. "It's business, Cassie. Bluff and counterbluff. And somehow it is connected with Glabro and the Visitors' Disciples, with all the pseudo-religious fervor in the world. Belief, Cassie. Control belief and you control the world. Christ, false information in some areas can cause mob violence, war, or worse. You know that. What has the DLF got? How are they connected with Glabro? Why does Millet want that crystal?"

"I didn't know he did." Cassie was hesitant, angry, and baffled at the same time. "I don't even know why you want it so much, unless it's because Millet wants it. And I don't understand why you came up here. Why don't you talk to your Glabro. She works for you, doesn't she?"

Brockhurst touched her on the shoulder then. "My dear, he is here partly because of Madame Glabro. There is a Visitors' Disciples settlement at the mouth of the valley. Our prophet of doom will be there by now, reconciling the failure of the world to end with the beliefs of her followers. I'm afraid that what usually happens in cases like this is going to happen again."

"What usually happens?" Buddy wanted to know.

Brockhurst ignored him, but Arnold answered. "The conviction becomes stronger, the efforts to gain converts more vigorous. As she had gained an international following, articles in *Time,* and so on, there is going to be a mess about this."

"I guess so. Well, well. In that case, Phil, I suppose we'd better get going."

"What?"

"Let's go, Phil."

"What about the . . ."

"Let's go, Phil." Buddy threw Cassie a comic look. See, I told you. Overeager and stupid.

She watched them vanish into the trees; then she looked down at the jar she still held. Nothing had changed, the crystal was still milky, translucent, and inert. Selenite. Moon.

"Now, Dr. Deleuw, I believe you can help us." Brockhurst, fatigued as he was, seemed to be, Cassie searched for the word, *gleeful*. Yes. Glee.

"Okay," Arnold gestured to Izzy, who had stepped back and had watched the mysterious interchange with a faintly tolerant expression on her fine features. Another day at nursery school, the kids learning how to socialize. She followed Arnold.

"Where are we going?" Cassie's voice was lost in the spaces. Brockhurst now had a grip on her forearm, and she found herself leading him, following her sister and Arnold.

There was a rumble from the elephant, and Brockhurst gave her an affectionate swat as he walked by, accurately aimed.

"She's enjoying herself," he murmured.

Arnold answered. "There's an old logging road along the northwest slope of the valley," he said over his shoulder. "It's long gone in the meadows, but I think I can find it through the woods here. We are going, I presume, to the Visitors' Disciples."

The elephant melted away into the trees, without a sound. Cassie caught glimpses of her gray sides through the trunks of the firs, then nothing.

"Hey, I thought you had never been up here before. How do you know all about this logging road?"

As she asked, they found it, two overgrown ruts cutting through the trees. They were on it before it was clear that this had once been a road.

"This way," he said, turning left. "You knew I collected guidebooks. Did you think I never read them?"

They moved slowly. Brockhurst dragged his feet, the jaunty and gleeful air dissipated. She was walking also the long trail up the mountain to the oracle as the day's heat increased. The Persian army was moving too, endless coils of soldiers out of Media and into Thrace. The dust of their passage filled the sky. Great changes were taking place, borders altered, languages shifted, customs changed. Only ambition remained the same.

Through lowered eyes she saw the feet of the suppliant before her, moving back and forth along the road. Someone else with questions; personal questions, perhaps. Should I marry? What will my child be? Should I move to another city, another country? Or were the questions more grand: Should we invade, develop our navy? To whom should the succession go?

A valley warmth breathed up at them as they walked, a miasmic heat thick with moisture. It moved among the trees that surrounded them like an animal breath, a carnivore breath, replacing the mountain cool. Seeds popped and flew away under their steps, insects scattered in the grass. The borders of the track were thick with poison oak, the dim pine darkness alive with mosquitoes. Spiders worked between the limbs, strand by strand, traps for the unwary, deceptively lovely. The gods were far away, preoccupied.

She carried the jar. Her feet moved without awareness, and the old man, light as gossamer at her side, moved with her. He seemed as they walked to be leaving his flesh as the gods had left the world. She felt that leaving as a loss of something unnamed, something she did not want to name.

The sun climbed high as the great planet turned, and they came to a meadow. Across from them they could see the cluster of strange buildings that made up the outpost of the CoreLight Mission. Cassie realized she was hungry.

They approached the buildings slowly, through thick orange blossoms of California poppy, the papery petals scattered under their steps. There was no one around, although on a square redwood tower a parabolic mirror rotated, sending a beam of sunlight back into the air, invisible. It was the only motion outside themselves.

"No one home," Izzy said.

"They're here," Brockhurst answered. He groped toward a door and slapped his palm against the wood.

While they waited, Izzy discovered three vehicles parked behind the far building and smoke coming from a stovepipe chimney; when she returned to report, the door had opened and Ronald Zsylk was gesturing them inside.

He said nothing. Cassie looked around. The walls were dense with astrophotography; nebulas, X-ray sources, galaxies, and double stars whirled and spun around the room. A huge *Voyager 2* photograph of Jupiter, bright Io crossing her disk, faced another of Saturn, the rings blanked by the shadow of the planet, an inky bowl of darkness across the right side. Saturn would be high and bright in the sky this night.

Some of the disciples believed the UFOs came from there, that Bibbles would be carried off to the ringed planet, given new, high-gravity bodies and a new, more perfect existence.

Ronald Zsylk was a believer. It was there in his expression as he gazed at the photograph, red lips pursed damply under his sparse moustache. His head gave a slight dip, a bow to the picture, before he turned back to his guests.

"I'm sorry it took so long," he said. "The others are in the meditation room." He didn't seem upset, or annoyed. He had about him, Cassie felt, that same assurance combined with discomfort he'd had on Monday at her house; a faint embarrassment mixed with arrogance, perhaps. Lack of social grace, confusion with strangers, security with his own.

She could hear the chanting. It was so distant and serene she hadn't noticed before, but now it carried through the walls, the floorboards.

She had heard that chanting before. Monk chant, orca chant, wordless music, polyphonic, the rhythms strange and staggered, low and sweet; she had heard it on the dirigible to La Jolla, had had it chanted to her by the orca. Now it was people's voices calling to the squat men of Saturn. The call was the same thing as that issued by the rotating parabolic mirror atop the tower, that message to the stars, planets, to the empty air: Help us. Help us. Tell us what to do.

We are waiting.

She turned to Ronald. "The end of the world? Today is the thirty-first. Did the world end, Ronald?"

But he nodded, his prominent Adam's apple bobbing the way she

221

remembered. His enthusiasm was undiminished. "Don't you feel it?" he asked. "You are a Bibble, you must feel it."

"Fire, flood. Black smoke everywhere?" Yet that music haunted her, as did the vehicles that shimmered in the air and swept her up into themselves. But she knew, now, what they were, those saucers. They were not from Saturn.

"A test," Ronald assured her. "The prediction was a test. We expected the end in one way, and it is the end; only the outer form is different. Not the important part. Madame Glabro *knows*. She has been told, you know."

"Yes." Cassie was thoughtful. "The telepathic network."

His head bobbed again, yes, yes, you know.

And she did know, remembered.

There were connections, of course, synchronous events, the chant in the meditation room was so close to the chant of the orca; the same visions time after time.

So she didn't laugh at Ronald Zsylk, though she thought him misguided at best.

The world had become far too curious a place, too open to the demands of a vague hunger—all that remained now the old gods were gone.

They had deserted the earth, left it in the possession of scavengers and hucksters, set up as gurus, leaders, saints, spiritual advisers. To fill the hunger. What she did at Investigate the Future was no different from the rest: We will tell you what will happen. Be reassured. Rest easy. Mineral chakra alignment, Tarot readings combined with psychoanalysis, levitation, Satanism, palmistry, exercise, diet, all are answers, ways to focus psychic energy. The crystal in her hand.

Yet the country was so filled with Sufis, fakirs, yogis, Tibetans, enlightened holy men, monks and phantom magicians, converted salesmen in the spiritual business, and they all had part of a workable answer; there were so many ashrams, temples, ontology parlors, gnostic centers, kundalini healing houses, astrocartography naturopathic and acupressure organizations, so many camps, retreats, meditation halls, mountain monasteries, paranormal universities, saucer communication towers; so much diversity and shucksterism that there were few trees of real wood in the forest of hope and yearning.

She didn't laugh anymore, not at the saucer freaks, the screwballs and misfits, the desperate or lonely who came together, joined hands, and worshiped minerals or Don Juan or sorcery, Bahai or Sufi or Tantra or Taoism, Tayu or Vedanta, vegetables or Mithra. Love or the devil. I Ching or Cabala, astrology or metempsychosis. But she knew things Ronald Zsylk did not know, and she wasn't sure that she should tell him.

There was a distant sound, a faint *crump* muted by forest and miles. She turned, about to ask, and saw Brockhurst nod, release a breath. "Ah."

It was Arnold who spoke: "What was that?"

Brockhurst moved by himself toward the door, fumbled for the latch, opened it. He pointed up the valley, toward the ghost town.

"Zeno," he said.

A column of black smoke rose straight into the still air, blossomed slowly into an ungainly black flower on a slender stalk as it hit a temperature inversion halfway up the cliffside. As they watched, the smoke began to dissipate toward them, down the slope of the valley.

Behind her, Ronald Zsylk said softly, "Burning, consuming, and thick smoke."

"What's that?" Cassie asked sharply, but Brockhurst answered a different question.

"The town," he said. "The hotel and saloon. Probably the helicopter as well." Up the valley, beyond the ridge, the cloud of smoke thickened as the flames spread, moved toward them, obscured the sky. Now the parabolic mirror sent a visible beam of light into that haze, struggled to penetrate, to flash beyond these suspended particles to the Visitors beyond. Failed.

"No," Cassie breathed.

He touched her arm, his thin, knotted hand on her elbow.

Behind them the chanting had stopped, and Cassie could hear the faint chattering of metal, hoops and bangles and rings of it. She knew as she turned whom she would see.

"Good morning, Wilbur," Renata Glabro said. Her voice was low, throaty, gracious. "And Ms. St. Clair. We knew you would be joining us. The Visitors have spoken of you often, as you know."

Madame Glabro smiled, her deep burgundy lipstick as careful as the intricate metalwork of her earrings and bracelets. Her smile was warm and genuine. She reached for Brockhurst's hand in a familiar way, pressed it between her own tough, pale palms. "You have been good to us, giving the Mission this place, allowing us to share this land with your elephant."

Brockhurst smiled at her, his awful white eyes gazing sightlessly toward her. "Not *my* elephant, Renata. She does not belong to anyone."

"Of course. But you must be hungry. Please come, there is food in the dining room. What we have is yours."

She swirled away from them with the tinkling of metal hoops sewn onto the hem of her skirt, her bracelets and earrings, all the precious metals of her gypsy affinities. But she was not gypsy; her accent was pure St. Louis, slightly affected but pleasant. She had as well in her manner a serenity, an assurance that gave her great authority. The failure of the end of the world had not thrown her off-balance at all.

"She's happy," Arnold said. "I didn't expect her to be so happy."

"Who is she?" Izzy asked.

As they went in to eat, Arnold tried explaining about the Core-Light Mission of the Visitors' Disciples, the end of the world predicted for this past Thursday.

"Oh, *that* Glabro. There was a big piece in *Time* about her. And that boy, his picture was with it too. Don't they think they are going to be carried off by flying saucers or something?"

Cassie silenced her sister with a gesture as they were placed at the table. The food was presented to them by other disciples, an old woman and a slightly younger man. Plastic dishes, simple food. Salad with dressing from a jar. Mayonnaise, boiled potatoes, canned vegetables.

"Do you grow any food here?" Arnold asked, looking at the supermarket cuisine.

"I've been living up here for over forty years," the old woman assured him. "We've never been able to grow much of anything. Soil's no good, winter's too cold for most stuff. Farther down the central valley, now, lots of farms down there."

"You've lived here that long? What do you do?"

"Wait," she said. "When I was young we lived in Albuquerque. The wind blew, the dust would rise up. One day there were lights. A voice told me to come here. It spoke here," she tapped her temple. "Inside my head. Like an angel. So I came. And now Madame Glabro has come too, and she can hear the voices. I have never heard them again, but Madame Glabro has."

There was no apparent regret in this last statement, only acceptance. She smiled then, and her face lost years in the expression. She too was happy.

In spite of its banality the food rapidly disappeared. Brockhurst pushed his plate away, tapped Cassie on the arm, and gestured her up. "Let us go meet Fritz. Then I must rest. We have busy times ahead of us."

She led him to the front door, wondering how he knew Fritz was coming, but he was, trudging across the poppy field to the camp. "Do you see him?" Brockhurst demanded.

"He's coming," she said.

The old man nodded.

Light played over the bright orange blossoms, moved in small ways among the delicate froth green of the leaves. Behind her back the sun started downward, toward the Pacific. The smoke had thinned, spread across the sky toward the west, a hazy layer of gray around which the oval of light from the mirror rotated. She watched that light pass across her vision to the east, and thought that if she squinted, the oval of yellow light could be a flying saucer, performing impossible aerodynamic feats. The thought made her smile.

"Sorry, sir," Fritz said when he arrived. "I had to walk. I guess you heard."

"I heard."

"The tank exploded. I think it was an accident, that they just

225

wanted to disable the bird, keep us here for a while. I'm afraid the burning fuel scattered all over the town. Caught the buildings."

"It's all right, Fritz. We won't be going back there again. It was a ghost town. Even ghosts must be laid to rest, eh? And now, my dear, I am very tired. Do you see a building over to the left? There is a bunk in there. Lead me. Go on in and get something to eat, Fritz." He turned away, and Cassie, once again, led him.

It was a simple bed and creaked slightly under his gossamer weight. He sighed. "I must be getting old," and then chuckled at his joke. His eyes closed.

It was the first time she had watched him in repose, seen those eyes covered by their wrinkled, reptilian lids. He was less alien, more vulnerable, and she wondered what drove him so, at his age. He should be dreaming in the sun.

He gripped her hand, lifted his head a bit, and whispered to her, without opening his eyes. "Remember. You are the pivot. You understand."

Then he dozed.

She sat beside the bed awkwardly, on her knees, his hand very slowly giving up its grip. Even when the stringy fingers had relaxed, given up their hold on her she stayed. Shadows pooled in his deep sockets, his hollow cheeks. His breath was shallow and even, frail as dream.

In the meditation hall the chant began again and wove through her memory, holding the world together with the symmetries of music, the immutable laws of harmony. She felt, in her own dozing, her own dream, the connections of all those rhythms: her husband, Arnold and Izzy, Anthony Malatesta and her mother, E. coli in her intestines, the intricate three-dimensional spiral of the DNA double helix.

The old man's hand stirred in hers, faint as the light from the edge of the universe. She squeezed back, matching his pressure. I'm here too. She saw her father, her stepfather, Buddy. Eyes, watching her.

In the daylight Saturn, the planet, rose, moved across the sky, invisible in the splash of light, the misting of woodsmoke, fuel smoke, dust adrift from the ghost town. Still, the chant she could hear, the double circle of these Visitors' Disciples seated in meditation, greeted the planet. They were dressed in silver, Ronald and Renata and the old woman, ten or twelve of them, chanting, draped in the color of astronauts, glittering and metallic: moon color, star color, cold fire; the high gloss of the Perfect Reflector; mirror of the soul.

As the planet moved, so the sun moved, down to the horizon, and the light began to fall. More shadows pooled in the sockets, under his chin, caught in the wisps of colorless hair around his smooth scalp. Outside, the smoke vanished from the sky, and the stars emerged, thronged tightly across all the visible heavens. The half moon hung up there, so far from the bright point of Saturn, gone down in the west as well.

Cassie's head had fallen against the side of the cot, and she moved in her sleep, made sounds low in her throat. She was listening to the ticking deathwatch beetle in the body on the cot, in her own body. She was hearing the small sounds of drying, of cracking, of slowing and swelling, the insect-teeth of time. Decay. Her own helplessness.

She lifted her head, looked around at the strange room, put her head down against the wooden side of the bed. The music had stopped, the early twilight had faded and gone, the dark reigned outside. There was no magic.

But she felt the vast gray shape moving through the trees in silence, felt it pause at the stream to pull water into the trunk, curl the trunk and drink. She felt the anticipation, knew what tomorrow was going to present her: the black-and-white shape, the smooth gray shapes, gliding through the waters. Her own body fell through the shadows, the warm buoyant water, the shafts of light and shade, the drift of plankton.

When she looked up, Renata Glabro was looking down. Beside her Fritz said softly, "Mr. Brockhurst."

Renata had on her silver caftan. Light fragmented off it, light from the doorway, from the moon through the window; shredded light, random light, that scintillated as she moved.

Brockhurst sighed. "It's you, is it Fritz? It must be time, then."

Cassie lifted her head, tried to speak, licked her lips and tried again. "You're awake." Her voice was muffled and uncertain. "What's happening?"

Fritz said, "There's a car coming. It'll be here in a few minutes."

"Wesley Millet," Brockhurst said, sitting up. "He's concerned about his report, Cassie. You haven't been available, and he hasn't been able to find L.R., either. So he is coming here. Everyone is going to be here soon. It's going to be a long night, my dear, and a short day tomorrow. We have a lot to do."

He swung his legs over the side of the cot, put his hairless dark feet on the bare wood. Light glinted off the terrible white eyes. "My dear, are you all right?" he asked. Her palms were cold and damp.

"A short day tomorrow?" she asked.

He smiled, his long yellow teeth visible in the yellow light from the hallway. "Never mind. Time will take care."

He put out his hand, and she stood, took it, and led him out, into the night. Renata, who had said nothing, strode away across the grass to the central building, where the meditation hall and dining room were, where the windows threw yellow trapezoids out on the new green grasses. Cassie could see shapes inside there, figures huddled together.

"Let's go," Brockhurst said, and it was the vision she had on Tuesday, when she went to see the orca, leading the blind old man toward the light, where the others were.

From the darkness of the meadow came the whuffling sound, a soft call. "Excuse me," Brockhurst said, pausing. He turned toward that sound, stepped away from Cassie, reached up. The wraith-gray shape moved silently toward him, the trunk extended as her pads rose and fell gently.

Behind him Glabro and Ronald and the others appeared, leaving the door open, an odd angular splash of light on the earth. They formed a rough circle behind the man and elephant.

She rumbled deep in her chest, and he rumbled back to her. In the darkness she seemed enormous, far larger even than in daylight, a shadow against the stars, a ghost of pale moonlight highlighting her back and sides.

The conversation was not, Cassie knew, an exchange of information. It was too late for news. This was only communion, a flow of feeling between the two. A farewell.

The disciples stood in the circle and watched. Brockhurst held the sinuous trunk in his wood-dark hands, and she writhed it in patterns, a

228

moving Braille, tactile signing. Cassie could hear the long breath rush through that double tube, a distant wind sound without end.

Then the gray shape turned and floated away across the field and was gone.

Car lights approached, swept across the group, brakes squeaked. The door opened, and Wesley Millet stepped out into the circle of disciples, facing Brockhurst, Cassie, Arnold, Izzy, and the rest. Beside him, Buddy too climbed from the car.

"It took a hell of a long time to get here," Millet complained.

No one answered.

"Well. I presume you know why I'm here?" Millet asked. Again, no answer. Finally Brockhurst took Cassie's arm, reached for it unerringly in the dark, and pressed her toward the door of the hallway. She led him in, and the others followed.

Inside, the hallway, dominated by that vast swirled circle of Jupiter, the delicate blues and oranges, yellows and whites of the upper atmosphere, the old NASA photo, was drenched in yellow light. The stars, despite the broad skylight, were no longer visible. Saturn drowned. The mirror up there still circled, but the reflected light was faint, moon and starlight.

"Jesus, Wilbur," Millet said from the doorway. "You lead us on a chase, don't you? But here it is, Saturday night. We are making our announcement Monday, and I do need some assurances from you. We do."

There was a quality to the confrontation between the two men, a ritual air, as if it were preordained and circumscribed. Cold air flowed into the room through the open door, and Millet's breath plumed cold and white as he spoke. Cassie felt the chill of it.

"Yes," Brockhurst replied slowly. "I suppose you do." His eyes moved restlessly around the room, unseeing, and he licked at his slack lips with a nervous tongue. He seemed uncertain, and Cassie felt a stab of fear, sharp and abrupt, and quickly gone.

"What are you going to announce?" she interjected quickly. "You know our report was going to be meaningless without knowing that."

Millet turned to her. "No, you still don't know, do you? You should have figured it out by now, although we tried to keep it from you, of course. Still, an organization like IF has influence, respectability. With an endorsement from you our effect could tip things the right way, you understand."

"Endorsement?" That was Arnold, surprised.

"Ah, yes, well of course you wouldn't see it as an endorsement, would you? You don't endorse, you merely report. Objective, scientific, detached. You wouldn't try to influence events." His lip was twisted in an odd way, revealing the crooked discolored teeth behind.

"It *is* complex," Arnold began, but Millet cut him off.

"No, I'm not interested. We are running out of time. Even my friend from NASA here, Mr. Rapaport, is growing impatient. We need Cassie now, not IF. Since Renata has gone off on her own, shall we say, we need someone with talent. As you say, Dr. Deleuw, this is a complex matter. And we all know that the old rationality is not going to help us. Not your computer, not your economic and social analysis. Only that right hemisphere of yours, Ms. St. Clair."

She backed away. "Uh-uh. No. My right hemisphere is not going to help you, Mr. Millet."

"She means, Wesley, that her talent is not quite what you think it is," Brockhurst said quietly.

"I also mean I don't want to help him. I don't trust him," Cassie flared.

Phil Rodgers appeared in the doorway behind Millet. "I have the jar," he said. "Found it in the other building over there. On the floor."

Millet nodded. He looked at Cassie. "You see? We have it now."

She shrugged uneasily, though still not certain the crystal meant anything. "It's just a crystal."

Buddy came over to her. "Cassie. Don't you see? We have something fabulous, something really important to us, to all of us, you and me, everyone. We need you." He spoke earnestly, looking into her eyes with an almost shocking directness, trying to compel her by his look.

Brockhurst wandered away from the group as though cut loose from his mooring, and everyone looked at him, even Buddy. There was an elevated section of floor, a low dais, before the two walls with the huge photographs of the planets. He stumbled awkwardly against the edge, felt his way around to sit on it. A vast weariness seemed to sweep over him, and Cassie hurried to his side, afraid he was going to collapse.

He waved her off.

"There are three worlds," he began, and stopped, chewing at his lips. "Three worlds." His eyes moved blindly around, restless in their sockets. "Wesley doesn't understand." His lips worked. "You do, don't you, Cassie?" This time it was a question.

230

"I'm not sure," she had to say. The figure of three worlds raced across her mind, but there were so many trios, so many possible triples, sectors, primary colors, trinities.

"There is the realm of desire," he said, and his voice was faint, losing ground. "We all belong. And the world of form, too, see, in the unconscious. Dream. And the formless, too: infinity. Those are three worlds." He fell silent, his head slumped, chin against his chest.

Finally Wesley said, "Enough of your half-baked Oriental crap, Wilbur. This is the real world, right here. The DLF has been doing the only significant work in a world gone nuts over petty desires. 'Save me, save me,' people are crying all over the place. 'We've screwed it all up, save us, tell us what to do.' That's what they want. The Death-Life Foundation has been finding answers, has *found* answers. Real answers, in the real world, not this mystical nonsense."

"What real answers?" Arnold asked. "Life after death but not awareness; no consciousness? That doesn't sound like a real answer to me, although it will certainly upset some people."

Millet smiled. "Ah. But it's true. Life after death but no consciousness. As things are now. But we can change that."

Renata Glabro snorted then, a shockingly derisive sound. Cassie could feel the texture of connections in the room, the surface layer of polite, earnest conversation, attempts at persuasion; patterns of belief under that, of obstinacy, of the fear of change; alignments of mutual interest, temporary and mercurial; unconscious forces, among them her own fear and hunger, the sum of her experience that made up her life.

She drifted away as the talk went on. She felt herself very small, between her parents in the car so long ago on the turnpike, the swerve, the violent image of the sign shifting away and up through the rain, her mother writhing, constricted, in contractions. She had been cut loose then too, had drifted away through memory and imagination, through past and future; she could be the oracle at Delphi, a shaman in the pine woods of Japan, a young girl on her way to the festival of Apollo Delphinios, white wool wound in fillets around sprigs of olive clutched in a sweating hand. She could see armies clashing in the distance, dust rising in vast swirls, the cries of the fallen, the wounded, and never know that what she saw was a vision of reality or a metaphor for another kind of conflict.

She married, had no children, divorced, and did not know why, did not question why. She sat at her dressing table, struggling with an unruly curl, and her stepfather came into the room, and she threw her brush, shattered the mirror, fled down the hall, and did not know why.

Now she tried to discern the pattern unfolding here, to ask the question she had fooled herself into thinking she had always asked before: the why of things.

Realized she had always asked why of the events outside herself, as if they were not connected to her. As if they were completely external, and she were detached.

The week past had proved her wrong. And she knew that Brockhurst had been trying to tell her something with his apparent rambling talk of three worlds.

There were three worlds of intelligence, of consciousness, and they were mountain peaks on the planet. Cetaceans, humans, and elephants.

And she could see that beneath the entreaty in Buddy's voice, the persuasive wheedling in Millet's, there was a threat to those three worlds. A blind hunger from one of those worlds to make itself the only one. To exclude the other two.

Abruptly she interrupted. "Give me the crystal." She glared at Buddy, and at Rodgers, unsure whether she was putting on an act or really meant it.

Rodgers said, "No."

Buddy shook his head. "No, Cassie. We need you. Come with us, and you can have it. But we need your help. We know the UFOs have something to do with this, and that the DLF is trying to change the world. We need to know, and soon, what the connections are. For a while we thought Renata was going to help us, but as you know . . ." He trailed off with a shrug. She did know.

And glancing down at Brockhurst, she saw him smile.

He approved.

She hesitated a moment longer, though. This was the moment, the pivot, but she couldn't see clearly what it would mean. If she did not go, would she stop the DLF? It didn't seem likely, though it would hinder them. If she went, would she be able to understand what they were about to do, what the world would become in time to influence it? Again, it wasn't clear.

What was clear was the texture. This was a crucial moment in the weaving of the pattern. A new element was needed.

The three worlds must be put together, and she was the only one who could do it. So in that moment, she took the step, committed herself, took from Brockhurst the mantle.

232

"All right," she said quietly. "I'll go with you."

She stepped forward before anyone could stop her, heard Arnold's protests, Izzy's surprise, Glabro and Ronald murmuring confusion, shut them all behind her as the door closed. She got into the car quickly, and the four doors slammed as the other three, Buddy, Phil, and Millet, got in. They moved quickly off, down the rutted road toward the highway, and high overhead the half moon glimmered, the planets wheeled, the processes of chemistry and physics went on, unperturbed.

The car was swallowed up in the darkness. Behind her, she knew, the old man was smiling, some of the weariness leaving him. For now.

SUNDAY

THE LONG HABIT

8:1 *And when he had opened the seventh seal, there was silence in heaven*

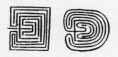

Gray sea, oily calm, lead foil.

Cassie St. Clair, sleep waxed at her eye corners, skin drawn tight across her cheekbones, which are high and Slavic despite her French name, hair tangled, the gray, seal-colored among the brown; clothes collecting salt crystalized out of the sea-humid air and clammy with it; feels the poisons of fatigue and hunger seep through her body, dying from birth. Before her the sea, stretching all the way to Dan-no-ura, to Sekigahara, to the Rashōmon gate, to Genji's court, to Komachi's ghost wandering without rest. At Dan-no-ura were burning ships, black smoke thick in the air, the water red with samurai blood.

Behind her the coast range, faintly gray in this filtered dawn light, and beyond the hills more ridges, central valley, and then, very small on any map, Zeno Valley, the burned town, the Visitors' Disiples, Renata Glabro, her own gray St. Louis eyes watching the sky with hope and contentment, the serenity of the absolutely assured. Lights will move in the skies, will hum there, land beside her, carry her and all Bibbles to another planet, appropriate to their level of spiritual development. The sky, for now, is empty still, the stars, whose light is a billion years ancient when the world began, are fading. Cassie's history is now, this pier, at the edge of this sullen gray ocean, face-to-face with her own past.

Beside her Buddy Rapaport, whom she cannot think of as Tom, thickened by his own years, stares into the water, though his gaze cannot penetrate the surface, which reflects nothing, reveals nothing.

Sunday. No horizon, no limits to vision, no line between sea and sky.

Cassie has tried to care, but grit irritates her eyes, salt itches her skin. The damp weathered wood on which she sits is both hard and unpleasantly yielding, the grain furred with damp.

They are waiting. There is no line between past and present,

237

between present and future, just as there is no horizon. She hangs between one thing and another, between memory and anxiety.

Buddy staring out over the water also has a sense of suspension, as if all roads have led here, as though those shoes exploding in the green gray New Jersey twilight, with soft gray rain falling on the soft gray Gothic buildings, the cement walks, and the aglets too falling through the trees had been a clear step on a precise path, and not the random Brownian motion it seemed at the time.

"I can't help you, Buddy. You must know that." She didn't look at him, but breaking the silence started time again, and sequence. The world was created moment by moment again.

"I can't accept that, Cass." He did look at her.

"The situation is delicate, as you know. We are not well liked in the world, Cassie. America, I mean. Perhaps we have too much, I don't know. But what we do have is a kind of momentum. It's there in our research, our technology. It can't be stopped. All we can do is try to ride it, ride the whirlwind."

"Technology?" She lifted her head, waking slowly.

"Yes."

"It is related to the DLF, some kind of biological technology, something to do with consciousness." She spoke to herself, as if it were abstract musing, nothing crucial.

Buddy answered. "In a way, perhaps."

She paid no attention. "How long has it been, anyway? Twenty years?"

He understood. "Almost. Seventeen, eighteen. A long time. How have you been?"

She shrugged. "Okay. Got married, divorced. You know all about that, I guess."

He nodded. "And Arnold?" There was a catch in the question, but she couldn't identify its source. Not jealousy, certainly. He seemed genuinely interested.

"I don't know. Perhaps. Maybe. Possibly."

He smiled. "Ambivalent, eh?"

She grinned back. "Yes and no."

"I've thought of you from time to time. You were my first, you know."

She stared. "No. I didn't know."

"I was terrified. It seemed important to be . . . masterful. Ouch. In those days, anyway."

238

"You're kidding. You must be kidding."

"No. Terrified." He grimaced. "I wanted to talk to you about it, really. I guess I didn't know how."

"I'll be damned."

"I hope not."

Cassie reached out, touched his shoulder. Her mouth moved, Buddy, but said nothing. The hand dropped, gripped the edge of the pier, and she swung her feet over the water; there was no reflected motion on the greasy surface.

"So here you are." Wesley Millet walked with a jaunty air down the wooden planks toward them. The long night's drive did not appear to have disturbed his equanimity. He had the crystal, and with the crystal he had Cassie.

Buddy climbed to his feet, giving Cassie's shoulder a squeeze as he did. "Here we are. Where's Phil?"

"Up at the house. The drive seems to have tired him out. He's asleep." Millet rubbed his hands briskly together, gazing out over the flat sea-surface. "Well."

He was wearing a quilted down jacket with dove patterns sewn into it. The yellow hat shaded his narrow face, but from her viewpoint his eyes twinkled in the shade.

"Here it is, Ms. St. Clair. Your magic crystal." He handed her the jar.

"It doesn't do anything," she insisted.

"I know. I tried it. But you know how to use it, so you are here. You came with us, remember? Please. We need a little help with this."

"You'll have to give me a clue. I don't really know what the DLF is after. We tried to figure it out, you know. But we didn't accept that life-after-death-but-no-consciousness suggestion, and no one came up with a better one. Except some kind of consciousness technology. A parapsychology technology, perhaps. Telepathy, remote viewing. Contact with the dead?" Cassie shrugged, dispirited.

"I will explain." Millet sat on the pier cross-legged. Carefully he put the jar down before him, next to Cassie. "We did start out that way, trying to interest people in death research." He made a rueful gesture with his mouth. "That's the reason for that tacky name, the Dead Liberation Front. There were masses of people out there, lost, cynical, despairing, unhappy people. They had been through decades when they tried political action, social reform, self-improvement. All of it was staving off the end, death, the void. It no longer was working for most of them. They had affluence, they had guilt for being affluent. Then they had inflation, the high cost of energy, international tensions about it, mass starvation in the world, and guilt about that. The millennium was coming, and they began to look toward it—apocalypse, Armageddon, astrology, magic. Flying saucers, Jesus, dangerous sports. 'Technology has failed us,' they said. 'Let us turn inward.' So they did, and most of it was nonsense, but all of it helped stave off that big fear."

He smiled. "To quote Sir Thomas Browne, 'The long habit of living indisposeth us for dying.' An organization that promised to investigate death, in all its aspects, attracted a great deal of attention, members, money. Prominent people were interested, as well as the everyday, the disaffected, the kooks even."

"You had people out in graveyards, with earphones on, listening for psychic residues. My mother, for one. Those are the kooks?"

"I suppose so. But as a group, people were willing to try anything, no matter how bizarre, if it showed any promise."

"And did the dead talk, did their residues register on those instruments? I never heard that they did." Curious, despite herself.

"No. They didn't, not really. Oh, there were some promising or perhaps I should say, tantalizing results. Nothing definitive, though. But of course, that was not the only avenue we were pursuing. Not at all. We had connections with many research facilities, many approaches. NASA, for one. Several approaches began to converge, to blend together. New avenues opened up. The momentum grew, gathered an inexorable weight."

"Yes," she said thoughtfully. "Ride the whirlwind. But what whirlwind have you mounted?"

"Ah." He said, and fell silent, thinking it over.

"'Indisposeth us for dying,'" she repeated. Chemicals washed through her mind, neurons fired or inhibited, thoughts moved together, diverged, a few molecules crossed minute gaps, locked on to receptor sites, made connections. Mind followed.

"You've developed some kind of longevity technology," she said softly, as if the sound of her words would shatter something important.

"We think it is near-immortality, Ms. St. Clair. We think that we can extend the human life indefinitely. Yes. So you understand why we have had to be cautious, to move carefully. It's a momentous discovery."

"What's the catch?"

"Eh?" He was surprised at her lack of enthusiasm. "No catch.

240

None at all. Indefinitely extended life-span. The answer. We were hoping, and we had people at the National Science Foundation who were hoping as well, that Investigate the Future could give us a forecast"—he was careful to use the proper word there—"of the effect of an important announcement without telling you exactly what the announcement was. It's too bad that didn't work out. Really a shame. Now we need your help." He gestured at the jar, the crystal.

She shook her head. "You're out of your mind."

He held up his hands. "Please, Cassie. This is not a melodrama. Not a conspiracy. We have something of incredible importance to the human race. We have to know how to handle it. It will be impossible to keep it a secret."

"You don't know everything, do you?"

"Perhaps not. But enough."

"No," she said. "Not nearly enough."

He stood up. "We don't have much time. Please think it over, Ms. St. Clair. An hour, say? Then we will just have to go ahead, you see. Momentum. Too much momentum." He turned and walked back up the pier, toward the steps cut into the soft sandstone bluff, toward the house out of sight over the crest of the hill.

Cassie touched the corners of her eyes, rolled the grainy sleep out. She thought briefly of reaching down for some water, to splash her face, then thought better of it. There was still no reflection in the surface, no clue.

"Cassie," Buddy said, behind her.

"Yes."

"Don't you want to live forever?"

She thought about that. She could see Brockhurst's face, the lizard eyelids closed over those ghastly white eyes, the prominent bridge of his nose, the flare of his nostrils. She had thought last evening that she could smell death around him, could hear the ticking of it in his body, and in her own. Her palm rested on the deck of the pier, and she could feel the texture of the white cellulose fur the damp had raised up, the nap of the wood. Almost, it was a living substance.

"I don't know," she said at last. "There's a catch."

She didn't know if she could hear his sigh behind her, but he said nothing. Yes, there was something.

Finally, "Will you think about it, Cass? Please."

She hunched her shoulders, partly against the chill of the morning, perhaps. Her boots were dirty, she noticed, curling her toes up, stretching them. Grains of sand clung damply to the edges of the soles. From the cliff behind her, when she had walked down here with Buddy. The sensation of curling her toes, stretching them against the pressure of the boot toe, was pleasant. She clung to it.

She nodded.

"Buddy," she said, after a moment. He turned, halfway back to shore.

She turned around, pressed her back against a piling, hugged her knees. "Do you know what day this is?"

"Sunday."

"Yes. April first." She laughed, a small sound that fell flat to the oily surface. "April Fools' Day."

She stared at the jar. It rested square on the gray fuzzed planking and picked up no special light. Yet there had been a moment, in the cave above the valley, when she'd had the illusion of something, a flow of pale silver. What she had seen by that light had nothing to do with the interplay of life and death, of politics and power.

Beyond her knee the water level rose, a thick metallic surface grasping at the pier's pilings.

Her talent had given her fugues, vague forebodings, glimpses of events in which she could not disentangle her own wishes from truth. The crystal would be no help.

She could create scenarios, assign percentages to the probabilities of events, assume the continuation of current trends, a linear progression. The DLF announcement could be phrased to pass almost unnoticed, or dramatically, for maximum exposure. The social results could be calm acceptance, riotous joy, disbelief, or panic.

She shook her head, salt-stuck hair stiff and sculpted. Scenarios would not help, either. Fatigue pulled at her cramped muscles, stiff joints, frozen awkwardly all night in the car. An alteration in the light distracted her, and she turned in place. Not a change in quality, but intensity. Still no sun, wreathed in eastward mists. Here the coast swings northeast, then in, and the pier extends, narrow, ancient, a bit north of west at right angles to the shore. If she were to reach out her right hand, she would point at the sandy bluff, the scrub, a Monterey pine tortured by years of incessant wind, now becalmed, bare branches combed back from the sea. Pickleweed filled the marshy, narrow beach, and the changing tide began to cover the dark mud that extended a third of the way out the pier.

Briefly she imagined rescue, she the aging maiden in the dragon's lair, the sacrifice. Arnold would walk, serene and pure, through a fusillade—impervious. His steps would thump sedately on the decking of the pier; he would sweep her up, carry her back through smoke and fire. This delicate vision—towers and graceful curves, half despair, half hope—made her smile. Almost, she could hear the bugle call.

But she was here on her own, had come to this coast, Sonoma or Mendocino, voluntarily, and it was time to concentrate. She picked up the jar, as if cupping her hands around its cool curve and staring into the coiled serpentine crystal would force some answers from it. Through the milky substance she saw the ocean, a gray blur that merged with gray sky.

What would a longer life mean in the world?

More people. More than the billions that teemed now over the surface, replaced the elephant's broad migrations with farmland, neatly laid out and sensitive to the depredations of those vast gray beasts who had no clear human sense of property or propriety. Fields that must be protected in order to feed those billions who would now live on and on, indefinitely. Billions and more billions.

Looking through the facets of the selenite, she saw the sea as if through an X ray, saw the whale pods, the herds, move through the waters, through clouds of plankton and krill, scything the protein crop, tons a day consumed as the smooth bodies moved. Saw that here too competition would rule, and these minds must give way. And that, she knew, was not possible. Could not be allowed.

There was more. She tried to look through this inert matter with her mind, not her eyes. Everything known about longevity, aging, the program in the genes, the beetle tick in the structure of molecules, complex acids, and enzymes. It could be reversed, perhaps. But at what expense?

Who would pay? Besides the elephants and cetaceans, who would pay?

Behind her an egret stalked the mud flats. Avocets, three of them, scythed upward-curved bills through the mud, long legs prancing through the shallows. The orange and swollen sun formed a pale circle in the mist, and the mist burned away, leaving a milky sky, a milky haze at the ocean's edges, and the tide climbed smoothly in rising swells up the rock-strewn mud, and the tiny barnacles opened up to the water and waved frond-feet in pulsing rhythms, feeding. Living and dying.

Cassie was alone at the end of the world. The sun turned yellow, then white, dried salt-damp on the planks, the pilings. A crisp, tacky frost of salt crystallized in the grain of the wood.

In the depths of the gypsum gray phallic shapes glide. Creaks and clicks, screams and buzzes form echo-images, dome-shapes, torpedo-shapes, shark and jellyfish and schools of sardine or salmon. Dolphins turn, roll, dance in courtship, nuzzle one another, play erotic permutations on the game. She could sense in there as well the dry odor of elephant, and hear the long wind of her breathing. In a savage anger she threw her brush at the mirror, and it shattered. Her life fell into the fragments of memory, each shard a partial vision of herself.

A reptilian fascination uncoiled in her dreaming, a slow, endless slither from the dark, a cold light that glinted on scales that were tiny, hard, and polished: mirror-bright.

Her dreaming through the gypsum makes the world. She is outside of time, in the dreaming. Smoke twists and coils, reveals and hides. Mist forms and burns. From far away, across a landscape devoid of details, a desert landscape without water or rock, flat, bright, dry, a figure is walking toward her. It is surrounded with light, the figure, as if the sun is behind it. Only when it comes closer can she see that he has his hand outstretched, toward her, entreating or commanding. She can hear an insect shrill in the rock behind her, can see now that the flat earth has striations, layers, sediment, and subtle shades of color, pale tan, brown, something close to vermilion. This is primal land, first earth, volcanic and nearly alive.

Brockhurst is standing before her, and beside him is an irregular stone taller than he. The stone has a cap, or lid, that extends out on all sides, as if placed there as a signal of some kind. She cannot read it, but is reassured.

Brockhurst reaches out to her, mouths words. The insect shrills in the rock, too loud. She can't hear the man, can only see his mouth move, his hand reach out to her, reaching in the same way, as a memory intruded, her stepfather had reached toward her.

The sound grows louder, the light brighter. Brockhurst, in slow motion, as though hampered, underwater, sweeps his hand in a circle, toward the light. Another figure is there, legs apart, with shafts of sun dancing with dust all around it, through it. She can hear a voice, distant and indistinct, from this new figure. The voice says "Father."

When she turns back, Brockhurst is under the cap of stone, seated cross-legged, hunched, mummified, his hands folded across his chest. He has been there, dried in the sun, for thousands of years, cycles, the days and nights a flicker. He is made of stone, carved from this primal rock, part of the rock. Now she can no longer distinguish him from the stone, his form merged with the rock, in the shadows, as the shrill sound swells and falls in a slow, febrile, irritating rhythm, meaningless, almost insane.

Steps crunch on the gravel, the dry river bed. The second figure approaches: Wesley Millet, his narrow face, dark lips, keen eyes. Looking up at him, she knows he is the one who spoke, who said "Father." He reaches down, takes her hand, and standing, she looks out over the dry landscape, dotted here and there with strange rock formations, but otherwise empty, harsh with the sun glare.

She tries to make cities rise up out of those plains, this hard desert. She imagines them, imagines lifting stones, placing one atop another, carving them, fitting them together, but they are too heavy, fixed in place, immutable, and eternal. There are no cities.

This is eternity. This is indefinite life.

This is dreamtime, the landscape half-formed, fetal, unborn. Gradually she realizes that she is looking through the crystal at the flat sea, through the hard stone land, the stone land is the sea, is flat, and gray, and, shifting slowly as the tide moves, rhythm reasserts itself; yet it is filled with life and movement, beneath the surface. It teems with generations, hydrodynamic and impossible shapes.

Reassured, she slips back, through the crystal, into the desert, where the human figure is dwarfed by the vast, unending plain, the empty sky; dwarfed, and petrified, frozen lava, congealed magma, planet-matter caught halfway. Time recedes, winks out, and timeless dream returns, although in the thought of *return* there is time, the evil, the ticking death, end, beginning, the gleam of light skipping across the crystal's face, event, moment, separation. Wesley Millet, stone face as if melted and solidified again, speaking through that high-pitched whine, that shrilling, has said, "Father," and she knows in the same moment that he has spoken not to her, but through her, to Brockhurst, who has become, since she looked up, stone, a piece of the landscape, and yet a consciousness that gives meaning to this empty, meaningless land.

Millet moves, his legs swing back and forth, he is walking toward her yet coming no nearer, the ground is flowing back with each step, and he cannot approach. It is important that he be close, that she see him as he is, not this silhouette against the empty, pale-milk sky, but fleshed, given form and detail, fine as the detail of barnacles clinging to the pilings, their frond-legs sweeping microscopic particles into their mouths.

She realizes it is her move, that he can come no closer on his own, that she must stand, and walk, and approach him, and in the thought is the action; she comes closer, peers into his face, and it is as if she is not there, as if she is made of the air itself, for he looks through her, beyond her, at the place she was. So she turns, with his look, to see where she has been, and where he is looking now.

And there is her own father, George St. Clair, blinking his nearsighted eyes against the harsh light. Something leaps in her, he is not dead, not here in this dreamtime, where the world is making itself. She tries to call out his name, finds herself saying "Father" to him, aware that she is standing now where she saw Millet standing, and that Millet is no longer here, that she has become his shape against the light, and that her father cannot make out her form against that dazzle.

So she begins to walk, toward him, and the land itself flows backward with her every step, each step taking her nowhere, in a desert where there is no *where,* no place distinguishable from another, except where he is standing at this moment, now, near the shapeless stones, on layers of primal stone. It is up to him, now, to move toward her, but he does not do so, peers instead uncertainly around as she calls to him, "Father. Father," her own voice lost in that overwhelming shrill of insects in the dry unalterable plain.

There is, then, a deep bass rumble in the land, a shaking so slow, lethargic, cosmic that it is a dream movement of its own generation, its own carrying and termination, without reference.

She heard, from that same vast distance without measure, a casual sound, an egret scream, and watched it gather take-off speed across the shallow tidewater, watched as the wings flapped slowly, and the pure white bird sailed out of sight around the point, dazzling against the sandy shore. She looked down, and the avocets looked up once, all three

246

together, in unison, as though in close communion, toward the bluff, then bent back to scything the sea, in unison.

The rumble was shaking the pier, very gently, barely audible, like an elephant speaking; then the sound died away.

The avocets' legs scissor as they walk, swinging their upturned bills back and forth, back and forth, turning over the silty bottom, neatly taking what they need. Their eyes are small, blank, and alien. They do not look at her.

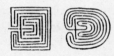

There was silence over the world. Tiny ripples, the mere shimmer of vibration, surrounded the pilings. She can see them, the disturbance of surface that gives detail, and with detail, a kind of life, to the water. Nothing has changed. The avocets continue their comic walk through the shallows, small heads swinging back and forth. Around their legs, the wavelets make confusing patterns of the greasy swells.

Buddy walked down the steps to the pier, looking back up the bluff from time to time as if pursued. Yet the earth was quiet again.

"Strange day," he said to her, looking down. Behind him the sun lit his hair, and shafts filled with dust fell through his legs, arms, around his neck.

She felt a shock, seeing him like that, as if this were not a pier over the ocean, but flat rock, desert dreamed out of chaos.

She nodded. "No wind at all."

The rumble returned and brought her fully into the material world, for the pier shook more violently: earthgrowl. Buddy looked, worried, back up the cliff, where runnels of sand sifted down erosion gullies on the bluff, dry and fragile. The avocets took to the air without hurry, followed the egret around the point.

"Earthquake weather," Buddy commented. Under his feet, under Cassie, seated against the piling, the earth stopped its complaining.

Beyond the dunes a puff of yellow smoke rises, smears across the sky, staining the pale blue with sulfur yellow.

"What the hell . . ."

"Yes," Cassie said. Gravity was stronger here, at the edge of the sea, and pulled at her with unnatural force.

"Eh? Oh, hell, yes. I see what you mean. That looks like sulfur, doesn't it? Some kind of gas released by that tremor, I would think. Odd."

The land stopped moving, restored. The sand stopped sliding down the twisted gulches in the bald face of the cliff. Buddy stared up there, waiting for something, someone, to appear. Cassie turned back to the water, the flat glare.

Here was movement, a swift stirring of the surface, and the shape rose, blew with a swift spray and intake, the huge head, only a few yards away, side toward her; the small eye almost invisible in this strange light, winked at her, and she felt a rush of recognition. Then the black-and-white shape rolled, slapped the dorsal fin as it vanished beneath the surface, leaving behind large swells and smaller waves to rush against the pilings, against the shore.

The sound brought Buddy around. He started to speak, but the head reappeared, the mouth opened, and that disturbingly pink and human interior flashed at them. It almost seemed as if the orca were going to stick out his tongue, instead light glinted off the conical teeth, the whale screeched and was gone.

"Was that . . . ?"

"Yes. The same one." She made the sounds of the orca's name.

Millet and Phil Rodgers were picking their way down the rough steps set into the bluff. Above them, the yellow had faded, blended with the mist, as if it had never happened.

Millet was frowning. He held his hat in hand, by the side of his leg, and a film of perspiration dewed his forehead at the hairline. "No damage done," he muttered. "Scared the hell out of Phil, though." Behind him Phil hunched, a dark look on his face.

"What was that smoke?" Buddy asked.

"It stinks up there," Phil said. "There's no wind, so that stuff just sits over the house. I don't smell it down here."

"Enough of this," Millet said. "What happened?"

Cassie shook her head.

He repeated his question.

248

"You really don't understand," she said. "Things do happen when I concentrate."

"I told you," Millet cried, looking at Buddy.

"But not what you think," she went on. "I get images, impressions, but they have nothing to do with politics; there are no predictions. I'm sorry."

"Dammit, enough. Tell us!" Millet was angry; a surge of exasperation rose visibly in his face.

Cassie held up her hand. "Please. I'm trying. I get impressions of relationships. But they are mixed up with my own family, my own relationships. There isn't much of a clue what belongs to me and what to you. For example, I get something between you and Mr. Brockhurst. Do you know where this crystal came from?"

"No."

"It belonged to a medicine man. It was never used for divination; it was used to see sickness."

Millet stared at her, nonplussed at the shift in subject and what she seemed to be telling him. At last his eyes shifted, and he was staring out over the ocean, as the swells rolled toward them, toward the shore, surged up the dwindling beach, and slid back in silence.

"Sickness." It wasn't a question, Millet's word, but a thoughtful statement. "That's very interesting," he turned back to her. "But tomorrow the world is going to learn that people can live forever. That is going to be disruptive, and we need to know how to counter it."

"The world," Cassie said slowly, "is going to learn that *some* people can live a long time. *Some* people are going to have the resources, the wealth, access to the technology to live a long time, although forever might be a little too long for most. That means of course that some other people are not going to live such a long time. Among those others are elephants, and whales, am I not right? I don't know what technology you have developed, but someone is going to control it, and the resources it requires. The government? The government along with the DLF? Someone is going to have to make the decisions about who the people are who will be given the choice of living a very long time. Will you be making those decisions? Mr. Millet? Buddy? Mr. Rodgers? No wonder you're worried. But I repeat, I can't help you. IF can't help you, not anymore. As you say, the future is already here. If you want an opinion, rather than a forecast, I would say this technology is completely wrong. It's on the wrong track, it emphasizes the wrong

249

things, it does the wrong stuff. It's no good, period. Furthermore, I think you know it."

In the silence that followed, Cassie wondered why she had changed the subject so quickly after mentioning the connection she had seen between Brockhurst and Millet: Wesley had been calling "Father," to Brockhurst.

In part she was afraid it was wrong, a projection of her own, for she too had called "Father."

He had not seen her. Not then, in the dreaming, not before, in the car, driving through rain beside a sign that crackled, swerved, and sailed away, into the dark sky.

So she roused herself and tried once again. "What is the connection?" she asked, and in response to the blank look, she continued, "between you and Mr. Brockhurst. Are you his son?"

He turned abruptly, a small, neat, outlandish figure in this curiously flat light, and walked back up the pier, without answer, without comment; yet in that gesture she knew the answer.

Rodgers hesitated for a moment, then followed. Cassie smiled, and hunched her shoulders up, taking a deep breath, pressing her hands hard against her thighs, stretching. She released the breath in a long sigh and felt some of the fatigue leave her.

Something had happened in that brief moment, a subtle shift in the balance, and it seemed right. Out there in the water, she knew the smooth, sleek shapes were moving, converging, fixed smiles concealing nothing now. The dolphins, the orcas, the others, that vast, incomprehensible presence she had sensed in her visions of the orca calling across the Pacific, all the way to the Mariana Trench, would give approval and thanks. A millennial barrier was falling.

"That's it?" Buddy asked her.

"Oh. Yes, that's it."

Buddy shook his head. "No, he won't give up so easily, Cass. You've shocked him. I didn't know they were related, and it looks like he didn't want anyone to know. So there are reasons for all this that have nothing public about them, eh? But he'll come back."

She nodded. "Yes. What about you? You've been used, too. Are you still with him?"

"I don't know. What did you see with that crystal, anyway? What are your visions like?"

She laughed, then, and more fatigue dissolved from her. She stood up, put her palm on top of the piling against which she had been resting, and felt a warmth in the thick grain of the wood, a vibrancy and light. "You persist in misunderstanding, all of you. I don't have visions, I can't see the future, any more than you or Millet can." She looked him full in the eyes and spoke more quietly, intimately.

"Buddy, something really wonderful, filled with wonder, is about to happen. To me, to the world. We have to let it happen, don't you see? All these visions, theta images, dreams, the crystal, they show something else. Not the future, although there is some overlap, some *correspondence* between the two. Yes, like coincidence. We are people, and we have to think like people, so we stick our own symbols on things that are alien, that we don't understand. I've been doing it all my life."

"I don't follow you."

A faint sound, growing louder, swept toward them across the open sea. She looked out over the flat, featureless water and saw, where the horizon would have been if there was any horizon, a dark shape, a point, that swelled with the sound it was making. A boat. She turned back to Buddy with a smile. "I know," she said. "A long time ago, something happened to me, something that has haunted me all these years. Before we took the train to Trenton, Buddy; before we both made love for the first time. I was brushing my hair, and my stepfather came into the room. I don't know," she shook her head, "but I thought he was looking at me in a strange way. Seductive, almost evil, maybe. I was trying to make it curl in a certain way, here," she touched her temple. "He reached toward me, and I thought . . . well, you can imagine what I thought."

The boat approached swiftly, and now she could see the wake of it, parting to either side, long, slow ripples at this distance widening north and south, endlessly. Her robe was open at the breast, the brush slithered through her hair, the sound of it loud in her ear. She was watching the curl in her mirror, and as she lowered the brush, the curl too collapsed, followed the movement of her arm and shoulder down.

His face was there, in profile, in the left-wing mirror, the fleshy tip of his nose, the huge, sweating bulk of him, Anthony Malatesta. "Now, now," he said.

"What?"

"Don't talk like that." He sat beside her.

"I can't get it to curl right." She thought she should reach up, close the gap in her quilted robe, yet did not.

His head was tilted to one side, appraising. She felt fear. A thrill of

251

fear, like a shiver down her ribs. "I see that," he said softly. "You want it to come here, over the ear." He reached toward her, his fleshy fingers hooked.

She drew back, clutched her robe tight around herself, lifting the brush. He was watching for that gap in her robe, the breathing loud in his thick nose, *then*. *Now*, twenty years later, after she had thrown the brush, shattered the mirror, he was reaching for the curl.

"It would look very nice," she heard him say. "Like that." Then the mirror shattered, his startled face broken into a thousand fragments, never healed, never brought back together again.

"We never spoke again, Buddy. Not really. It was if I had killed him. It was stupid, Buddy. Really stupid. My own symbols, you see. My own interpretation, and my own actions. Stupid. I don't want that to happen again. Do you see?"

He nodded, his face serious. "I think so."

The shape, the sound, were close, swinging in an arc to come broadside to the pier. Arnold waved to her. They slowed, drifted against the wood with a thump, the engine off and silence filled the air again. Cassie waved, smiling, as they threw Buddy a rope. Izzy climbed out of the launch and gave Cassie a hug.

"Hi."

"Hi, Izzy." Cassie held the hug an extra moment. "I'm glad to see you."

"It's been a long night," Arnold said.

"He told us it would be," Cassie answered, responding to his white smile. "And a short day."

"Mm." He bobbed his head back and forth, a maybe gesture. "Shall we?" He indicated the open boat. "He's waiting for us."

"The *Dreambridge?* His boat?"

"Ship, more like," Arnold said. "Hey, if a man has watery eyes, would you say he had rheum with a view?"

Cassie rolled her eyes. "Gods," she said. From the boat, she turned back. "Buddy? Want to come with us?"

He grinned. "Not this time. I think I'd better sort some things out."

"Okay," she said. "Next time. See you soon."

"Is that a prediction?" Buddy asked, still grinning.

"Nope. It's a forecast."

Arnold pointed into the wind of their passage. "There it is."

Cassie followed his finger, and the boat swung a bit, correcting course. There was a smudge in the faint gray shade that passed for horizon. The smudge grew slowly larger.

"How long?" she asked.

Arnold shrugged. "Twenty minutes. A bit more. Took us three quarters of an hour to get to you with the whale leading."

Ahead, the swift wake of the black-and-white orca led them on. From time to time the great shape rose to blow, subsided once more, leaving broad ripples in the endless gray swells of the open sea. She shook her head, wondering. "How did he find me? As if I didn't know."

"The question is rhetorical?" Arnold asked, rhetorically, and Cassie laughed.

"Look," Izzy said, pointing toward shore. A small shape, dark against the faded low line of bluff, and the vanishing series of ridges inland. "They're following us."

"Of course." Cassie leaned back and closed her eyes. She imagined she was on a ship, a Cretan vessel moving slowly into the harbor at Itea, below Delphi. Sleek gray shapes of dolphins rose and sank through the small waves alongside. The harbor would be thick with god-presence. The dolphins were god. She was the dolphin, sleek in the water, quick with intelligence. The ship would turn to, the sails luff in the wind, clatter down. The oars would be shipped with a quiet exchange of words, hushed in awe of this holy spot.

She was not on a sailing ship, though, and opened her eyes again to look behind them. Wings of spray rose to either side of the following speedboat, visible now as it drew closer to them, narrow and sharp-prowed.

Cassie laughed at a sudden thought.

"What?" Arnold was looking back at her.

"I had been imagining a last-minute rescue, back there. And then you appeared. I was Iphigenia, a sacrifice. There was no hope. I guess it was because there was no wind, and the fleet needed wind. But you saved me. I was laughing because it was so undramatic, so calm and ordinary."

"Ah."

They followed the orca, over the swells, and the motion was a soothing, soft rocking. Cassie relaxed, muscle by muscle, slowly letting go. Her neck relaxed, and her head bobbed without mooring as the launch lifted and fell with the swells. A quiet drone from the engine sang to her, and she drifted back to Delphi, delivered ambiguous words to the priest, who carried them out to the light, the suppliants, carried them up, out of the dark narrow space in the earth, where the vapors still twisted toward the opening in the rock. Trance came and went, seized her from without, released her from within. She was medium and voice, carrier and message.

She was a bridge, a connection between two peaks, separated by abyss.

The abyss was time, and more than time; it was understanding, and more than understanding. It was as though for thousands of years the two sides of the abyss had tried to connect, had thrown cables, strands, words across the abyss, and they had always fallen short, failed to reach.

Now the connection had been made. She was the connection.

"Cassie."

"Yes?"

Izzy was holding the jar in her hand, against the pale sun. Light fractured through the crystal, prismatic with pale fires. "Brockhurst told us about the crystal. The swallow carved on the bottom."

"He got it from an Indian," Cassie said.

Izzy nodded. "And the Indian, a Hopi medicine man, got it from a white man. It had a long history. He traced it down, I don't know how, but it's fascinating. Geologists told him the gypsum came from Utah, which would make sense for a Hopi medicine man. But the swallow was carved in England, and in the fifteenth century. Which doesn't make sense. There's something about the patterns of the cuts that makes it typically British. And there was a man named Roger Bolingbroke who tried to kill Henry VI by witchcraft. He was hanged for it. At some point he ordered this crystal carved, but never took delivery. Even then the crystal had an old history, well before the New World was discovered. So how did the crystal get to Europe?"

254

"That's the wrong question," Arnold put it.

"What do you mean?"

"You should ask why the crystal got to Europe."

"Okay. Why did the crystal get to Europe?"

"So Roger Bolingbroke could order a swallow carved in it," Cassie murmured.

"So the Indian could get it back with goodwill for all," Arnold said.

"So Brockhurst could acquire it and give it to Cassie," Izzy said, laughing.

"So Wesley Millet could chase it," said Arnold.

"And I could look through it."

Izzy shook her head. "I give up."

"It's simple, really," Cassie said. "The universe wanted that crystal, which happened to be in Utah, to gather the necessary karma, so the universe organized a trip for it."

"Oh. The universe organized a trip for it. The universe is now a cosmic travel agent?"

"Izzy! A joke?"

"Yes, and no. What's the answer?"

"The answer is, yes. The universe is a cosmic travel agent. And no, it is not."

"You must admit that is a lot of coincidence, isn't it? The crystal gets to Europe, gets carved, fails to save Bolingbroke, is brought back to America, is used by Indians, gets to Brockhurst, and then to you. And it was all so you could look through it? It do strain credulity, it do." Izzy shook the jar gently.

"An old law of magic. Once is accident, twice is coincidence; three times, and Someone is trying to tell you Something."

"Now, Cassie, where did you pick up the laws of magic?" Arnold wanted to know.

"An old gypsy," she said softly. She listened carefully to the metallic jangling behind her, saw the gypsy smile, and dismissed the fear she had felt then, on the road back to Athens. A friendly smile, the gypsy's; two people meeting on the road from Eleusis, nothing more.

The abyss between them was in her mind. She was the bridge; she was coming home.

Before them, the *Dreambridge* widened, stretched its broadside to them, sleek and low to the calm water. The bowsprit was rakish and graceful. Cassie thought she could see the old man seated up there, out on the point, over the water. For a moment, in a brief throb of the engine, she thought she could hear him singing in his low rumble, and the whale's broad black back, slick and shining, broke the surface. He rolled sideways and sounded, gone.

"*Dreambridge* is a funny name," Izzy mused. "For a boat."

"It's from Japanese, an old image. The poets use it a lot, to describe life, a bridge of dreams, from eternity to eternity."

There were figures along the rail, and as they got closer she could see L.R. As they swung sideways to the side of the ship, Reggie leaned over the rail and called to them. Arnold waved back, and the three of them climbed the ladder to the deck.

Sounds were quiet out here, solemn, only the gentle bumping of their launch against the side, the soft footfalls on the wood decking, the subtle creak of wooden joints, the clack of metal fixtures on rope. Cassie greeted everyone, feeling good despite the grit of salt and fatigue.

L.R. leaned on the rail, one foot on the lower rope, and watched.

"Did you know?" Cassie asked him.

He filled his pipe thoughtfully, and she realized this was one of the rare times she had seen him actually put tobacco in it. He stuck the pipe in his mouth and chewed for a moment before lighting it. Then he leaned forward and puffed smoke into the pale sky. "If you mean, did I know what we were supposed to be doing about the DLF project"—he gestured to Millet as his launch approached the ladder—"the answer is, partly. I did know that the DLF was doing something that could be dangerous, but I knew no more than you what it was. Mr. Brockhurst told me to go along with them, so I did. Besides"—he looked at her, not smiling, but with a twitch at the corner of his mouth—"we do need funding."

"L.R.," she chided.

"Well. Anyway, I also knew you were important, but not in what way. I still don't know. I suppose all I really knew was that Mr. Brockhurst wanted to slow the DLF a little." He seemed content, there, sending cloud after cloud of aromatic smoke into the sky. It was out of his hands.

In the distance, the whine of the following boat grew louder, yet no one hurried. The big battles were over.

Millet's boat circled the *Dreambridge* as the launch was hoisted up.

"Wilbur," Millet called. "I want to talk."

L.R. waved Millet in. "Come on up. He's been expecting you."

"What?"

L.R. waved again, and turned away from the rail. "I'll go up front and get him," he told Cassie.

Buddy's head appeared over the railing.

"Hi," he said. "You were right, of course. I'm surprised, I must say; I didn't expect him to be so eager to chase after you." He swung his leg onto the deck and turned to help Millet up the ladder.

"Where is he?" Millet demanded. "Where's Wilbur?"

Cassie tossed her head toward the bow. "He'll be here." She turned to Buddy, her back to Millet. "Is this the Second Coming?"

"Oh, that's a joke." He laughed a little. "I guess it is, now you mention it. A millennial joke."

"What does he want?"

Buddy shrugged. "Wait and see."

Millet was tapping his foot impatiently as Brockhurst, led by Dr. Hubletz, appeared around the corner of the forward cabin. He was slow, his walk a shuffle, painful to watch. Cassie stepped forward to help, and Brockhurst's grip on her forearm was firm, as always, but weaker, much weaker, than before.

"Ah, my dear, how good to see you," Brockhurst said without irony. His ghastly eyes stared at nothing, and his voice was more feeble than ever. She could not have heard him singing to the whale, not over the engine noise.

He turned his head to Millet, as if seeing him. "Wesley. The war is over, thank the gods. There will be a delay in the DLF announcement. A long delay. As you know."

"Wilbur, I . . ."

Brockhurst held up his hand. "It's been too long, and I don't have much time left. Discussion on that subject would be futile. Don't waste what we have."

Millet sagged, all the tentative bravado of his posture, the flashy eccentricity of his manner drained out of him. "All right," he said quietly.

Brockhurst reached out and took his wrist. It was a gesture of great delicacy, not only because of the gentleness of the touch, but because of its unerring aim, the complete assurance of it. As if he could see.

"Come on," he said. "Let me explain some things."

They walked together, back around the cabin, to the bow, and talked.

She looked out over the flat water, the swells on the calm surface invisible from here: they could not move the ship. In the distance the shoreline was a blue gray edge, ruled on the bottom, indefinite on top, a vague gathering to distance. Beyond was the valley, the Visitors' Disciples settlement, where the chanting would continue. To some it would appear futile, that chanting, misdirected belief. Cassie was no longer so sure.

"What do you see?" Izzy asked, beside her.

"Nothing." Cassie turned and smiled. "Right now, not a thing. Soon, though. Izzy, I'm glad you're here. We can't let this happen again, this silence."

"No. We can't. We won't."

They looked down at the water, side by side. The water looked back with their faces as the sun rose higher, or the earth fell away.

Finally, "I've got to ask your question again, though. How *did* the whale find you? How did he know where you were?"

Cassie thought a moment, sighed. "You'll see. Soon. It's nearly time. Just wait."

Izzy looked hard, started to speak, caught herself. "All right," she said shortly.

Behind them Arnold cleared his throat.

"Look," he said, pointing. A school of dolphins broke the smooth surface together, coming toward them. Beyond that school, another, approaching. Suddenly the water was quietly alive with gray bodies, in absolute silence.

"I still don't get it," Izzy said.

"There's a . . . gathering. Can't you sense it? An excitement, a tension. Something is about to happen, yet is waiting."

"No. I don't feel anything."

"Don't worry, Izzy. You'll see."

"Hey!" Arnold said. "Remember that statue in New York? The one with the missing arm?"

"Yeah, I remember."

"It seems the arm was found. It was in the news this morning. A vegetarian cult from Canada had it. It was found in their headquarters, sticking out of a wall, holding a plate of hothouse tomatoes. They had cut it off with a small industrial laser, at night. That was probably the light everyone thought was a UFO."

" 'They don't want us,' " Cassie said. " 'They want our vegetables.' "

He nodded. "That's the one."

Gray heads, pointed beaks, toothy grins, filled the waters around the ship. *Tursiops gilli,* the Pacific dolphin. They could hear the sharp, quick inhalations of their breathing; nothing else.

"It's getting strong, the feeling . . . tension." Arnold's banter was gone.

"Does it have something to do with them?" Izzy gestured at the alien faces in the water, the small eyes looking directly, unblinking.

"Yes. And them." Cassie nodded toward the pod of orcas rising through the swells, black backs shining with the moisture.

A small crowd was collecting at the railing. Buddy was there, looking out in silence over this gathering. Reggie stood next to him, a bemused expression on his face.

Arnold touched Cassie's shoulder and she leaned against him, a gesture so slight as to be invisible to anyone else.

"No!" The cry came from forward, around the cabin. Millet's voice, lifted in anger. He appeared around the corner.

"You," he called Cassie. The distance was awkward, neither conversational nor public, but something in between. He came closer. "Wilbur tells me you know something more. Something I need to know. What is it?" It was an order; a demand.

"Yes," she murmured. "It's time."

"What's that?"

Izzy was holding the jar. Cassie took it, smiled thanks, and walked toward the bow, this motley crowd following her.

Brockhurst was seated near the bowsprit, his back against a metal post. She felt his weariness and sat next to him, facing the water.

"I'm glad you are here, my dear," Brockhurst whispered, his deep rumble a papery rustle now. The bridge of his nose arched, pinched and waxy looking; his nostrils flared, as if his face were shrinking away from it. Cassie touched his wrist, took the jar into her lap, sighed deeply. "It's time," she repeated. Brockhurst nodded.

"Yes."

She held the jar cupped in her hands, frowned down into its milky surface, glimpsed the movement inside, purposeful, rhythmic.

"The crystal is a focus," she said. "I needed it, before. And didn't know it. Now I don't need it."

She put it down at her side. Brockhurst gave a slight inclination of his head, a nod she did not notice.

Her eyes were closed. Softly she called the orca's name, the whistles and clicks of it. Very softly. He could not possibly have heard her voice, but the broad expressionless head lifted at that moment from the water below. "Cassie," he puffed, the syllables nearly perfect despite the absence of vocal cords.

She fell into meditation, hands forming the cosmic mudra, the breath circle before her center of gravity, an inch or two below her navel. Her breathing deepened.

She spoke into her head. Hello. It's time, it's time. Yes, an answer, from her own mind, perhaps, yes, it's time. From a great distance she heard someone else say "Look!" and ignored it. She knew what there was to see. The sea was alive, a gathering of clans and families; she said, can you call him, call to the Mariana Trench? Yes. I can call.

The orca sounded, dove deep. The alien intelligence behind his expressionless face. Thoughts of what things were manifest and what things were not; what was potential and what was inevitable. Thoughts that were a song, intricate, complex, asymmetrical, unavoidable: death, its gradual manifestation coalescing out of dream and imagining, making real; birth, and the bloody arrival of it, nudging the newborn to the surface for the first breath, the first staggering inhalation. And now, expansion, inclusion, the leap of a spark across the abyss.

At the temperature interface, where cool and warm met, the orca screamed, and the sound, propelled by density and temperature, shot at tremendous speed the thousands of miles across the Pacific. A request.

Time was confused now, event happening even as it was thought, considered, manifested. Out beyond the growing numbers of dolphin shapes, the glow began, the hum, the shape rising from beneath the waters, breaking the surface, the vast and incomprehensible oblong shape, a hundred feet in length at least, the water running in cascades down its sides, fragments of obscure technology, and the glow, the glowing light.

It rose into the air. Cassie opened her eyes and saw inwardly and in truth, the great shape, the mother ship, the whale, the huge sperm whale itself, rise into the air.

She spoke, and her voice was mantic, not her own, the Sibyl voice, the orphic voice, the oracle speaking the truth. "For thousands of years they have tried to speak, to talk to us. They have spoken in their own voice, the world of sound, of echoes, and we have heard in the world of vision, of sight. They have shown us their world, the sea, three-dimensional and filled with strange shapes, torpedo shapes, jellyfish shapes, shark shapes. We have seen our own shapes, the shapes of our own myths: fairies or angels, fiery chariots or flying saucers, technological spaceships bringing visitors, guardians, brothers from somewhere else. But they are here, in the oceans, not in the sky. The visions they sent, to those who were sensitive, were visions of the sea. That is Leviathan." She pointed.

The glow deepened, and the sound. The shape turned serenely in the air, water still pouring down its flanks. It drifted toward the *Dreambridge,* slowly, slowly, the glow throbbing now, deep yellow, deep orange as if in sonar pulses, testing the world around it.

"Is it real?" someone asked behind her. She did not answer. High up, very high, stratosphere high, dome shapes drifted, trailing white gossamer: jellyfish shapes, the Portuguese man-of-war. From the west, from the open sea, where Cassie faced, a shimmer. It sped toward them, changed direction to the south abruptly, changed direction again, impossible aerodynamics, the shimmer altering shape as it altered direction, going now up at impossible angles, now down, now right or left. It could have been a craft of some kind, those could have been portholes or windows, the shapes indistinctly seen inside could have been human.

"These are images, directly impinged on consciousness, of the echo patterns of the sea," Cassie said, and fell silent again. And all the while the shapes moved in the sky, more shapes gathered in the sea, dolphins, Beluga whales, all the toothed whales of these waters, filled the surface of the sea, which had fallen flat and calm, without swells. The surface was thick with fins, flukes, beaks, mouths and melons, blowholes huffing.

Three yellow shapes reappeared, shot across the sky from northeast to southwest, reversed and shot toward the ship. Again, as she had seen it before without understanding, the dark shape rose from the depths, engulfed the yellow shapes, merged with them, and raced away, abruptly gone.

She heard someone say "Shark," and did not reply. It didn't matter, shark or whale or sea lion. The shapes moved, shattered, showered, coalesced, split, and rejoined. The sky, from shoreline to western horizon, was filled with shapes, moving in their own ways, about their own purposes. The shimmering group, the school of silvery fish, approached the ship, split in half on either side, and glided by, rejoining on the shoreward side, to as abruptly alter direction, head north, vanish over the horizon into the vague blue haze.

More colors appeared, darted around the vast glowing yellow whale shape hovering a few hundred feet off the port bow of the *Dreambridge*. Pilot fish, groupers, squid shapes moved as well, some fast, some slowly.

Beneath the surface of the sea, other shapes began to glow and to pulsate, fires of life burning in the waters. The dolphins and whales, gathered thickly around the ship, ignored them, turned instead toward the group of humans on deck. Light flickered over the ship, reflected off the deck's polish and metal fixtures. Hums and buzzes, and the deep throbbing sound Cassie had heard before, filled the air with sounds. Soon creaks, screams, buzzes, and clicks were overlayed on the hum, and the air was alive with sound as well as light. Some of the shapes swirled, rotated rapidly as they hummed, shot lightning-flickers into the air, a confusion of colors, a bounty and kaleidoscope of the visible spectrum and beyond to colors no one had ever seen before, subtle hues that shot in spirals, waves, intricate curves, circles, helices. They were the tracks of subatomic particles curving away from the site of interaction, loops and whorls, meringues of shape and color.

The sky grew thick with color and shape, overlapping, densely textured, merging. Light flickered on the hull, the sides, in the cabins of the ship. Static crackled through the air, electricity discharged from the radio masts, along the metal rail aglow with Saint Elmo's fire. Hair stood out on the neck; Cassie could feel it pucker her skin, shimmer over her flesh, throb in her bones. She was deep in trance yet fully aware, fully conscious, in a way she had never been before. A great intensity filled her.

She was aware of the joke. She was not hypnotized, though she was joyously amused: the wonderment of childhood, the fireworks and music in the air.

The colors deepened, emeralds, maroons, vibrant blues, violet nearly black, thick red, dense orange with fountains of brilliant yellow emerging from the center. The shapes that could have been metal or flesh spun, whirled, danced, jigged, flashed, raced, shot, zagged, fizzed, merged, and split in increasing tempo, until there was a full orchestra of color and shape centered on the vast whale-shape near the boat, still motionless, as if amused at all these antics, patient and serene and completely alien.

Other sensations began to shoot through the human bodies on the deck: fears, elations, numbness. Lapses of memory, drowsiness, the feeling of cool water flowing over skin. Bugles in the blood. Vapor behind the eyes, warm then cool. A powerful seizure in the throat, as if someone else were trying to speak through it. Music that tasted like lemon juice, that had the texture of plums, the aftertaste of sole. Fever. An odor like onions or asphalt. Fragrances that felt like sandstone. Loss of balance. Hot wind. Emptiness. Death and loss. Fierce glee.

The wooden deck began to tremble, a small vibration growing in intensity until it was nearly intolerable, then dying away.

The light began to fade, subside, and with startling swiftness there was only that one huge glowing shape remaining, hovering over the surface of the water without motion.

Then it, too, turned gracefully and receded, not as if moving, but as if shrinking, dwindling in size, vanishing to a point, gone.

Silence. The pale yellow sun in a pale blue sky. The surface of the sea.

Then a chattering as the dolphins shook their heads, up and down, shouted, raspberries, burps, hollers of noise; they began to dance, to leap and splash, fall sideways on the surface, twine over and under one another, leap straight into the air, twisting two, three, four times in the air before falling back with tremendous splashes. The orcas, too, raced in circles, increasing speed, sending waves shattering against the side of the *Dreambridge*.

Cassie was smiling, and tears flowed down her cheeks.

The sea was in constant turmoil. The dance went on and on, this exuberant, intricate weaving, thrashing, the thunder of bodies falling and twisting, but there was never an accident, not once did two dolphins collide.

It was a long time before anyone noticed that they were beginning to drift away. At the edges of this enormous school a few would plunge into the water and not reappear. In the distance, from time to time, groups could be seen, porpoising through the water in unison.

Gradually the crowd thinned around the boat, the shrieking and

263

burping sounds diminished, faded away, and at last, only the orca remained.

Cassie clung to it, outside of herself; let it go. Looked around.

Brockhurst's chin rested on his chest, lifted very slightly by the
small motion of his breathing. The rest stood in an irregular grouping,
apparently in shock.

Slowly she stood up. Her muscles, her tendons, her bones worked
harmoniously together, complete with health, life. She walked slowly
through the group, and no one moved, no one noticed her. It was as if
they were frozen and she were a shadow.

She knew it was an illusion, an aftereffect. Arnold had lost two
hours on Thursday, when the UFO had taken her. He would not lose
this time; he would remember it all, but as a dream.

On the other side she looked out at the distant shore. Had Renata
Glabro seen this display, the lights in the sky? Behind her, Arnold said,
"My god," in hushed tones, and she turned.

He was looking at her, though the rest seemed to be sleeping still.
She smiled, took his hand.

"So that's it," he said.

"That's it."

They stared at each other for a long time, in the quiet, on the deck
of the ship, on the surface of the sea, at noon. Then the others began to
stir, to move around, to breathe once more. There were murmurs, heads
shaking as if to clear them, and Cassie heard Izzy say, "Did you see?"
and Reggie said, "Yes. It happened."

"It happened," Cassie said. "And it has happened before. See." She
pointed to the orca, his head lifted above the surface, reflected sharply in
the clear water beneath him, two heads, one up, one down, two dorsal
fins the same. "That has happened before, Arnold. I feel it. It's like
coming home, it *is* coming home. Déjà vu."

Of all the population in the sea, only the orca remained, his head quite still, reflected in the glassy mirror of the water; the only motion was the rise and fall of that head with the slow swells, a rhythm so subtle and easy it was nearly beneath notice.

Wesley Millet was in shock, his wet lips slack and expressionless. Buddy sat beside him, hands clasped in front of his knees, and watched Cassie.

"I don't know what to do with him," he said softly. She smiled.

"Don't do anything," she said. "When in doubt, do nothing."

Millet's eyes stared vacantly at the vacant water. His breathing was rapid and shallow, as if feverish, though he had no fever.

"It will pass," she said. "Patience. Leave him alone."

"Patience," Buddy repeated. "I've never had much of that." He, too, stared out at the vast and empty sea.

The sun overhead was undefined, a vague stain of white heat across half the flat heavens, remote and unreal.

Cassie was drawn away from the others, into some interior distance of her own.

Her body moved only through its time, but her mind was not so bound, and now it roamed through all it knew. She was Nii-dono who carried her grandchild, the young emperor Antoku, into the water, to their capital beneath the waves, at the battle of Dan-no-ura, the ships burning, banners aflame and falling into the red waters, blackened as they sank twisting out of sight, and the air was thick with cruelly barbed arrows that hummed as they flew. Great deeds were being done, futile and grand. The smell of the air was sour and full of death.

She was walking the hot road from Eleusis past olive groves, gray green leaves faded with road dust, her mind thick with the fumes of sacred wine, still shaken by the mysteries revealed in the blinding sunlight when it broke through the roof into the dark temple. She was walking stiffly, holding her sprig of olive wound with wool, through the shadow of the Acropolis to the temple of Apollo Delphinios. Above her was the Parthenon, the high city, the texture in time of the gods.

Very far away, but extremely clear, with fine detail, resolution, Brockhurst and Millet revolved about each other, a two body problem, the tension between them a minor eddy in the rush of headlong time, in the cycles and waves of it. She could see them revolve, become perturbed, alter momentum, switch charge, grow heavy with grief or triumph or fear; achieve parity.

No one could have been touched by the events she had just summoned up, and not be altered.

She knew that Brockhurst was there, behind her, and she turned to take his hand. Beyond him, Buddy was looking at her again. She smiled at him, and he nodded slightly. As she and Brockhurst walked past him, he said, "You did that, didn't you? You called them?"

"Yes."

Brockhurst heard, tilted his head toward Buddy, rumbled in his strange, reedy voice, "He will recover."

"All right," Buddy said. "I'll wait."

"I want to talk to you," Brockhurst told Cassie. She felt his arm, how frail it was, how the light bones were so close to the surface, hollow, nearly weightless, yet somehow dense, as if collapsing inward. She could see the deep wrinkles around his mouth and eyes, the cheeks sunken, leaving their points, their bones more prominent under the ridge of the brows, the bridge of the nose. Even the awful eyes seemed emptier today, more inward-looking.

She walked carefully, leading an invalid.

They sat at the stern, a comfortable three-sided bench inside a sunken cockpit arrangement that supported Brockhurst's back. He relaxed with a deep, very faint sigh. He closed those eyes, and she saw how deep and hollow they were with that milky white hidden.

Long moments passed in silence. There appeared to be no movement, but finally she saw it, the slight rise and fall of his breath, very slow. She watched.

"My dear," he said.

"Yes?" She took his hand; it was light and dry, the knuckles lumpy and arthritic.

"You know it all, now, don't you?"

"Not all."

266

He smiled without opening his eyes, without moving. "No," he agreed. "Not all. But you know why I sent you to La Jolla."

"Yes, I know that. Empathy. The orca said look below the surface. Where the connections are."

"Ah." He sighed, still without moving. His head was tilted back against the cushions, and full sun flooded the parchment skin of his face, the sunken cheeks and eye hollows. "Good," he whispered. "Do you think of me as a powerful man?"

"Yes. I do."

He nodded slightly, without lifting his head. "Do you think of me as a good man?"

"I don't know. I think so."

There was at the corner of his mouth the faintest thread of a smile. "That might put you into a minority. But I am a person. Perhaps that is a complicated thing to be, in this world, anyway. But power, that is based on reputation, and reputation is based on belief. You understand all that. Someone to hate, someone to worship, that is the magic that moves the world. Possession does not give meaning; only the measure against something else. Do you follow me?"

"I'm not sure."

"Wesley has power, he has power because he has knowledge, and with that knowledge he can manipulate beliefs. He can offer people magic. To live forever. To have infinite time. To have consciousness. To know everything, even the purpose. You see?"

"Yes," she said. "It is the wrong understanding of time. There is no point in living forever if you can't live right now."

"Even the elephant couldn't have said it better. Do you know what the shortest measurable unit of time is?"

"No."

"The past. I want you to listen carefully, I don't have much time left."

"What do you mean?" She knew what he meant. She could see it in his face, the increasing shallowness of his breath.

He didn't answer. "My notes, at Calaveras. Plans, all the plans. You'll have to make your own, now. Things have changed. I suspected you were the one, I suspected that the cetaceans . . . but I didn't know. Now I do. It will be up to you."

"What?"

"Ask Fritz. He will help you. The earthquake earlier, the smoke. To

267

move Wesley. You'll see. There will continue to be fear in the world, and need. People will still want to live forever. All you have to do is move an inch, and you can change reality with viewpoint. To fight the fear."

He was silent.

The sea was silent too, and calm. Off the bow, the orca hung in the water, buoyed by small movements of his fins and flukes, by the rush of air into his lungs.

He squeezed her hand. "Now back. To the bow. Please." The last word was drawn out, a hiss of breath in his teeth. She frowned as she helped him back. He was wandering; she felt afraid of what was about to happen.

Millet was awake, aware, visibly shaken. When he spoke, it was from very far away, absently, as if he were thinking about something that eluded him.

"We're going. I don't know what is going to happen." He shook his head.

He climbed down the ladder to his launch. Buddy followed him, and then Phil Rodgers, who paused at the top to give her a look. She was frowning and ignored him. Finally he too vanished below the deck. The engine started up, and she watched as the boat gathered speed, dwindled away, leaving only the faint sound of its wake lapping against the side of the *Dreambridge*. It vanished finally into the haze over the water, and the sea was empty once more.

Brockhurst was still clinging to her forearm. "My dear," he whispered. His touch was an insect landing on her arm, gossamer light. "It's almost time."

Pain shot through her, sudden, sharp. A sorrow.

He was so calm, though. "What's it like?" she asked, wished she hadn't.

His face did not change, the eyes drowsy looking, half-closed and hollowed; his head was fallen forward, chin to chest. But there was a faint humor in his whisper. "Scary. I've never done this before."

She didn't laugh, but felt the smile contest her grief a moment. As she led him forward again, she heard him say, "So tired."

The others were there, L.R. and Arnold and Izzy. Fritz stood off to one side, leaning against the railing on his crossed arms, gazing out to sea. They were all motionless, vague shapes barely recognizable, limned in a nimbus of misted light. At the bow he indicated he wanted to go further, out onto the sprit, where the platform was.

There was a narrow metal catwalk out there, just enough to edge along, and the going was difficult, since she had to help him along from behind, but at last he was seated facing the sea. Below him the orca waited, the double image of its head and fin sharp and rich, perfectly matched pairs. His eyes were just above the surface, mirrored, small and expressive. She could see, even from the height of the bowsprit, the small trail of tear-stuff at the corner, down into the water, where it met its reflection.

Far away, over the shore, a triangular dirigible floated northward serenely, toward Portland-Seattle, a remote speck against the pale blue. It was filled with people, going north on business, to visit relatives or friends, go to a wedding. Or a funeral. Or vacation, Easter in Seattle.

She could hear the slow trickle of water finding its way down through rock, the sound of the Castalian spring, the sacred spring in the deep gorge at the eastern side of the Phaedriades, the Shining Ones, the twin eight-hundred-foot rocks at Delphi, bare and gray.

Far below she could imagine the sound of the Plistus River, winding through the deep valley to the Gulf of Corinth, at Itea, where the Cretan ships rocked gently at anchor. She knew it was nothing but blood in her ears, the thread of heartbeat through the narrow channels of her veins, but it didn't matter. It was also a spring, falling through granite.

The dirigible moved on out of sight. She was not oracle, not Pythoness or Sibyl, and could read nothing in the blank heavens, the empty waters. She knew what was about to happen, and could do nothing. Only wait.

Brockhurst sat calmly, without moving, hands completely relaxed as if forgotten in his lap, eyes closed, she thought, though she couldn't see them from behind. She did not move, as if afraid to wake him.

She could feel the others at her back, though, watching. Arnold and Izzy. L.R. And somewhere on the ship Fritz waited for her. She realized, still without moving, that she had not seen one crew member since she had boarded the *Dreambridge*. They must all be below.

Slight motion appeared in the water. Another orca rose beside the first, breaking the surface without stirring it. They floated side by side for a time. Cassie did not move yet. There was no sound. Two more orcas appeared, then another, and gradually the waters around the ship filled with shapes, the orca pod, thirty or forty of them, or more. She stopped counting. They all floated, watching the bow without moving. The mood was completely different from before, as they watched the old man.

Her eyes filled, unaccountably. Tired. She was tired. From time to time the faint sound of their blowing came to her, and a frail jet of mist hung over their blowholes for a moment. She could see muscles moving in those holes, opening and closing, the sharp in and out of air.

The old man shifted slightly, lifted his hand, beckoning.

She leaned down. "Yes?"

"They're there, aren't they?" he whispered.

"Yes."

"I can feel them. Please take everyone aft. I want to be alone with them."

"Are you sure?" she found herself asking, also in a whisper.

His hand groped blindly for hers, squeezed it. "I'm sure," he rasped, and she thought she could hear the pain in that effort. "Take everyone aft."

While she hesitated, opening her mouth to speak, protest, or say good-bye, her thoughts were drowned in a sudden rumble, a prolonged thunderous roll across the sky and water, a booming that rose and fell, faded and renewed itself endlessly, like distant artillery or thunderstorms on the horizon, though the horizon was empty, the air utterly calm, though filled with this awful noise, coming from every direction at once.

The hair on her nape stood up, as though the static electricity had returned; this time, though, she had not called it, did not understand it. She looked around, could see nothing.

The sound faded, died away.

The old man spoke. "Brontides," he said. "There may be another earthquake coming. Go now, quickly."

The thunder returned, went on and on, a continuous rumble that troubled the surface of the water with an agitated shimmering, and in it, the orcas, also troubled, began to move. They rose and sank, blew more frequently. But they stared up at the old man without pause.

She turned, made her way along the catwalk, back to the deck. She waved to the others without saying a word, and wordlessly they followed her, around the cabin, toward the stern where she had sat with him just a few minutes ago as time telescoped, collapsed, fluid.

Cassie spoke softly to herself. She said, *"And I heard a voice from heaven, as the voice of many waters, and as the voice of a great thunder."*

"What's that?" her sister asked. She was shivering.

"Revelation 14:2. Are you cold?"

The answer was lost in thunder. Izzy held her hand, clung to her, a child. Booming filled the air, shook the rigging, the masts, the sides of the ship; everything trembled in that vast sound.

Even from here they could see orcas, gathering, moving in the water. Small waves began to splash against the sides as they circled and sounded.

The five of them huddled in the stern, stricken. The booming went on.

"What is it?" Izzy shouted finally. "What's happening?"

"He called them something . . . brontides." Cassie spoke in an undertone, but they heard.

L.R. nodded. "Sometimes they're called *mistpoeffers*. Means 'fog-belchers.' A rare phenomenon, but not unheard of."

"But what are they?"

He shrugged. "Earthquakes. Gas vents, mud-volcanoes, temperature inversions that carry the sounds of thunder or artillery. Nobody knows. Lots of theories."

The fantastic rumbling went on. Izzy pointed. "There. Look."

The dolphins were back, thousands of them it seemed, porpoising smoothly through the water, all around the ship; the water was boiling white with sleek gray bodies.

The brontides died away, and the air fell flat and still once more.

271

The weather had not changed, there was not a cloud anywhere. Only the gurgling sounds of the dolphins' bodies breaking the surface came to them. Yet there was a change, a sharp alteration in the quality of the world. They could feel it, from the motion of the dolphins.

"Something's happened," Izzy said.

They moved toward the bow, along the cabin, came around to the foredeck, and looked out to the bowsprit.

It was empty.

Brockhurst was gone. Cassie ran out along the catwalk to the platform where he had been sitting. She shouted, an inarticulate cry.

One of the orcas turned, lifted his head, and called her name. In spite of the alien voice, the hissing syllables, she felt the intensity of grief in that word. And then the pod of orcas, followed by all the dolphins, sounded and vanished beneath the water.

Her hands gripped the railing around the platform as she stared into the empty surface. Her own face looked back at her far below.

Images passed before her. Vague shapes moved in the water. Events began, flourished, resolved, and vanished, replaced by others, equally lacking in detail, definition, clarity. Some of the events were galactic: plumes and jets of ionized hydrogen, formaldehyde, carbon dioxide, so vast it took light a thousand years to traverse them, extended, slowed, froze in place; stars collided, merged, erupted unimaginable energies. Or the events were microscopic, cilia waving rhythmically in water, single cells dividing, mitochondria, the replications of virus; or on the human scale: in Africa a hunting lion leaped on an elephant calf in the Sud or in the Serengeti, raked its claws over the tender neck, and the calf died; in a DLF laboratory in St. Louis a new combination of amino acids formed inside the DNA of a mutated bacterium; in Goshen, Indiana, a mother wept; a black-and-white cat walked over the roof of the IF building in Menlo Park.

The sun moved on, a darkness gathered over the water, turned the sky to pale violet; deepened; Venus appeared out of the increasing dark, a brilliant flare on the horizon. The stars followed. The sky filled with them, and as the mist retreated, they became sharp and clear and impossibly distant.

Finally she moved, shrugged, a small, inoffensive gesture, and made her way back to the deck, to where the others had gathered to talk, sporadically, of nothing.

When she appeared, Arnold asked her. "Did you see it?"

"See what?"

272

"The sunset. It was very strange, a kind of gray green."

"No, I didn't see it."

She picked up the glass jar from the table in the cockpit. The milky crystal glowed faintly in the starlight. She noticed then a warmer glow from the cabin windows, the human world. The crystal clinked very faintly when she shook the jar. She hugged it to her for a moment. Carved into the soft mineral the swallow sailed on, wings outspread. Good will of all.

Sounds resolved themselves, waves lapping at the waterline, small sloppings. There was around her a palpable, crafted reality: chairs, cushions, deck, fixtures. People breathing.

"Izzy, we will have to do something about Martha. Can we bring her out here?"

"I think so. I'd better talk to her." Her voice was there, in the velvet dark, soft.

The chop of water increased, the sound of it against the sides rhythmic and melodious now. The planet turned, stars wheeled overhead. Venus was below the horizon. Gemini hovered just above it.

"We're going to miss you, Cassie. At the office." L.R. spoke out of the dark.

"I'll be around. Often. Fritz, where does this ship usually berth?"

"Half Moon Bay."

"How long would it take to get there? If we go slowly?"

"As long as you want. We could time it to get there by morning."

"Are there enough cabins for everyone?"

"Of course."

"Then if anyone is hungry we should eat, and then sleep."

Fritz opened the cabin door, and light flooded the deck. Izzy pressed Cassie's hand, went inside. The others followed.

Cassie took Arnold's hand before he entered, and he stopped, turned to her. He breathed, she could feel his breathing, as he stood, half in the light, half in the star-filled darkness. His fingers closed on hers, his other hand rested on her shoulder. A miracle of tendons and bones, of joints, veins, and skin, the half-moon nails of his fingers, the pale follicles of down on the back of his hand and wrist: all were infinitely precious. With the back of her head and neck she could feel, as she leaned back, the hollow of his shoulder, and could sense the strands of muscle, the knotted collarbone, the sheath of fascia around those sheets of muscle.

"Are you all right?" he asked her, quietly.

"Yes. Tired. And . . . sad."

"Yes."

He hugged her to him. Once more she recited from the mad Saint John, a low murmur Arnold could barely make out. *"And I saw a new heaven and a new earth: for the first heaven and the first earth were passed away; and there was no more sea."*

"No more sea," he repeated softly.

She turned inside the circle of his arms, a need rising in her, in him.

A breeze sprang up, the first breath of long voyage across the Pacific, all the way from Japan. A gray lock stirred on his forehead.

Deep inside, the engine hummed to quiet life. The anchor chain rattled softly, and they began to move, very slowly, a ponderous turn back toward land.

Neither of them spoke. She lifted her face to him, trembled slightly in his arms. Kissed him. Her arm closed around his neck. She sagged against him.

"It doesn't make sense, does it? Doing this?"

"No. Yes."

She laughed a little. "He said today would be short. For me it has been long, the longest of all. I'm tired."

"Oh?"

She looked up, shoulders pushing against the undersides of his arms, around her neck. She rested her cheek against his collarbone.

"What's the point?" he asked her. "All this uncertainty."

She thought about the Portland-Seattle dirigible, drifting northward along the coast, filled with people. Other people. Other lives.

"It keeps on going," she said. "It all goes on, anyway." She looked at him again, her smile playing with him. He saw it and slipped his arms around her waist, held the small of her back, the swelling flesh below, the softness. The current of need passed between them.

"I'm tired," she repeated. "But not that tired. Shall we find the cabin?"

"Yes," he said.

Cassie falls into waking dream once more, her arm reaching upward, head resting on it. She tries, and seeks through the dark, and makes the contact she desires. Beside her, Arnold sleeps.

The fire was still smoldering when the elephant arrived. Only the stone chimney stood, smoke blackened, against the milky sky, tendrils of dark particulate rising straight up from the ruins.

The booming had started some time ago, a distant continuous rumble that had paused once and then begun again. As soon as she heard it, she set out for the village, her huge body shambling through the underbrush, ignoring the paths and logging trails. A mile or so after she began, she caught the scent of smoke spiced with burning hydrocarbons and gasoline. The smell of man, heavy in the air.

Her trunk extended straight ahead, her ears attentively swiveled half-forward, listening carefully to the forest sounds, that distant rumble. There was almost no wind, so the scents had to have diffused through the air, which meant the fire had happened long ago, in the night. She jogged on, ignoring the small trees and brush in her path, trampling them under her flat heavy feet. Her trail would be easy to follow if anyone was there and cared.

She passed not far from the CoreLight Mission settlement, lofted her trunk, and twined it in the air, testing for their scent, familiar but wary. She understood vaguely that they were interested in the night sky, that they watched it, and waited. She knew they were not interested in her, and would not harm her, but she kept a distance, circling in the meadow.

The booming went on and on, and its wavering intensity made her feel something close to panic. Her pace increased, her feet thudding through tender spring branches and shoots, mashing new buds to paste. She broke into a run, as if she had to arrive at the town before the booming stopped.

She didn't make it. When the sound stopped abruptly, so did she, dead in her tracks, confused and disoriented. Her trunk seemed to wilt then, to test in a dazed manner at the soil by her feet, to quest up her leg, reach into her mouth to take the taste of her own tongue. She stood, baffled a moment in that sudden silence, before the sounds of the woods came back to her, the birdsong and rodent scuttle, the crackle of deadfall underfoot as something, a bear perhaps, moved away.

Then she bellowed, a long, drawn-out, harrowing cry, riven with grief. She began to shamble forward once again, without the panic-driven hysteria now. Her small, solemn eyes were half-closed, as though drowsy, but she was not tired. Her bellow echoed away through the boles of oak and fir, fragmented, shattered by the confusion of obstacles. She left it behind her and made only the sounds of her breathing and her footfalls on the needle carpet.

At last she arrived at the clearing, watched the smoldering town from across the road. Everything was gone, the ancient mining town buildings, and beyond them, up the slope, the lodge. She stared at the smoke rising straight into the air. The road was desolate without buildings to give it meaning, just a bare stretch between trees. Slowly she moved across it, as inevitable as nightfall, toward the lodge, turning aside momentarily to test the old saloon foundation from a distance. His smell was there yet.

In the clearing before the lodge the blackened remains of the helicopter slumped to the ground, rotors half-melted, warped, the plastic cabin shattered, a door here, and the other beyond the foundations, resting against a tree. She walked carefully to it, sniffed loudly in its direction. Puffs of sooty debris rose at each breath and fell back. The seats were burned out, coils of springs like the growth of symmetrical climbing vines toppled haphazardly, spilling from the seat frames. She tested each one, looking for him, but the fire had taken it all into the sky long ago.

The wreckage was cold, dead, meaningless, instrument panel a fused mess of glass and metal, the control links, wiring, the engine just lumps, rods, dead nerve. The rains in the fall would turn it all to oxides, red rust, a subtle mound in the earth. She moved on, toward the house.

His smell was strong here, and remembered conversations passed through her large, slow-moving, complex brain. She remembered the stories she had told him of her family history, her genealogy, the migrations around Africa and Asia and America, collected in her mind. He had spoken back to her, his deep rumble small compared to hers, and had twined his arm against her trunk. There had been a terrible sadness in him, and it was this memory that made her stop now stock still before the house and lower her enormous head. She lay the tip of her trunk on the ground, rested it there, before her feet, and did not move as the burned wood smoldered before her.

A rafter, resting across two other beams, collapsed with a soft ashy sound, but she did not move. A shower of sparks went up, twisted in the air, fell back. Two or three landed on her back, burned there briefly and died to ash, taking with them a few of her coarse hairs. She did not move. The air flowed in, through the long tunnel of her trunk, making to her ear a very faint roar, a rushing sound; then it flowed out once more, and the ashes before her stirred slightly, eddied, fell back without sound.

She stood that way, indifferent to bird calls, the thrash of jays in the branches, the returning rustle of field mice in the new grass, indifferent even to the scent of ash everywhere; indifferent to the smoke that still rose, black and heavy with particles, and dwindled, thinned, scattered.

The sun moved westward, taking its vast nimbus of brightness with it, and the air over the mountain peaks to the east grew darker, though the peaks themselves, which she could not see, were bright on their western faces. Finally she stirred a bit, as if rousing from a trance, and walked carefully around the foundation, testing everywhere with her trunk, inhaling the smells, unpleasant ones of burned petroleum and melted plastic, the acrid smell of metal appliances, and the other, the smell of him, the old man, thick with the memories that flocked in her mind.

With that came the awareness of something else, of the dreamer with her, the empathy: Cassie, dreaming the elephant's grief. Cassie, making a note to herself to send people here, to come herself. Develop this communication.

The elephant lifted her trunk then; it rose into the air above her head, made a vertical S in the air, and she trumpeted, a shrill, powerful blast into the twilight, and lowered her trunk.

She could smell his grief and despair, his hope, and as she sniffed around the heat-cracked stones of the chimney, she rumbled deep in her chest. It sounded like the booming sound that had brought her here, and continued, on and on, one with Cassie's waking dream, filled with grief.

He was gone. She knew it. He had told her yesterday that he would never return, that he was old, old. Someone else would come. But she was a social being, and in this vast preserve of hers, she was alone. She felt it in her mind, and deep in her lungs, and in her thickly muscled heart. She began to pace restlessly around the charred ruins, to rove her trunk tip over the foundation, faster and faster, trying to draw into herself whatever might remain of him, whatever lingering odors might remind her of him, for soon the ashes would grow cold, and with them the scent; he would fade from this place and be gone finally and forever, and would exist only in memory.

For a time even Cassie's presence could not console, stricken as it was too, and her heavy head moved back and forth, back and forth, trunk twisting more and more rapidly, coiling and uncoiling, breath coming in quick jerks that held before being released. Her ears were listening for his step, his voice, and from time to time it seemed she heard him.

But she did not hear him, and when at last she had taken into her mind and lungs all that there was of him there, she turned and walked, slowly and with a vast dignity, past the ruined foundation and into the wood, where she found the trail up the valley to the sacred junction of vertical and horizontal, where the rocks formed a hollow, and the smell of the woman who would come soon to talk to her was still strong and clear.

And there she rested.

22:10 *The time is at hand*